2005

W9-DFM-696

Grounds for Agreement

Grounds for Agreement

The Political Economy of the Coffee Commodity Chain

JOHN M. TALBOT

ROWMAN & LITTLEFIELD PUBLISHERS, INC.
Lanham • Boulder • New York • Toronto • Oxford

ROWMAN & LITTLEFIELD PUBLISHERS, INC.

Published in the United States of America
by Rowman & Littlefield Publishers, Inc.
A wholly owned subsidiary of The Rowman & Littlefield Publishing Group, Inc.
4501 Forbes Boulevard, Suite 200, Lanham, MD 20706
www.rowmanlittlefield.com

P.O. Box 317, Oxford OX2 9RU, UK

Copyright © 2004 by [author or Rowman & Littlefield Publishers, Inc.]

All rights reserved. No part of this publication may be reproduced, stored in a retrieval system, or transmitted in any form or by any means, electronic, mechanical, photocopying, recording, or otherwise, without the prior permission of the publisher.

British Library Cataloguing in Publication Information Available

Library of Congress Cataloging-in-Publication Data

Talbot, John M., 1951–
    Grounds for agreement : the political economy of the coffee commodity chain /
    John M. Talbot.
        p.   cm.
    Includes bibliographical references and index.
    ISBN 0-7425-2628-3 (cloth : alk. paper) — ISBN 0-7425-2629-1 (pbk. : alk. paper)
    1. Coffee industry.   I. Title.

HD9199.A2T35   2004
382'.4566393—dc22

                                                                    2004011297
Printed in the United States of America

⊛™ The paper used in this publication meets the minimum requirements of American National Standard for Information Sciences—Permanence of Paper for Printed Library Materials, ANSI/NISO Z39.48-1992.

382.4566393
T131

$870.00

B & T

4/25/05

For Mom, Dad, and Luis

Contents

Figures

Tables

Abbreviations

ACP	African, Caribbean and Pacific Countries (beneficiaries of the Lomé Agreements)
ACPC	Association of Coffee Producing Countries
ANRPC	Association of Natural Rubber Producing Countries
ATO	Alternative trading organization
CPA	Cocoa Producers Alliance
CFTC	U.S. Commodity Futures Trading Commission
CIPEC	Council of Copper Exporting Countries
CSCE	New York Coffee, Sugar, and Cocoa Exchange (futures market)
EEC	European Economic Community
FAO	UN Food and Agriculture Organization
FAS	Foreign Agricultural Service (agency of the U.S. Department of Agriculture)
FNC	Federación Nacional de Cafeteros (Colombia)
GATT	General Agreement on Tariffs and Trade
IBA	International Bauxite Association
IBC	Instituto Brasileiro do Café
IBEC	International Basic Economy Corporation
ICA	International Coffee Agreement
ICC	International Coffee Council, governing body of the ICO
ICO	International Coffee Organization
IFOAM	International Federation of Organic Agriculture Movements
IMF	International Monetary Fund
IPC	Integrated Program for Commodities (part of NIEO proposals)
MMC	Monopolies and Mergers Commission (U.K.)
NAC	New Agricultural Country (H. Friedmann)

NAFTA	North American Free Trade Agreement
NCA	National Coffee Association (U.S.)
NCD	National Coffee Department (Brazil)
NIC	Newly Industrializing Country
NIEO	New International Economic Order
OPEC	Organization of Petroleum Exporting Countries
PACB	Pan American Coffee Bureau
SCAA	Specialty Coffee Association of America
TPC	Trade Policy Committee (interagency U.S. trade policy committee)
UNCTAD	UN Conference on Trade and Development
UNCTC	UN Centre on Transnational Corporations
UPEB	Union de Paises Exportadores de Banana (Union of Banana Exporting Countries)
USAID	U.S. Agency for International Development
USDA	U.S. Department of Agriculture
USTR	U.S. Trade Representative (agency in charge of U.S. trade policy)
VAT	Value-added tax
WTO	World Trade Organization

Acknowledgments

This book is the product of over ten years of research, thinking, and writing about coffee, a subject that continues to fascinate me. As is the case with any project this large, there are numerous people and organizations that have assisted, supported, and even inspired me to keep at it and eventually finish it. I can't thank all of them by name, so let me begin with a blanket thank you to everyone who helped me with this project, not elsewhere specified.

Beyond the intellectual debts to those whose work I have built on, who are acknowledged in my notes and bibliography, my main intellectual debt is to my original dissertation committee from the University of California at Berkeley. Peter Evans, who was the chair, was the ideal thesis advisor, and has continued to help me to think strategically about research, writing, and my academic career. Laura Enriquez was a very careful reader who helped me to develop my ability to state my arguments clearly and consistently. Brian Wright helped me to clarify my economic thinking and to make my sociological and political arguments more intelligible to economists. Philip McMichael, though not a member of the committee, has consistently supported and encouraged my research in this area. Finally, I would like to thank all of the members of the Political Economy of the World-System section of the American Sociological Association, and of the International Sociological Association's Research Committee on Food and Agriculture (RC–40), who have commented on my various papers and presentations on the coffee commodity chain over the years. Any shortcomings of this book are probably due to my decisions to ignore sound advice from these people.

I would also like to thank all of the people who gave their time to help me with the research that went into this book. First and foremost are C. P. R. Dubois and his able staff at the International Coffee Organization. They opened their library to me during the initial stages of the research, and have continued to take the time to provide me with the documents and statistics I needed to update my analyses. I also interviewed several key people involved in the coffee commodity chain in various ways, who gave me many insights into how it worked. Jim Reynolds of Peet's Coffee and Bert and Elmer Fulmer of Gold Mountain Coffee gave me the perspectives of the specialty coffee roaster and the coffee trader, respectively. Neil Rosser of ED&F Man provided the perspective of the TNC traders. Salim Janna, at the time the United States and Canada representative of Colombia's *Federación Nacional de Cafeteros*, explained Colombia's marketing operations in North America. Ted Lingle, Executive Director of the Specialty Coffee Association of America, and George Boecklin, at the time the Executive Director of the National Coffee Association, provided insights into how their organizations worked and helped me to understand the overall structure of the U.S. coffee industry. I am particularly grateful to Nestor Osorio, now the Executive Director of the International Coffee Organization, who, at the time I interviewed him, was Colombia's Permanent Representative to the ICO, and a key player in the 1989 and 1993 negotiations. He spent a great deal of time discussing these negotiations and Colombia's positions in them, helping me to understand how the International Coffee Agreements (ICAs) worked, and ultimately failed. Finally, a source close to the 1993 negotiations on the U.S. side, who wished to remain anonymous, also provided valuable insights into the process. Obviously, none of these people bear any responsibility for the uses I have made of, or the interpretations I have placed on, the information they provided; but without it, I could not have completed this project.

This book is the culmination of a long process of research and writing, and during that time I have published a series of articles about coffee. Some findings and conclusions from each of those articles have been incorporated into this book, in many cases in significantly revised and updated form. I would like to thank all of the publishers who allowed me to use this previously published material here. Greenwood Publishing Group published my first article, "The Regulation of the World Coffee Market: Tropical Commodities and the Limits of Globalization," in Philip McMichael's *Food and Agrarian Orders in the World-Economy* (Praeger, 1995), parts of which appear in chapters 1 and 3. The *Berkeley Journal of Sociology* published "Regulating the Coffee Commodity Chain: Internationalization and the Coffee Cartel," in Volume 40, 1995–1996, parts of which are used in chapters 3 and 4. *Latin American Research Review* published "The Struggle for Control of a Commodity Chain: Instant Coffee from Latin America," in Volume 32, 1997; parts of this article appear in chapters 6 and 7. *Studies in Comparative International Development* published "Where Does Your Coffee Dollar Go?: The Division of Income and Surplus along the Coffee Commodity Chain," in Volume 32, 1997; the bulk of chapter 7 is a revised and updated version of this paper. "Information, Finance, and the New International Inequality: The Case of Coffee," was published in the *Journal of World-Systems Research*, Volume 8, 2002 (http://jwsr.ucr.edu/index.php). Material from this article was used in chapter 5, and also in chapter 4. I would particularly like to thank Eric Titolo of *JWSR*, who made figures 4.1 and 5.1 look much more professional than the original graphs I sent him. Information about the effects of the coffee crisis, in chapter 5, and an earlier draft of my proposal to end the crisis, in the Conclusion, were published by the *Georgetown Journal of International Affairs*, Vol. 3, 2002. Finally, some of the theoretical discussion of commodity chains in chapter 1 was taken from my article "Tropical Commodity Chains, Forward Integration Strategies, and International Inequality: Coffee, Cocoa and Tea," published by Routledge in *Review of International Political Economy*, Volume 9, 2002 (www.tandf.co.uk). Last but not least, I would like to thank my brother, Peter J. Talbot, for his expert editing on the cover photo.

This book is dedicated to my parents, James and Margaret Talbot, who have supported and encouraged me through the entire process. Without their love and understanding, I doubt that I could have finished it. The book is also dedicated to my good friend, Luis Arturo Betancourt, who first got me interested in coffee as a subject for political-economic analysis, and introduced me to the production end of the chain in Colombia. I wish that he had lived to see this final product.

Introduction

When you drink a cup of coffee, you are completing the final link in a global chain of activities that made that cup of coffee possible. The coffee had to be grown, picked, processed, shipped, and roasted before it could get to your cup. That simple act of sipping your coffee connects you to peasant farmers in Colombia and Indonesia, to dock workers in Sao Paulo and Mombassa, New Orleans and San Francisco, and to many others in between. Literally millions of people work every day to bring you that cup of coffee. Although you rarely think about it as you sip your fresh brew, the way that this global chain of activities is organized has enormous implications for the millions of people involved in it, and the societies in which they live. The organization of this chain and its global implications are the subject of this book.

Coffee is a tropical crop. That is, there are only a limited number of places on the planet with the right combination of soil, sunlight, temperature, and rainfall in which the coffee tree will thrive, and all of those places are located within the tropics. Almost all of those places are located in developing countries, and many are located in the poorest countries of the world. Meanwhile, most of the world's coffee drinkers are located in developed countries in the temperate zones of the planet. So the chain of activities that brings you your cup of coffee is also a direct link between what used to be called the First World and the Third World, between the North and the South, the rich and the poor.

This link between North and South is a legacy of colonialism. Coffee was one of the earliest products in the colonial trade, along with others such as tea, cocoa, sugar, and tobacco. The spread of coffee cultivation from eastern Africa, where coffee originated, through the tropical zones of the world was a project of European colonizers, and they spread it to feed the insatiable desire for the strong black brew back home. As a result, these tropical zones were first integrated into the world economy as suppliers of coffee, and some became stuck in that niche.

Coffee is also a valuable crop. It is the most valuable agricultural product exported by developing countries, and the second most valuable raw material overall—second only to oil. In a very real sense, the world economy may run on fossil fuels, but it also runs on coffee. So the organization of the chain of activities that brings you your coffee has enormous financial implications as well. When you buy coffee—whether it's a can of Maxwell House in the supermarket, a pound of single-origin specialty beans from Peet's Coffee, or a tall skinny latte from Starbucks—the organization of this chain determines where your coffee dollar goes. Does most of it go into the coffers of Philip Morris (owner of the Maxwell House brand) or does most of it go to the farmer in Kenya or Costa Rica, who tended the coffee tree and picked the beans? Because coffee is such a valuable crop, the answer to this question has a great impact on the chances for development of the coffee-exporting developing countries.

These questions of how the chain is organized, where your coffee dollar goes, and what this means for the development of coffee producing countries, are the central questions addressed in this book. I hope to demonstrate that, under today's conditions, a "free" market in coffee really means that giant corporations like Philip Morris get to decide how the chain of activities is organized, resulting in cheap, poor quality coffee that impoverishes the farmers and their countries and destroys the environment. As we will see in chapter 7, the average coffee farmer today is receiving about 41 cents for tending and harvesting one coffee tree for a year. The issue is not whether or not the market is "free"; instead it is who organizes this chain of activities, and who benefits from it?

I also argue that we can do something to change this situation. If we look at the history of the coffee commodity chain since World War II, we see that periods of a free market have alternated with periods when the world market was regulated by international agreements. This history demonstrates that, all things considered, a politically regulated market is better than a free one, *at least for coffee*. During the periods of regulated markets, prices were more stable and returns to coffee producers were greater than during the free market periods. I argue that a return to a regulated market is urgently needed, because the free market has currently driven world market prices to historic lows and coffee growers all over the world are suffering greatly because of it.

I also examine the recent growth of organic, shade-grown, and fair-trade coffees. While these are welcome developments, they will not significantly affect the organization of the chain through which most of the world's coffee is sold. I argue that a properly managed world coffee market is the best way to produce high quality coffee that is good for the environment, at a fair price for consumers, and to ensure that the workers who set the whole chain in motion are justly compensated for their efforts.

The book is organized as follows. Chapter 1 lays out the theoretical and methodological grounds for the analysis. It reviews the literature on commodity chains and international commodity agreements. It also argues that the evolution of the coffee commodity chain has to be placed in the larger context of the evolution of the world economy, and draws on two theoretical approaches to do this: food regimes and systemic cycles of accumulation. Finally, it discusses the methodological approach of incorporating comparison, which is used in this analysis.

Chapter 2 lays out the material and historical grounds for the analysis. It considers the nature of coffee as a tropical crop, and demonstrates that the ecology and the economics of coffee growing and processing influence who controls the successive stages of the chain, and how the benefits from them are divided up. The chapter also sets the stage for the analysis that follows, by presenting a brief history of coffee up to World War II.

Chapter 3 covers the history of the coffee chain from World War II through 1972, the year when the second International Coffee Agreement broke down. It focuses on how coffee producing countries, some just emerging from colonialism, banded together and tried to regulate the market. It explains why the United States, the hegemonic power and the world's largest coffee importer, decided to cooperate with these efforts. It also explains why the resulting international agreement to regulate the market broke down in 1972, in the aftermath of a series of crises of U.S. hegemony.

Chapter 4 covers the period 1973–1989. After the coffee agreement ended, producing countries once again engaged in collective actions to raise prices. The devastating Brazilian frost of 1975 intervened, causing a price boom followed by a price crash. Further collective actions by producing countries resulted in the restoration of a regulated market from 1980–1989, despite the fact that the United States was pushing to free markets everywhere. However, the 1980s were marked by chronic overproduction, with a variety of causes, which eventually undermined the international regulatory regime. The crucial vote that led to the end of the coffee agreement is analyzed, showing clearly that U.S. intransigence was the major cause of its demise.

Chapter 5 analyzes the ways in which the coffee chain was reorganized in the globalization of the world economy through the 1980s and 1990s, leading to persistent coffee crises during the 1990s and into the 2000s. World market coffee prices have been pushed to historic lows, causing incredible economic hardship for millions of people, and contributing to a host of barbarities, from the genocide in Rwanda to the civil war in Colombia. It looks at attempts by producing countries to reimpose regulation on the market, and explains why they have not been successful.

Chapter 6 analyzes an alternative strategy used by coffee producing countries to increase their returns from coffee production. They attempted to add value to their exports by producing instant coffee, and exporting it directly into the consuming markets. The chapter shows how the market power of the major coffee companies, backed at times by the political power of the U.S. government, severely limited the gains achieved through this strategy.

Chapter 7 evaluates the outcomes of these struggles over control of the coffee chain by asking the question, "Where does your coffee dollar go?" It demonstrates that the International Coffee Agreements achieved a reasonably equitable distribution of benefits between coffee growers and producing countries, and the major coffee companies. This balance was upset by the reorganization of the chain and the demise of the coffee agreements, leading to a highly unequal distribution of benefits in the 1990s and beyond. It also shows how the benefits from instant coffee production were limited by the market power of the coffee companies.

Chapter 8 considers the rise of organic and fair-trade coffees as possible solutions to the coffee crises. It describes how globalization and the reorganization of the chain caused a decline in the quality of coffee, setting the stage for the rise of specialty coffees. Specialty coffees, in turn, helped to open the door for organic and fair trade. However, organic and fair-trade coffees are caught in a number of contradictions, because they are also products of the globalized market, and by themselves, cannot solve all of the problems it has created.

The conclusion summarizes the results of this analysis and makes the case for a return to a regulated world coffee market. It considers what will be needed to achieve effective regulation in the conditions of the early 2000s. It also draws out the implications of this analysis of coffee for the further development of commodity chain analysis.

Chapter 1

Theoretical and Methodological Grounds
for the Analysis

Theoretical Grounds: World-Systems and Commodity Chains

The production system that brings coffee, or any other commodity, from where it is produced to where it is consumed can be thought of as a chain. For coffee, it starts with the planting and maintenance of a coffee tree somewhere in the tropics during the three to five years that it takes to begin producing coffee. It encompasses all of the intermediate processing stages that are needed to transform the coffee from a red cherry on the tree to a beverage in the cup; and all of the transactions that move it from the grower to the exporter to the importer to the roaster to the consumer. The chain conceptualization highlights the connections between all of these different transactions and processing stages, which happen in different parts of the world. These connections establish social relations between the people involved in the different stages. This way of conceptualizing production systems as chains has been formalized as the commodity chain approach, and this approach provides the framework for the analysis of the coffee production system presented in this book.

The commodity chain approach has been developed within the framework of world-systems analysis. World-systems analysis, originally developed by Immanuel Wallerstein and his colleagues in the 1970s (e.g., Wallerstein 1974), contends that a capitalist world-system, which began in Europe in the sixteenth century, has expanded to incorporate the entire globe. A basic premise of the approach is that this world-system is a unitary social system with a single, capitalist division of labor. World-systems researchers are explicitly critical of the use of nation-states as the units of analysis. As Chase-Dunn and Grimes put it, in their review of world-systems analysis (1995, 389), "it is the whole system that develops, not simply the national societies that are its parts." However, this theoretical orientation creates some practical problems for the researcher, for it implies that there is only one unit of analysis, the modern world-system.

The commodity chain approach presents one way out of this dilemma. A commodity chain is an intermediate unit of analysis, bigger than the nation-state but smaller than the entire world-system. A commodity chain is the interrelated system of production processes and economic transactions that creates a commodity such as coffee, and brings it to the point where it is purchased and used by the final consumer. If we think of the world economy as being made up of thousands and thousands of chains like these, for every product that is produced and used on the planet, then, in Hopkins and Wallerstein's apt metaphor, commodity chains form "the warp and woof of [the] system of social production" (1994, 17). They link together globally dispersed production processes that are carried out within the borders of many different nation-states.

Approaching the study of coffee production from the perspective of the nation-state, we might compare several different coffee producing countries and investigate the impact of coffee production and exporting on their economic development. We could look at how coffee production was organized, how much income the exports generated, and how this income was distributed. Studies like this are valuable, but they tend to obscure the positions of individual countries within the global production system, and the transnational system of social relations within which local actors are enmeshed. Nation-states as units of analysis divide up the world into a set of discrete, non-overlapping territorial units, and the natural tendency of a researcher using these units of analysis is to begin to conceive of them as independent and self-contained. Commodity chains are fundamentally different kinds of units of analysis. They are interwoven. The commodity chain that produces coffee, for example, is intimately linked to the chains that produce ships and the fuel to run them, because they are essential for getting the coffee from the grower to the consumer. It is impossible to analyze the commodity chain as an independent, self-contained unit, without considering the whole world economy of which it is a part. A change in the structure of any individual chain will have repercussions for all other chains it intersects, and thereby for the world economy as a whole. And since the world economy is nothing more than the totality of all commodity chains, it is impossible to conceive of changes to the structure of the world economy in the abstract. A change in the structure of the world economy must mean a change in the structures of one or more of its constituent chains.

The introduction of the commodity chain concept shifts the focus of the analysis away from the way in which a particular nation-state is linked to the world economy through a particular commodity market, and toward the global organization of production, processing, and distribution of a particular commodity. The unit of analysis shifts from an individual nation-state to the interlocked network of chains for a particular commodity. Individual nations can be located with respect to this global structure, and the types of stages of the chains that are located within their borders can be identified. But the commodity chain as unit of analysis also incorporates the political and economic relationships among all nation-states involved in the production system. These relationships can be specified based on the types of stages located in each nation-state, and the nature of the commodity flows between them. As states attempt to exert control over these flows, they develop political alliances and conflicts with other states involved in the global chain.

The fabric of the world economy that emerges from the interweaving of commodity chains has a hierarchical structure with three distinct strata: the core, where the most dynamic and profitable stages of major commodity chains are located; the periphery, where the simplest and least profitable stages tend to be located; and an intermediate stratum, the semiperiphery, which includes a mixture of these stages (Arrighi and Drangel 1986). The coffee chain reproduces this structural feature of the world economy; the simplest stages of the chain, coffee growing and initial processing, are located mainly in poor, peripheral countries, while the most dynamic stages, such as the development of new coffee beverages for niche markets, are located mainly in the developed countries. This consideration brings us back to nation-states again, because the stages, or specific production processes, that constitute the chains have specific geographical locations, within particular nation-states; at the same time, however, they are intimately linked to stages or processes located in other nation-states. The commodity chain thus reproduces another of the fundamental characteristics of the world-system as a unit of analysis: the contradiction between the global unity of its economic system and the territorial fragmentation of its political system of nation-states. The states try to regulate the production processes that occur within their borders, but they are constrained because these processes are linked to others located in different nation-states.

If we look at the world economy as being made up of thousands of interwoven commodity chains, we can see that the territory of any given nation-state will encompass a wide variety of stages of many different commodity chains. In theory, any given nation-state could include the simplest and least profitable stages of some chains (e.g., coffee growing) and the most dynamic and profitable stages of others (e.g., the design and marketing of fashion apparel). Empirically, however, the core activities of many different chains tend to cluster together in certain nation-states and the peripheral activities of many different chains cluster together in others.

The key to understanding this empirical regularity—the clustering together of core and peripheral activities in different nation-states—is to understand the process through which different areas of the world were originally incorporated into the world economy. The core areas of the world economy are those where capitalism as a mode of production and accumulation first took hold. They are the areas where the modern industrial production system was invented. They drove the expansion of the system to encompass the entire planet, initially through military conquest. The peripheral areas were the conquered. Their initial role in the world economy was to supply the raw materials needed by the industrial production system, and to consume some of its products. These strata have

remained remarkably stable over time, with very little upward or downward mo-
bility between them (Arrighi and Drangel 1986; Korzeniewicz and Martin
1994). As new products have been invented, and new commodity chains developed, the core areas of the world have used their economic, political, and military power to control the core stages of these chains, and to shift most of the
peripheral stages to the same areas where all other peripheral activities are concentrated.

The commodity chain approach thus grew out of the broader world-systems
approach, as researchers sought a way to analyze the structure of the world
economy and its change over time. Gary Gereffi and his colleagues (e.g., Gereffi
and Korzeniewicz 1990, 1994) were instrumental in the early development of
this approach. The chain metaphor captures the separate, yet interdependent,
nature of the linked production processes that are needed to produce a final
commodity for consumption. "Each successive node within a commodity chain
involves the acquisition or organization of inputs (e.g., raw materials or semi-
finished products), labor power (and its provisioning), transportation, distribution (via markets or transfers), and consumption" (Gereffi, Korzeniewicz, and
Korzeniewicz 1994, 2). At each stage of the chain, the analysis focuses on how
production is organized (e.g., technology and scale) and who organizes it, particularly on the forms of labor control used and the ownership of the surplus that
is produced. It also focuses on the nature of the commodity flows to and from
each stage, and the geographic distribution of the flows.

According to Gereffi (1994), a commodity chain has three main dimensions: an input-output structure; a geographic distribution of production, and a
distribution of production among different sizes of firms; and a governance
structure. In a later formulation (1995), Gereffi divided the third dimension, the
governance structure, into two separate dimensions, which he called the governance structure and the institutional framework. I prefer the earlier formulation,
because the latter one overemphasizes the roles of transnational corporations
(TNCs), and de-emphasizes the roles of states. Gereffi's earlier formulation de-
fines the governance structure as "authority and power relationships that determine how financial, material, and human resources are allocated and flow within
a chain" (1994, 97). In his later formulation, the governance structure is defined
as "authority and power relationships *between firms* that determines how financial, material and human resources are allocated and flow within a chain" (1995,
113, emphasis added). The additional dimension, the institutional framework,
"identifies how local, national, and international conditions and policies shape
the globalization process at each stage of the chain" (1995, 113). In the latter
formulation, it seems as if the firms (TNCs) determine the structure of the commodity chain, and the only role for states and other social actors is to create the
conditions under which the firms make these decisions. This is an artificial and
unnecessary separation of the roles of states and firms, both of which can directly influence a chain's structure. Indeed, some of the most important power
and authority relations shaping commodity chains are between states and firms.
In Gereffi's earlier formulation, all authority and power relationships that di-

rectly affect the rules and the structure of the commodity chain are included within the governance structure. This conceptualization is more appropriate for the coffee chain, because, as we will see, states can impose rules that have a direct impact on the structures of all stages of the chain.

Much of the recent work on commodity chains, particularly that of Gereffi (1994, 1995, 1999), has focused on the governance structures of chains, the sets of rules that determine how the different stages are structured, how the commodities flow between them, and how the income and profits are divided. Gereffi has sketched two ideal types of governance structures: producer-driven and buyer-driven. Producer-driven chains are usually found in capital- and technology-intensive industries. In these chains, TNC manufacturers coordinate production through a vast network of subsidiaries, suppliers, and subcontractors. The TNCs assemble the components provided by this network, and control the forward linkages into distribution and retailing of the finished product. The automobile commodity chain exemplifies this type of governance structure. Buyer-driven chains are usually found in labor-intensive consumer goods industries. Here, the leading firms that organize the chains are TNC retailers and marketers, who often do not actually manufacture the products they sell. They specialize in design, branding, marketing, and financial services, and contract out the actual production to a network of independent firms that obtain inputs and organize production according to designs supplied by the TNCs. They rely on flexible production and global sourcing, and control the markets for their products through advertising and globally recognized brand names. The apparel commodity chain, which has been extensively analyzed by Gereffi, exemplifies this type of governance structure.

While these two ideal types of governance structures are useful for analyzing chains for many manufactured goods, it is less clear whether they are generalizable to other kinds of commodity chains. For instance, Clancy (1998) argues that they are inadequate to describe the governance structures of chains for tourism services such as hotels and airlines. Agricultural commodity chains offer a further challenge to this typology. The coffee chain has some elements in common with both producer-driven and buyer-driven types, but neither is adequate to describe its governance structure. The coffee chain has large TNCs that rely on global sourcing, and control markets through advertising and brand names, as in Gereffi's buyer-driven chain. But, as in Gereffi's producer-driven chains, these TNCs assemble components (different types of coffee) provided by a global network, manufacture the final product, and control forward linkages into distribution and marketing. Finally, Gereffi's two types are inadequate for describing the governance structures of the production and initial processing stages of the coffee chain, which are located in the coffee producing countries. Actors such as state coffee agencies, marketing boards, locally based firms, and peasant unions can all very directly affect the rules and structures of this portion of the coffee chain. They are difficult to fit into Gereffi's two types, because his types focus primarily on the TNCs that dominate the major consuming markets. This is another aspect of his overemphasis on TNCs and de-emphasis of states in the governance structures of chains.

Gibbon (2001) has recently proposed a third type of governance structure which, he claims, is found in many "traditional" primary commodity chains: the international trader-driven chain. The organizing firms in this case are giant TNC trading houses that typically trade in a variety of commodities. They obtain supplies of commodities from all over the world for other firms that process them into final form for sale to consumers. They exercise a loose and indirect form of governance over their suppliers, based mainly on price, volume, and reliability. They make their profits on the huge volumes of commodities that they trade, because per-unit profits are very low. They specialize in logistics, including knowledge of where to find supplies of different commodities, and of how to ship and insure them; and in financial services, including access to large amounts of capital, and the ability to protect themselves from risk and increase profits by playing the commodity futures markets.

Gibbon's international trader-driven type is an important addition to Gereffi's typology, because it captures the central role of international trading TNCs in the coffee chain. Although the governance exercised by global traders is loose and indirect, it can still have a direct impact on all earlier stages of the chain right down to the direct producers. However, since his type also focuses primarily on the role of TNCs, it suffers from some of the same problems as Gereffi's typology. It doesn't fully incorporate the roles of other actors, such as states, in the governance structure of the early stages of the chain. For example, as Gibbon admits, some of the rules that are enforced by the TNC traders, such as those governing the grading and classification of coffee, are developed by state coffee agencies and marketing boards. Further, it says nothing about the role of the TNCs that manufacture coffee for the final consumer, which are separate from the trading TNCs that bring the green coffee into the consuming markets. The TNC traders exercise almost no governance over the portion of the chain that begins where the green coffee leaves their warehouses. In trying to fit the coffee commodity chain into the Gereffi-Gibbon typology, it becomes clear that each of their types applies to only one segment of the entire commodity chain. Gereffi's two types omit the extraction of the raw materials that go into the manufactured goods (e.g., the production of wool or cotton), while Gibbon's omits the production of the final product (e.g., coffee roasting). In fact, most commodity chains probably do not have a single governance structure. Rather, most chains are probably divided into a few segments, each having their own governance structures. Further, these governance structures may overlap and come into conflict. The best example in the coffee chain is overlap and potential conflict between the rules of the international traders and state policies in the producing countries, which both impact the growing and early processing stages of the chain. Therefore, in order to properly characterize the governance structures of commodity chains, we need to examine the flows along the entire chain, from the raw material to the final consumer, and all of the authority and power relationships that shape them.

One thing that is clear from this discussion of the governance of commodity chains is that it is a very complex phenomenon, and needs to be closely examined on a case-by-case basis for each commodity chain, and within the chain at each individual stage. It must also be related to Gereffi's other two dimensions of the structures of chains: the input-output structure and the distribution of production. Once we have completely described the structure of a chain, the next task is to analyze how and why it changes over time.

Using Gereffi's three dimensions, this could involve change in its input-output structure. New products might be invented, or new processing technology developed. This could add new stages to the chain, remove old ones, or alter the way the commodity flows between stages. For instance, the invention of the modern technique for producing instant coffee added a new strand to the chain, with a different type of product output. New inputs, different types of machinery and packaging materials, were required, creating new linkages to other chains. A second type of structural change might involve changes in the geographic location of certain stages of production, or in the types and sizes of firms doing the production in a particular location. The development of instant coffee production in coffee growing countries illustrates the former kind of structural change; the rise of small specialty coffee roasters in the 1980s illustrates the latter. Finally, there might be change in the governance structure, the authority and power relationships that set the rules for production, and for transactions along the chain. One very important change of this type in the structure of the coffee commodity chain has been the rise and demise of the International Coffee Agreements.

All of these types of changes in the structure of chains are ultimately the results "of the complex and diverse strategic choices pursued by households, states, and enterprises" (Gereffi, Korzeniewicz, and Korzeniewicz 1994, 11). In other words, all participants in the chain are struggling to improve their positions, relative to other participants in the chain; and the collective outcome of all of these struggles determines how the chain will change over time. Since these three dimensions are interrelated, change in one dimension may precipitate changes in the others. For example, the invention of instant coffee, a change in the input-output structure, opened the possibility for a geographic relocation of instant coffee production to the periphery. And because of the linked nature of the chain, change at any one stage of the chain can reverberate along the chain in both directions from the point of the initial change, causing additional structural changes. For example, the rise of the small specialty roasters changed the way that some coffee was grown and processed. This aspect of commodity chain analysis makes it a powerful tool for connecting the global and the local. The production processes that constitute the individual stages of the chain are local. They are carried out by people in particular places. At the same time, these local processes are linked to the other processes that constitute the chain, and the chain in turn is an integral part of the world economy. The commodity chain approach thus enables us to analyze how changes at the global level impact individuals "on the ground," engaged in particular economic activities. At the same time, we can understand how the outcomes of struggles over particular production processes at the local level can change the structure of an entire chain, and even of the world economy.

One aspect of this struggle by participants to improve their position in the chain, which has received significant attention in the literature, is "upgrading," or what I will refer to as forward integration. Forward integration is a strategy of extending one's control from a given point on the commodity chain to processing stages located further along the chain, toward the final consumption end. Because many commodity chains, particularly those for primary commodities like coffee, were established in the colonial period, the raw material ends of the chains have involved peripheral, low-profit activities, and the final consumption stages have been the ones where the most value is added, and the greatest profits are made. Forward integration has thus been a strategy employed by actors in the commodity producing regions, to increase their shares of income and profits. For coffee, this meant, first of all, gaining control over the growing and initial processing stages of the chain, up to the point where the green coffee was shipped out of the country. Then, it involved moving into the more advanced processing stages that prepared coffee for final consumption, which have typically been located in the consuming regions.

For Gereffi, "upgrading is a process of improving the ability of a firm or an economy to move to more profitable and/or technologically sophisticated capital- and skill-intensive niches" (1999, 51–52). It involves the ability of a firm to move up the learning curve, to acquire the kinds of skills necessary to successfully compete with the firms already established at the more advanced stage of the chain. Gereffi (1995) identifies three types of strategies that have been used to promote upgrading. The first is policy and institutional reform. This includes macroeconomic reforms by states, as well as changes in the institutional environment, such as improved infrastructure, education and training, and financial systems. It also includes adaptive and organizational innovations by individual firms, which increase their ability to take advantage of changing conditions in the world economy. The second is new relations with capital, involving the ability of states both to attract and manage foreign direct investment to promote development, and to enhance the abilities of local firms to compete globally. The third strategy involves participation in regional economic blocs. Here again, we see Gereffi's overemphasis on firms as the key actors that shape chains, with states playing a facilitative role.

These strategies seem specific to the commodity chain that Gereffi has focused on, the apparel chain, and to the region in which the most upgrading has occurred, the East Asian region. It is not clear whether they are generalizable to other types of chains or to other regions. Further, Gereffi does not identify factors which would help us to explain why some regions or firms are successful at upgrading and others are not. Gereffi (1995) does suggest that moving to more advanced processing stages is "perhaps the most successful strategy" open to countries dependent on raw materials exports (123), but he does not analyze this strategy. In his categorization of export roles, countries move from primary commodity exporting to various types of manufacturing export orientations unconnected to the primary products they export. In fact, it is only recently that the determinants of success in this strategy of primary processing-led industrialization have been analyzed in any detail.

Owens and Wood (1997) examined whether the processing of primary commodities offered an alternate path to export-oriented industrialization. They found that primary processing was similar to other types of "narrowly defined" manufacturing, and that the key factor was the skill of a country's labor force. A country with a rich endowment of natural resources would have a comparative advantage in primary processing if it also had a high level of skill per worker, measured by the average years of schooling in the adult population. Cramer (1999) argued that this factor alone did not provide an adequate explanation of successes or failures in particular cases, and identified additional factors such as state policies, external market conditions, and the relative strengths vis-à-vis one another of domestic and foreign capital and the state. But he also argued that country- and commodity-specific factors were important, and that the balance of all of these factors needed to be determined in particular cases. Schurman (1998) focused on the changing structure of international industry, particularly strategic decisions by leading TNCs that altered the profitability of different stages of the chain. She stressed the necessity for states to analyze the nature of their raw materials sectors in order to ascertain the feasibility of a forward integration strategy. This implies that the characteristics of different commodities and their chains also influence the chances for success at forward integration. Gellert (2003) also pointed to the characteristics of the commodity as one factor influencing outcomes of this strategy. He emphasized the importance of political alliances between states and local capital in the commodity exporting regions, as well as alliances between local and transnational capital, in determining the success of efforts to "move up" the chain.

Gibbon (2001) contrasted the type of upgrading that has been analyzed by Gereffi in the apparel chain, and by analysts of the fresh fruit and vegetable chain (e.g., Dolan and Humphrey 2000), both of which are buyer-driven, with the type of upgrading likely to occur in international trader-driven chains. The former chains, he argued, have been characterized by a process of externalization, in which the lead firms have spun off lower-profit operations, such as garment assembly or packaging of fruits and vegetables for final sale. This is part of the larger process, noted above, through which the most profitable activities in chains have been retained in the core areas, while the least profitable have been located in, or relocated to, the periphery. In the buyer-driven chains, Gibbon argues, firms located in peripheral countries have been able to upgrade by picking up these operations that the lead firms no longer wanted to perform. In the international trader-driven chains, there has been no such tendency toward externalization. This makes forward integration much more difficult, and makes state action to enhance the abilities of local firms to compete with the TNCs much more important, in these types of chains. Gibbon concurs with Schurman and Gellert that the structures of the individual chains also strongly influence the chances for success in this strategy.

However, there is another form of struggle through which actors located in the producing regions have attempted to increase the benefits they derive from participation in the chain, which has been overlooked in commodity chain analysis and in world-systems research more generally. This is what I call the strategy of collective action. It involves states in the producing regions banding together to try to change the governance structure of the chain, and it has been prominent in the coffee commodity chain, as well as in other tropical commodity chains. For theoretical insight that will help us to analyze this aspect of structural change in commodity chains, we need to turn to a body of work that has been developed primarily by political scientists, on the formation of international regimes.

Regime analysis grew out of the reactions of U.S. political elites and political scientists to the multiple economic shocks of the early 1970s, in particular, the success of the Organization of Petroleum Exporting Countries (OPEC) at raising the world market price of oil (Strange 1983). Krasner (1974), in an initial attempt to explain this success, set out seven conditions that enhanced the likelihood of collective actions by commodity producers. The first two were demand and supply unresponsiveness to price. These basic market conditions meant that producers could raise their income by restricting supplies, and that new supplies could not easily be found, at least in the short run. Third was a small number of producers, making coordination among them easier. Fourth was a lack of resistance by consumers; this factor took account of the collusion of the oil TNCs with OPEC, which Krasner viewed as crucial to its success. The final three conditions were that the producers shared a common experience, had the ability to take a long-term perspective, and shared values. However, this set of conditions dealt only with explaining why producers of a particular commodity might act collectively. The sweeping proposals for a New International Economic Order (NIEO), and its centerpiece, the Integrated Program for Commodities (IPC), presented by developing countries at the UN Conference on Trade and Development (UNCTAD IV) in Nairobi in 1976, were much more ambitious (UNCTAD 1978). They aimed to change the rules governing international trade in most of the primary commodities on which developing countries were heavily dependent. In response to these developments, political scientists began to broaden their thinking from the factors which would explain collective action by Third World states to the factors which would explain how international regimes were established and maintained, and why they broke down.

Krasner stated the generally accepted definition of regimes as follows:

> Regimes can be defined as sets of implicit or explicit principles, norms, rules, and decision-making procedures around which actors' expectations converge in a given area of international relations. Principles are beliefs of fact, causation, and rectitude. Norms are standards of behavior defined in terms of rights and obligations. Rules are specific prescriptions or proscriptions for action. Decision-making procedures are prevailing practices for making and implementing collective choice. (1983, 2)

Regimes are defined by their norms and principles; rules implement the norms and principles, and decision-making procedures allow for changing the rules within the regime. The norms and principles of a regime generally define a set of rights and obligations of all states. Thus the rules of a regime prescribe certain types of behavior and proscribe others (Haggard and Simmons 1987); they place limits on state action. Krasner (1976) argued that during periods in which there was a hegemonic power, trade tended to be free and open, while in periods of hegemonic decline, tariff barriers rose and regional trade blocs appeared. But once a free trade regime had been established, it tended to continue into the period of decline until brought down by a crisis. In other words, regimes were established by hegemonic states, but then tended, like most social institutions, to take on a life of their own.

Regime analysis was criticized on a number of grounds. Strange (1983) argued that it had a static and conservative bias, and ignored other types of institutional actors which govern international relations or international political economy, particularly TNCs. Haggard and Simmons (1987) criticized regime analysis for treating states as unitary actors and ignoring the effects of national political forces on the pattern of international conflict or cooperation. Ruggie (1983) criticized its narrow focus on maximization of power as the overriding goal of all states.

Ruggie (1983, 1992) attempted to extend and modify regime analysis to deal with these criticisms, through development of the concept of multilateralism. He defined multilateralism as "an institutional form which coordinates relations among three or more states on the basis of 'generalized' principles of conduct" which "logically entail an indivisibility among the members of a collective with respect to the range of behavior in question" and "generate among their members . . . expectations of 'diffuse reciprocity'" (1992, 571). The generalized principles of conduct exist prior to the establishment of a particular regime, whereas for Krasner, the establishment of principles and norms is a part of regime creation. For Krasner, principles and norms are established by groups of states pursuing a common interest; for Ruggie multilateralism influences the ways in which states define their interests. For Krasner, regimes are intervening variables between power and interests on the one hand and behavioral outcomes on the other; for Ruggie they are background variables which determine how interests are defined and how actions by other states are perceived (Kratochwil 1993).

Ruggie distinguished between international orders, international regimes, and international organizations. International orders are the broadest category, describing the general principles which govern entire domains of international activity, such as the international economic order. Regimes are sectoral components of international orders; thus norms and rules governing commodity trade in general or the world coffee market more specifically could be conceived of as regimes with varying issue-scope. Regimes may or may not be associated with formal international organizations. In this regard, Ruggie argued (1983) that the post–World War II economic order is best described as "embedded liberalism."

That is, it was a liberal or open economic order, but embedded in a social system in which state intervention in the domestic economy in order to achieve domestic stability was seen as legitimate. He argued that "the United States after World War II sought to project the experience of the New Deal regulatory state into the international arena" (1992, 592). Although Ruggie rarely referred to the Third World in his analyses, multilateral efforts to promote development were clearly consistent with the norms of this economic order. Underdevelopment posed a threat not only to the internal stability of Third World nations, but also to the international security order. In this case, concerted state interventions in world markets could be justified as efforts to stabilize the situation; demands by Third World states for the creation of international regimes to counteract the devastating effects of the declining terms of trade and market instability could be seen as legitimate.

Given the origins of regime theory, it is not surprising that political scientists began applying it to the analysis of commodity agreements, international agreements between producing and consuming states that regulated trade in various commodities. Finlayson and Zacher (1988) used a regime analysis to study the attempts to negotiate commodity agreements for the eighteen commodities included in the IPC. This included analysis of the five agreements which were concluded (for sugar, coffee, cocoa, natural rubber, and tin), as well as the unsuccessful attempts for copper, iron ore, manganese ore, bauxite, phosphate rock, tea, jute, hard fibers, cotton, bananas, tropical timber, oils and oilseeds, and bovine meat. They noted that developing countries have maintained remarkable unanimity on general principles and basic proposals for change. This unanimity stems from a common belief system: that the rules of the international economic order are biased against them; in particular that they generate unstable but declining terms of trade for primary commodity exports which damage developing economies. As a result the Third World is justified in taking collective action to remedy this situation, by forming cartels or negotiating agreements. Developed countries, which benefit from these biased rules, have an obligation to compensate the Third World, through commodity agreements that raise prices, or through other forms of compensatory financing. Despite this agreement on general principles, it has been much more difficult for producers of specific commodities to agree on regulatory measures and to persuade developed countries to go along. One of the main problems has been disagreement among producing states over market shares. Established producers want to retain their shares; new producers want to expand theirs. Another problem is caused by the price fluctuations which cooperation is intended to alleviate—it is much harder to hold a consensus on rules together in periods of rising or high prices. Finally, it is often difficult to apply sanctions against producers who violate the rules.

In addition, developed countries have often been reluctant to agree to proposals for many commodities. In part, this is due to opposition from the TNCs based in the developed countries. Developed country states have also been concerned about the effects of commodity agreements on inflation in their domestic economies. A common complaint about existing commodity agreements is that they have been much more effective in defending price floors than in defending price ceilings. Thus, when developed countries have agreed to participate in commodity agreements, it has been primarily for geopolitical and foreign policy reasons rather than for economic reasons. As we will see in chapter 3, this was a major reason for U.S. support of the coffee agreements.

Under these conditions, the achievements of the Third World in commodity negotiations have been relatively modest. Finlayson and Zacher judge the global commodity trade regime to be a relatively weak one. Most agreements have given veto power to the largest producers and consumers, and thus have imposed only minimal constraints on the actions of these states. Developed countries have generally agreed that excessive price fluctuations have damaged Third World economies, and have sometimes agreed to forms of market regulation to mitigate them. But the goals of Third World leaders have been primarily to raise prices and only secondarily to stabilize them. This has resulted in compromise language in the stated goals of commodity agreements, such as the one for coffee, which states its main goal as: "[to] assure adequate supplies of coffee at fair prices to consumers and markets for coffee at remunerative prices to producers . . ." (ICO 1982, 2). Seen from the perspective of regime analysis, this compromise language is intended to smooth over some basic disagreements between the Third World and developed countries over the norms of the commodity trade regime. It allows both sides to make politically palatable interpretations of the agreements for domestic consumption. But these disagreements also make agreement on the rules and decision procedures of specific commodity agreements more difficult; and these disagreements came into the open and were at the core of the failure of the IPC negotiations. International organizations monitoring commodity markets have provided forums for discussion, made information on commodity trade more widely available, and probably served to curb some of the worst excesses of TNCs and developed states. But, Finlayson and Zacher conclude, commodity agreements "have not transformed the character of global commodity markets" (291).

One of the most trenchant criticisms of international regime theory has been its neglect of domestic political factors (Haggard and Simmons 1987). Ruggie attempted to respond to this criticism by tracing the roots of embedded liberalism to the domestic politics of the New Deal in the United States. But another strand of theorizing in political science has attempted to more fully integrate domestic and international politics. The most influential early statement in this literature was Peter Gourevitch's "The Second Image Reversed" (1978). Waltz (1959) had labeled regime-type explanations which took state interests as given "first image" explanations, while those that sought the roots of foreign policy in domestic politics were "second image." Gourevitch reversed the second image by analyzing the impacts of the international system on domestic politics. He viewed the second image and its reversal as two sides of a process of joint causation, concluding: "International relations and domestic politics are therefore so interrelated that they should be analyzed simultaneously, as wholes" (911).

Bates (1997) uses this type of approach in his recent analysis of the political

economy of coffee. He argues that the foreign economic policies of Brazil, Colombia, and the United States, which led them to support the coffee agreements,
were the result of domestic politics. In each case the policies were "the outcome
of the efforts of politicians to gain and retain political office within a structure of
domestic political institutions, sometimes to the benefit of particular interests,
and other times not" (12). For instance, in Brazil, while coffee growers and merchants controlled the state government of Sao Paulo in the early 1900s, they
needed to forge alliances with politicians from other states in order to commit
the national state to international economic policies to defend world market
prices for coffee. It was only after the centralizing revolution of Getulio Vargas
and the creation of the Estado Novo that Brazil became able to effectively intervene in the international market. And ironically, this effectiveness came because
the coffee sector no longer influenced policy; instead the economic technocrats
sought to raise world coffee prices so that they could tax the coffee income and
use it for other programs.

    Bates also recognizes that international factors can reshape domestic politi-
cal economy. He notes that the coffee agreements compelled producing states to
regulate their coffee sectors. Different states at different periods chose different
ways of doing this, and these choices created winners and losers among domestic political groups, which changed their abilities to influence the further development of coffee policies. But his primary focus is really on domestic politics,
and he sees that as the root of most international policies. In this respect, he
moves away somewhat from equal attention to domestic and international factors, and toward more of a second image explanation.

    These concepts of multilateralism and international regimes are clearly
helpful in understanding how the governance structures of commodity chains are
established and changed over time. The call for a NIEO was an attempt to
change the rules governing international trade in a broad range of primary commodities simultaneously. But it also built on earlier, commodity-specific attempts by groups of developing countries to change governance structures by
establishing international regimes, most notably, the collective action by coffee
producing states that led to the International Coffee Agreements (ICAs) beginning in 1962. This aspect of change in governance structures has been virtually
absent from commodity chain analysis. At the same time, as pointed out by its
critics, regime analysis was completely state-centric, and ignored the existence
of TNCs. By focusing on the nation-state as the basic unit of analysis, it fell into
the fallacy identified by world-systems analysts. It explained the formation and
collapse of international regimes on the basis of the attributes of individual
nation-states, most centrally, their relative military and economic power. It
failed to see one of the most important underlying factors: the way different
nation-states were linked together because of their participation in the different
stages of commodity chains. And by ignoring TNCs, it failed to account for the
ability of TNCs, through political pressure exerted on states, to shape the rules
of international regimes in their interests. However, the focus of regime theory
on nation-states nicely complements the overemphasis of commodity chain

analysis on TNCs and the insights of regime theory add an important dimension to commodity chain analysis. They enable us to explain more completely how and why the structures of chains change over time, as a result of the struggles of participants located all along the chain to improve their positions.

One of the most important objects of these struggles is, as one would expect in a capitalist economy, money. Actors located all along the chain attempt to increase the income and the profit they derive from their participation (Hopkins and Wallerstein 1994). The commodity chain can be viewed as a series of transactions, beginning with the sale of the raw product to the first stage processor, and ending with the sale of the finished product to consumers. These transactions may take place on a free market; they may be completely removed from the market, as in transactions between divisions of a vertically integrated firm; or they may be structured by oligopolistic sellers and/or oligopsonistic buyers using long-term contracts only indirectly affected by supply and demand conditions. Analysis of the structure of transactions all along the commodity chain is necessary to answer a fundamental question: who benefits? The amount of value added to the product at each stage of the chain, and who appropriates the profit from that stage, are determined by the structure of the chain: its input-output structure, its distribution of production, and most importantly, its governance structure. Participants in the chain thus struggle to change its structure in ways that will cause more profit to flow to them. In commodity chain analysis, the "excess" profits that result from these types of structural changes in chains are referred to as "rents."

Kaplinsky and Gereffi have both discussed the sources of rents along a commodity chain. Kaplinsky (1998) developed a typology of nine different types of rents. Gereffi (1999) used this typology to argue that lead firms in producer-driven and buyer-driven chains obtained different types of rents. Following this logic, and applying it to Gibbon's international trader-driven type of chain, we might expect that the TNC traders that are so important in the coffee chain have their own distinctive pattern of sources of rents. But as we have seen, there are other important actors who shape the structure of the coffee chain, and therefore influence the distribution of benefits. Each different type of actor obtains a different mix of rents. For the TNCs that manufacture coffee for sale to consumers, the main type of rents is product and marketing rents, based on "product identity, product differentiation, and product innovation" (Kaplinsky 1998, 25). These rents are derived from brand names and slogans, like: "Maxwell House—Good to the last drop," now owned by Philip Morris. These TNCs also earn technology rents, for inventors of new technology that improves productivity. But this might also include the invention of new products, such as Nestle's invention of spray-dried instant coffee. For the international traders, finance rents are the most important. According to Kaplinsky, these rents accrue to those who are financially innovative and able to secure access to capital on the most favorable terms. In the case of coffee trading TNCs, the major source of these finance rents is the coffee futures market.

There are several different types of rents available to participants in the coffee producing countries. First there are resource rents. Resource rents are based on differential costs of extraction or production. For coffee, owners of land that produced particularly high quality coffee, such as regions of Guatemala, Kenya, or Indonesia, would receive resource rents because their coffee would command a premium on the world market. But so would producers in Brazil, who have a very low cost of production relative to other producers growing similar grades of coffee. Related to this are infrastructural rents. These rents are based on a comparative advantage in transportation and communication technology that allows firms in some locations to compete more efficiently than firms in other locations. For coffee, this type is more of a "negative" rent that penalizes producers with particularly poor infrastructures, such as landlocked Uganda, which has to rely on an uncertain rail link through Kenya to Mombassa for the export of its coffee. Policy rents, which derive from political restrictions that protect or restrict access to markets, are also available to producing countries. Examples would be the protectionist policies associated with import substitution or the non-tariff barriers currently associated with phytosanitary standards. For coffee, and other tropical commodities, the most important trade policy rents have been associated with preferential market access, as under the Generalized System of Preferences, or the Lomé Agreement. These have generally benefited the poorest coffee producing countries. Producing countries have also received some technology rents, derived from developing coffee hybrids that mature faster, produce greater amounts of coffee, or are resistant to common diseases of the coffee tree. While it might seem that coffee producers are in a favorable position because there are so many different potential sources of rent available to them, we will see that most of these rents are relatively small, and they pale in comparison with the amounts of rents extracted by traders and manufacturers.

Kaplinsky includes rents generated by a cartel, through restricting supplies to raise the price, in the category of resource rents. This is in keeping with the classical political economists' usage of rents as deriving from scarcity (in their day, scarcity of productive land was most important). However, as we will see, this has been the most important source of rents for producers in the coffee chain, and it has derived not from a cartel, but from a negotiated agreement between producing and consuming states. For this reason, it seems more appropriate to put these rents, generated by market intervention, into a separate category, which I will call "regulation rents."

Finally, there is another type of policy rent that has been an important source of revenue for both producing and consuming states: taxation. This type of rent has been overlooked by commodity chain analysts, once again, because of their focus on TNCs. States in the consuming countries tax imports of green coffee, and also tax coffee consumption. In some European countries the value-added tax (VAT) adds significantly to the price of a cup of coffee. States in the producing countries also levy taxes on coffee exports, and this has been a major source of state revenues in many producing countries. In fact, these states can potentially capture large proportions of all of the rents discussed above as being available in producing countries. Since most producing states have historically very closely regulated their coffee production and processing sectors, they have determined who has received most of these various rents: small or large coffee growers, processors, middle-men traders, exporters, or the states themselves.

When commodity chain analysts have examined the factors that determine where the largest rents or the highest profits are located along the chain, they have focused almost exclusively on just one: the relative degree of monopolization or competition that exists at each stage of the chain. Hopkins and Wallerstein (1994, 18): "the most important question is the degree to which the box is relatively monopolized by a small number of units of production, which is the same as asking the degree to which it is core-like and therefore a locus of a high rate of profit (often misleadingly called the 'value-added')." Gereffi (1999, 43): "Profitability is greatest in the relatively concentrated segments of global commodity chains characterized by high barriers to the entry of new firms." Kaplinsky (2000, 126): "The central driver is the prevalence of competition which forces down profits by lowering barriers to entry, and which increases as producers in more and more countries enter global trade." While the degree of monopolization and competition is certainly an important factor, it is not the only one. As becomes clear once the insights of regime analysis are taken into account, states can impose rules on the chain that shift the distribution of income and profit independent of the degree of monopolization. However, as Kaplinsky (1998) emphasizes, this distribution of profit is dynamic, and participants along the chain are always searching for "the Nth rent," the next new source of additional profit.

Theoretical Grounds: Food Regimes and Systemic Cycles

The preceding discussion has focused on describing the structure of a chain and analyzing how it changes over time, at the level of the commodity chain as a unit of analysis. But as stated above, a commodity chain can't be analyzed as an independent, self-contained unit, because it is an integral part of the world economy. Analysis of the changing structure of a particular chain, such as the one for coffee, must proceed in parallel with analysis of the changing structure of the world economy. For this, we need to draw on two other areas of world-systems analysis: food regime theory, and systemic cycles of accumulation.

Food regime theory, originally developed by Harriet Friedmann, has analyzed the increasing industrialization and globalization of food production and trade. The recent work of Friedmann and McMichael (Friedmann 1991a, 1991b, 1993; McMichael 1992b; Friedmann and McMichael 1989) has identified and analyzed two distinct food regimes that have governed international agricultural production and trade. The first, established during the imperialist period (ca. 1880–1914), was characterized by the rapid increase of food production in the settler states, and by food exports from these states that competed directly with European agriculture. This new form of agricultural trade between nation-states supplanted the traditional colonial trade in tropical agricultural products as the most important dynamic shaping the world food system. The first regime broke down during the economic crisis following World War I, but the U.S. model of agriculture as an integrated sector of a national industrial-capitalist economy formed the basis for the second food regime, which was established under U.S. hegemony following World War II. This second regime was based on regulation of national economies by independent nation-states (Fordism in the United States and Western Europe, and state-led industrialization in the Third World), but was increasingly undercut by the rapid expansion of TNCs as the organizers of global production and trade.

Friedmann (1991a) identified three major agri-food complexes of this second regime, all of which were undergoing a process of transnationalization:
(1) the wheat complex, involving agricultural subsidy programs in the core which led to overproduction of wheat and other grains, and rapidly expanding grain exports to the Third World, led by U.S. "food aid" (Friedmann 1978, 1982);
(2) the durable food complex, involving import substitution by TNCs of ingredients produced in the core for "traditional" tropical imports from the Third World (e.g., beet sugar and high fructose corn syrup for cane sugar), for use in increasingly highly processed foods sold on core consumer markets; and
(3) the livestock/feed complex, involving transnational integration and industrialization of the commodity chains leading from agricultural products through livestock feed, livestock, and finally to meat products sold in core markets and increasingly to the rich and middle classes in the Third World (what Sanderson [1986] refers to as the emergence of the "world steer").

The second food regime was thrown into crisis by the combined energy-food-currency shocks beginning in about 1970. The increasing transnationalization of food production outlined above had undermined the possibility of national regulation of agricultural production. The debt crisis and World Bank/IMF policies of structural adjustment and export promotion began to force Third World producers, whose traditional exports had been undercut by transnationalization, into new specializations in "non-traditional" agricultural exports, also organized by the TNCs.

Friedmann and McMichael (1989) identified several tendencies at work in the struggle to create a new globally organized third food regime:
(1) the Uruguay Round of GATT negotiations, in which the United States sought to extend "free trade" to previously excluded agricultural markets, to enable U.S.-based agricultural TNCs to gain access to protected markets in Europe and Japan, in order to further extend their control over international agricultural production;
(2) the emergence of the NACs (New Agricultural Countries, a term coined by Friedmann), semi-peripheral industrial-agricultural exporters who could compete with the United States and Europe on increasingly liberalized world agricultural markets, leading to trade wars; and
(3) the introduction of biotechnology, increasing tendencies toward substitutionism, the diversification and standardization of agricultural inputs into the

industrial food system of the TNCs, and appropriationism, the introduction of new industrially produced inputs into the agricultural system, making all agricultural producers more heavily dependent on "proprietary seed-chemical packages" controlled by the TNCs (Goodman 1991).

Friedmann (1993) also identified a countertendency that could lead to a more democratically controlled new food regime. This arose from recent concerns about the relationship between diet and health, food safety, the environmental damage done by large-scale intensive agriculture, and the increasingly unequal distributions of incomes and access to food, leading to the spread of hunger, even in developed countries. This tendency was toward locally produced food for local consumption, using more organic methods, sensitive to local diets and environmental conditions, and under local control. Obviously, this tendency is less well developed than the one toward globalization, but as we will see in chapter 8, it has had an important impact on the coffee commodity chain.

More recently, McMichael (1996, 2000) has broadened this approach to analyze the change in the mode of regulation of the entire world economy, of which the breakdown of the second food regime was an integral part. McMichael characterizes this larger change as the shift from the "development project" to the "globalization project." The development project was an attempt to stabilize capitalism, to ensure a steady pace of capital accumulation, by putting the primary responsibility for managing national economic growth on the national state. Trade was used as a stimulus to growth, but was seen as subject to regulation by states, acting either individually or collectively. The model of national regulation was developed in the core countries (United States, Europe), and spread to the Third World as decolonization proceeded, where it became "developmentalism." Developmentalism had failed on its own terms by the 1980s, by failing to "develop" any but a handful of Third World countries. It was finished off by the debt crisis and the structural adjustments of the 1980s, and replaced by the globalization project. The roots of the breakdown of the development project can be traced to the multiple crises around 1970 that also ended the second food regime. The growth of the petrodollar market following the huge increases in the price of oil in the 1970s was the source of the funds lent by commercial banks to the failing Third World developmentalist states, which precipitated the debt crisis and structural adjustment.

These accounts of the second food regime and the development project are consistent with Ruggie's description of the regime of embedded liberalism. Although they differ in interpretations, they all agree that state regulation of the economy was a basic foundation of the post–World War II economic order. Ruggie would probably not agree, however, that this economic order ended around 1970.

According to McMichael, "the globalization project seeks to stabilize capitalism through global economic management—this time along the lines of specialization, rather than replication" (1996, 31). The development project, in which national development was managed by national states, and the agricultural sector was an integrated part of the national economy, attempted to replicate the U.S. model. The globalization project sought to create specialized agricultural sectors that were integrated into a global rather than a national production system. To do this, the globalization project restructured states, changed their role in the economy by reducing their capacity for economic regulation, and delegitimized state intervention in the economy more generally. State regulation became subordinate to trade promotion, and there was a move toward global economic governance, the creation of institutions that could enforce the withdrawal of states from economic regulation.

McMichael also sees a countertendency to this shift to global regulation, in the rise of "cosmopolitan localism," a term he borrows from Wolfgang Sachs, as referring to "the assertion of diversity as a universal right, and the identification of locality as globally formed" (2000, 269). McMichael uses the Zapatista rebellion as a prominent example of this tendency. The movement toward locally produced and organic food discussed by Friedmann is obviously a part of this larger movement.

However, coffee and other tropical commodities play a peculiar role in Friedmann's and McMichael's scheme of food regimes. What they call the first food regime is based on the export of food, primarily grains, from the settler states. It replaces a regime that came before, based on the colonial trade in traditional tropical products. Since this came before the first food regime, it must have number zero. This trade complex in tropical commodities is not analyzed as part of the first and second food regimes, nor as a part of the present crisis that may be coalescing into a third food regime. But as we will see, coffee and the tropical products more generally are still important parts of the world economy. Changes in the structures of their chains were part of the larger changes in the food regime and in the mode of regulation of the world economy. Because of this inattention to the tropical commodities, these analyses tend to overlook the poorer peripheral countries that are still major exporters of these traditional tropical commodities, many of which are neither NICs nor NACs.

The food regime and regulation approaches, like the commodity chain approach, focus on the central role of TNCs as organizers of global production. Unlike the commodity chain approach, they tend to conceptualize TNCs as an undifferentiated "global capital" which imposes its will through the multilateral institutions. Core states exercise control over these multilateral institutions, in the interests of "their" TNCs. But peripheral states are viewed as reactive. They attempt to find niches in the global production system, but they do not act to directly shape the regulatory regime. On the other hand, Ruggie's concept of multilateralism focuses solely on the role of states in creating international regulatory regimes, and ignores the role of TNCs. While Ruggie tends to give short shrift to less powerful peripheral states, his conceptual framework allows for the possibility that they can be directly involved in the construction of regimes that change the governance structures of commodity chains. Combining these perspectives gives us a more balanced framework with which to analyze the structure of the world economy of which the coffee chain is a part.

The periodization of changes in the world economy presented by both the food regime and regulation approaches, of a post–World War II economic regime that was fundamentally transformed by a series of crises around 1970, is put into an even broader framework of cycles in the capitalist world economy by Giovanni Arrighi's theory of systemic cycles of accumulation. Arrighi (1994) argued that the development of the capitalist world economy over the last five hundred years can best be understood as consisting of four systemic cycles of accumulation with similar structures: the Genoese, Dutch, British, and U.S. These cycles are designated by the hegemonic power that served as the center of capital accumulation during each cycle. Each cycle begins with a period of crisis of the previous regime, during which there is instability and increasing competition for capital. Then, a new regime is consolidated, initiating a period of material expansion, during which capital is rapidly accumulated by developing the means of production, under the direction of the new hegemonic power. This material expansion leads to a crisis of overaccumulation, initiating a new period of financial expansion, increasing instability, and renewed competition for capital, which establishes the conditions for the rise of a new hegemon.

The main achievement of the British cycle of accumulation was to draw the entire world into a single world market, or more precisely into a single social division of labor based on industrial production (Arrighi 1994, 250–53). The "discovery" of the rest of the world and the initiation of world trade in products such as spices, sugar, coffee, tea, and cocoa took place during the Genoese and Dutch cycles. But a single, integrated system of international inequality was the creation of the British "cosmopolitan-imperial" regime, which extended the division of labor to the areas that produced these products. As Arrighi states, "[u]nder the Genoese regime, the world was 'discovered,' under the British it was 'conquered'" (219). The essence of the division of labor established in the British period, then, is the roles assigned to the different areas in the world division of labor. The colonized areas became suppliers of mass quantities of raw materials to feed the industrial machine, and the new working class that operated it, in Britain and the other core countries of that period, and also served as markets for its products. The stimulants, such as coffee and tea, played an important role in the process, because they served to keep the working class sober and alert as they labored in the "satanic mills."

In Arrighi's framework, extensive cycles alternate with intensive cycles, so while the global division of labor was established during the British cycle of accumulation, it was consolidated under the U.S. cycle. During the crisis period dividing these two cycles, the colonial empires of the British period were broken up, and under the U.S. cycle the world economy was nominally divided into "national" economies. The newly independent former colonies received their own national states and nominal sovereignty within an interstate system; however, their roles in the international division of labor as suppliers of raw materials and markets for finished products remained essentially the same. The integrated national economy of the United States served as a model for these newly independent nations. But under the rubric of this model, U.S.-based TNCs became, in Arrighi's words, "so many 'Trojan horses' in the domestic markets of

other states" (294), reinforcing the positions of the former colonies in the consolidating world division of labor and international system of inequality. To be
sure, there were innovations involved. One of the most important was the spinning off of routine, labor-intensive manufacturing operations to the semiperiphery. But this was carefully managed by the TNCs and the U.S. state so as to
avoid creating any serious competition with the operations of the TNCs. The
convergence here with McMichael's development project, and Friedmann's second food regime, is clear; however, Arrighi focuses more clearly on the raw
materials exporters as a key part of the world economy.

The signal crisis of the U.S. regime occurred around 1970, marked by the
U.S. defeat in Vietnam, the breakdown of the Bretton Woods system of fixed
exchange rates, and the declining legitimacy of the U.S. anticommunist crusade.
This marked the beginning of a period of financial expansion. According to Arrighi, periods of financial expansion are driven by overaccumulation crises.
There is excess capital in search of profitable investments in the expansion of
material production and trade, driving down rates of profit. In response to this
development, capital is increasingly invested in various kinds of financial deals
and speculation, which yield higher profits than investments in production, as
well as preserving the liquidity of capital, so that it can be shifted quickly to
more profitable opportunities. One result of this financial expansion is a concentration of capital, but another is increasing instability. Arrighi argues that the
U.S. government response to this instability was to abandon the ideal of state
management of the national economy and to put its faith in the "self-regulating
market," in the hopes that this would preserve the competitive advantage of
U.S.-based TNCs on the world market, and maintain U.S. hegemony. But rather
than just benefiting U.S.-based TNCs, the new ideology of the self-regulating
market has enabled all core-based TNCs to tighten their control over production
located in the peripheral and semiperipheral regions of the world, through their
control over financial capital. This has enabled them to squeeze additional profits out of these regions to fuel their capital accumulation. Once again, Arrighi
provides a broader understanding of the crisis of 1970, and of the current period
of instability, than Friedmann and McMichael by grounding it in a larger cycle
of the world economy, driven ultimately by the search for profit and accumulation.

Arrighi draws here on Polanyi's (1957) concept of the self-regulating market, which according to Polanyi, generates a double movement. The extension of
the self-regulating market, that is, a market free of any political regulation, depends on the assumption that three "fictitious commodities" can be treated exactly the same as any other commodity; these are land, labor, and money. These
three must be freely exchanged on markets, with their prices determined by the
unrestricted interplay of supply and demand. Polanyi argues that the extension
of the self-regulating market on these terms creates tendencies that are destructive of human society. A free market in labor destroys the social relationships
that hold society together; a free market in land leads to environmental destruc-
tion that undermines the ability of a society to support itself; a free market in

money destabilizes any social organization of production. Hence, the double movement: the extension of the self-regulating market inevitably creates a movement for social protection against its ravages.

Polanyian double movements have figured prominently into the history of the coffee commodity chain during the period analyzed here. Typically, what has happened is that the extension of a free world market for coffee has unleashed the tree crop price cycle, described in the next chapter. This has led to low coffee prices, which have caused economic crises in the coffee growing regions. Coffee growers and others who depend on coffee for their livelihoods have then pressured the states to take action to protect them from the forces of the market. This has been one of the main factors behind the collective actions undertaken by coffee producing states, which have resulted in the institution of international regimes to manage the world market, under the ICAs. In the Conclusion, I argue that another of these double movements is underway during the current crisis of coffee, which could (and should) lead to a new agreement to regulate the market.

All of these theoretical approaches provide important elements for the analysis of the evolution of the coffee commodity chain since World War II, which is the task of this book. Changes in the coffee commodity chain have occurred in its input-output structure; in its geographic distribution and in the types and sizes of firms involved in production; and most importantly in its governance structure. All of these changes have resulted from struggles and alliances among the various participants in the chain, who have been trying to improve their positions, and the shares of benefits they receive from their participation. They have used forward integration and collective action strategies in their struggles. All of these changes have been strongly influenced by larger cycles in the structure and mode of regulation of the world economy, in particular, the shift from the period of U.S. hegemony and material expansion up to about 1970, to the period of hegemonic decline and financial expansion since then. But in addition to this larger cycle, there have been several cycles of Polanyian double movement, which at times have coincided with the larger cycles of accumulation, and at times have run counter to them. The evolution of the chain can only be explained by understanding the complex interaction among all of these forces over time and at all of the different stages of the chain.

The complex comparative analysis involved in applying this theoretical framework to the study of the coffee commodity chain requires methodological guidance. The method most consistent with this theoretical orientation is McMichael's method of incorporated comparison, discussed in the following section.

Methodological Grounds: Incorporated Comparison

Charles Tilly (1984) has identified four basic types of comparative-historical analysis. He classifies methods on two dimensions: whether they aim at propositions which cover only one or all instances of a given phenomenon, and whether they attempt to demonstrate that all instances of the phenomenon have a common form, or allow for multiple forms. Combining these two dimensions yields four types of analysis: individualizing, universalizing, variation-finding, and encompassing comparisons. These can be exemplified by considering how they might be applied to the study of coffee. Individualizing comparison focuses on the peculiarities of each case. This would involve comparing the coffee commodity chain to other commodity chains in order to clarify what is unique about coffee. Universalizing comparison seeks to find a general rule or theory that can explain all cases. This would involve constructing a general theory that could explain all commodity chains. While the latter type of comparison is far too ambitious a goal for this study, if it is even possible, the former is not ambitious enough; the other two types seem more useful.

Tilly's third type is the variation-finding comparison; this attempts to categorize cases into different classes and explain the differences between them. There is an element of variation-finding in the analysis presented in this book, in that it identifies tropical commodity chains as a unique class and attempts to explain how and why they differ from other types of commodity chains. But this is really only the starting point of the analysis, because it also seeks to use the analysis of tropical chains to say something about larger processes such as globalization and the growth of international inequality. Finally, there is encompassing comparison, which places instances at different locations within a larger system and explains their characteristics based on their relationship to the system as a whole. This method comes closest to the aims of this study, and involves understanding the nature of the coffee chain as a result of its location within the larger world economy. This is not surprising, as this is the method Tilly identifies with Wallersteinian world-systems analysis. However, Tilly also reiterates the major criticism that has been leveled at this method: "It leads effortlessly to functional explanations, in which a unit behaves in a certain way 'because of' the consequences of its behavior for the system as a whole" (125–26).

McMichael (1990, 1992a) seeks to overcome this problem by developing a method of incorporated comparison. The problem, McMichael contends, occurs when one begins analysis with a preconceived notion of what the larger system is and how it works. Then, once one has placed the instances being compared within the larger system, it becomes easy to commit the fallacy of deducing the characteristics of the instances from the assumed properties of the whole. But, McMichael argues, the specific instances together make up the whole, and therefore the whole cannot be known prior to comparative analysis of its constituent parts. The whole, or the structure of the larger system, emerges as a "self-forming whole" through this analysis.

McMichael identifies two forms of incorporated comparison. The multiple or diachronic form involves comparison across time of multiple instances or moments of a single world-historical process. Thus the struggles of coffee producers, oil producers, or bauxite producers were all instances of a larger historical process of Third World states trying to overcome their situations of underdevelopment within the world economy. This analysis seeks to understand the place of coffee in that larger process, through analyzing the similarities and differences between the struggles of coffee producers and those of the producers of other commodities. But more importantly, it seeks to understand the relationship among these struggles, how coffee served as a model for the producers of other commodities, and how coffee producers learned from other struggles. The larger historical process is the sum of all of these particular struggles, and cannot be understood prior to careful analysis of each of them. Similarly, globalization is a large world-historical process that is currently receiving much attention. But globalization occurs through the particular ways in which the commodity chains for coffee, apparel, or automobiles are reorganized within the world economy. Globalization can't be understood prior to an analysis of how coffee has been reorganized, how its reorganization is similar to or different from the reorganizations of other commodity chains, and how they are all interrelated. Thus through the use of the multiple form of incorporated comparison, this study contributes to our understanding of two of the major world-historical processes which have occurred (and are still occurring) in the postwar period.

McMichael's second form of incorporated comparison is the singular or synchronic form. It involves comparison across space of particular instances within a single world-historical conjuncture. In the case of coffee one of the most important conjunctures turns out to be the late-1970s coffee boom. But the boom was not a unitary process; it occurred as the sum of the forms that the boom took in each producing country, including the ways in which states and growers in each country reacted to it. The forms that the boom took in each country were all interrelated, because all countries, states, and growers were participants in the coffee commodity chain. The nature of the boom itself, and more importantly its implications for the future evolution of the coffee commodity chain, can only be understood after careful comparative analysis of these forms. McMichael argues that the best analysis emerges from creative combinations of these two forms of incorporated comparison, and that is what is attempted here.

The analysis presented below began with a detailed reconstruction of the evolution of the structure of the coffee commodity chain over the postwar period, paying particular attention to the roles played by producing states, consuming states, and TNCs. As I was producing this reconstruction, I was continually comparing it with the simultaneous evolution of other tropical commodity chains and of the world economy more generally. These comparisons revealed several important aspects of the particular case of coffee. For instance, collective action by coffee producers to increase their export earnings actually predated the actions of most other primary commodity producers, including oil producers. This suggested that the ICAs may actually have served as a model and an inspiration for later actions by other groups of producers.

I then began comparing different periods in the history of the coffee chain, focusing on how the structure changed over time, and particularly on changes in the distribution of benefits along the chain. These comparisons revealed key turning points in the evolution of the chain. Although I had gone into the study thinking that the most important turning points in the evolution of the coffee commodity chain were the changes in regulatory regimes, these comparisons showed that this was not necessarily the case. Certainly the beginning of the first ICA in about 1962 was a major turning point, but the end of the quotas in 1972, the signing of the third ICA in 1976, and the reinstatement of quotas in 1980 were not, for a variety of reasons. Some had to do with the situation in the coffee market, for instance the fact that prices were rising in 1972, or the fact that coffee producers were cooperating privately to regulate world market prices during the 1972–1980 period. Others had to do with the situation in the world economy more generally, particularly the early-1980s worldwide recession. Instead, the coffee boom of the late 1970s emerged as one of the key turning points, primarily because of the way producing countries reacted to it, and the seeds of overproduction and dissension among producers which these reactions produced. Also, the consolidation of control by the TNCs during the merger and takeover frenzy of the 1980s turned out to be a key development, which may have been equally important for the future evolution of the chain as the collapse of the ICA in 1989 and the subsequent price crash. The major features of the story of the coffee commodity chain that is presented below emerged out of these kinds of theoretically driven incorporated comparisons of selected key periods or locations in the history of coffee.

Chapter 2

Material and Historical Grounds
for the Analysis

Material Grounds: The Coffee Commodity Chain

The coffee commodity chain is a relatively simple one; it is depicted schematically in figure 2.1. The major participants in the chain are indicated by boxes; the transactions that move coffee from one type of participant to another are indicated by arrows. Coffee flows up the chain from the growers who start it to the consumers who complete it. Transactions that move the coffee from producing countries to consuming countries constitute the world market. The structure of the chain depicted in figure 2.1 and described below was typical during most of the period considered here; however, as we will see, there have been significant changes in the structure during this period, which will be described in more detail in the chapters that follow.

The ecology of the coffee plant is what makes it a tropical commodity.[1] Arabica coffee is actually a subtropical crop, requiring an average annual temperature between 17 and 25 degrees Celsius, but preferring an even narrower range around 20, with as little variation as possible through the day or the year. It requires a minimum of 1200–1500 millimeters of rainfall per year, evenly distributed over the year, except for a not-too-hot dry season of around 10–12 weeks. These fairly stringent ecological requirements are found only within the tropics, and at altitudes of about 3,000–6,500 feet, depending on latitude. Not surprisingly, these specifications describe the climate of the Ethiopian highlands where arabica coffee is thought to have originated. Robusta coffee, which is a different species of the coffee family, is a more tropical plant, native to Central and West African rain forests. Its average annual temperature requirements are in the range of 20–26 degrees Celsius, with somewhat higher rainfall requirements, and it is therefore grown at lower altitudes in the tropics, generally under

Figure 2.1: The Coffee Commodity Chain

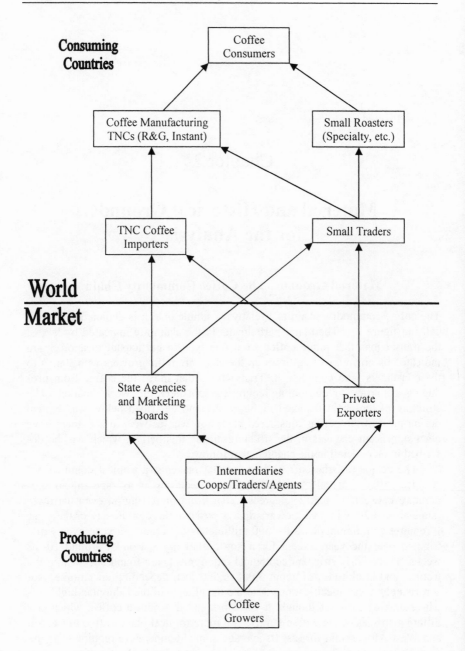

three thousand feet.

Coffee grows as a red "cherry" on a bush which grows to about six feet in diameter and can grow to over twenty feet high, but which is usually topped periodically to facilitate picking, and to stimulate the growth of side branches and flowering. This bush is generally referred to as a coffee tree, because coffee is a tree crop, that is, a crop that does not bear any fruit for three to five years after planting. Then, a coffee tree will continue to bear for at least another fifteen years, although many trees are stumped (chopped off to allow a new tree to grow) or replanted sooner than this, because the tree's productivity declines slowly with age after the first several bearing years. A mature coffee tree will produce, on average, enough coffee cherries per year to yield one pound of roasted coffee. Coffee trees generally produce two crops per year, one in the spring and one in the fall. The spring crop is usually larger, but which months this falls in depends on location, north or south of the equator. Coffee trees also tend to produce in a two-year cycle, in which a large crop one year is followed by a smaller one the next year, as the trees "rest."

Inside the coffee cherry are two seeds. These seeds are dried and the white seed coating (called the "parchment") is removed, yielding green coffee beans. Both parchment coffee and green coffee can be stored for several years under proper conditions without losing too much of their final coffee flavor, but green coffee is lighter and considerably less bulky. This makes green coffee the ideal form for the long-distance trade between the producing countries and the core markets. The arabicas, which account for about 75 percent of world production, have a larger bean, and are generally considered to have a superior taste. Robusta produces a smaller, flatter bean, which has a harsher taste considered inferior by most coffee drinkers. The robusta variety also has a higher caffeine content.

There are two general methods for processing the cherries into parchment coffee. In the dry method, the whole cherry is dried in the sun, and the dried fruit is removed by threshing. This method requires no special equipment, but produces an inferior flavor. In the wet method, the fresh cherry is removed by a depulping machine, which crushes the cherry and separates the lighter fruit from the heavier seeds. The parchment coffee, with a thin mucilaginous layer surrounding it, is soaked overnight; the mucilage is allowed to ferment slightly, and then is washed off. The parchment coffee is then dried, either in the sun or in electric dryers. The wet method produces a better flavor from the coffee, but requires more specialized equipment and careful handling. The cherries must be depulped within twenty-four hours after picking. Depulping machines are needed to do this, but they can be fairly primitive; small hand-cranked or gas-powered machines have been manufactured in many coffee growing countries for many years. Relatively large amounts of water are also required for the depulping, soaking, and washing. Most robusta coffee is processed by the dry method, since the taste improvement obtained is usually not worth the extra time and cost of wet processing. Arabicas are processed by both methods. The milling off of the seed coat or parchment is a more capital-intensive process, requiring larger, more sophisticated machinery to crack the hard shell and separate it from the green bean without damaging the bean. Since the wet and dry processing methods can both be done on a small scale with simple technology, they are more likely to be done by the growers, who, in most producing countries are small-to-medium size farmers. The processing into green coffee is usually done by large growers or exporters.

Arabica coffees (also called milds) are further divided into three subtypes, depending partially on the processing method used. Brazilian arabicas, about 40 percent of total arabica production, are generally dry processed. This subtype includes coffee from Brazil, Paraguay, and Ethiopia. Colombian milds, the second subtype, accounting for about 25 percent of total arabica production, are generally wet-processed; they are grown in Colombia, Kenya, and Tanzania. All other arabicas are included in the third subtype, about one-third of total arabica production, called the "other milds." These are mostly wet-processed coffees from Central America, Mexico, and other Latin American countries, as well as Asian producers such as Indonesia and Papua New Guinea. But this type also includes wet- and dry-processed coffees from smaller producers such as India and several African countries. Robusta coffees are grown mainly in western, central and southern Africa and in Asian countries (Indonesia, Thailand, Vietnam), as well as in Brazil and Ecuador. There are a total of about fifty countries that produce some coffee for export. The characteristics of these four types determine the kinds of "export niches" (Gereffi and Korzeniewicz 1990) available to the different producers on the world market: Colombian and other milds are considered best for fresh brewing and bring the highest prices. Brazilians are slightly lower priced and used extensively in TNCs' commercial blends, and robustas are lowest priced and considered less suitable for fresh brewing, but produce a higher yield of instant coffee than the arabicas.

Once coffee is in the green bean form, it must be moved from the producing regions to the consuming regions by ship. This involves a transaction between an exporter in the producing country and an importer in the consuming country, who typically makes the shipping and insurance arrangements for the coffee. Who the exporters are varies by country. In Latin American and Asian countries, there is usually a mix of private exporters and state coffee agencies. In some countries, the state agencies just regulate the private exporters through export tariffs, export licenses, and minimum export price requirements. In other countries, the state agencies export some of the coffee themselves. In African countries, there is a mix of state marketing boards and agencies along with some private exporters. In Anglophone countries, there are usually state marketing boards that have a legal monopoly on coffee exporting, although some allow private exporters to operate as well. In Francophone countries, there are state agencies that regulate the internal trade in coffee and set export prices. They may export the coffee themselves, or leave it to private exporters. The coffee importers buy the green coffee either on order or for their own account. On order means they have an order for a certain type and grade of coffee from a coffee roaster, and they buy the coffee to fill that order. In this case, the importer transports the coffee to the roaster as soon as it arrives. "Own account" buying means that the importer buys the coffee and holds it in their warehouse, and then offers it for sale for immediate delivery to roasters.

Once the green coffee arrives in the consuming country, the only processing required to make it ready for consumption is roasting and grinding. But there are several different strands to this segment of the commodity chain. For the period under consideration here, the most important one is through a large roasting company that roasts, grinds, and packs the coffee and then sells it wholesale to a retailer (supermarket, food store, or large discounter). A more recent strand is the specialty market, where the green coffee is sold to a smaller roaster who roasts and packages the whole beans to sell in their own retail outlets. In the food service strand, the coffee is roasted and usually also ground, and sold to a company that sells brewed coffee (restaurant, hotel, etc.). Then there is office coffee service, in which a large roaster supplies not only coffee but also brewing equipment to a business that provides free coffee for employees, for the ubiquitous coffee break. All of these strands involve the same process: the roasting (and possibly grinding) of the green coffee. Over the period considered here, roasting has gone from an art that required long training to a computer-controlled industrial process, although the specialty coffee roasters have brought back "art" roasting in small batches. The other important strand at the consumption end of the coffee chain is instant coffee. For the production of instant coffee, the green coffee is roasted, ground, and brewed in an industrial system designed to extract the maximum amount of soluble coffee solids from the roasted coffee. The resulting extra-strength coffee liquid is processed by spray- or freeze-drying to obtain instant coffee, and then wholesaled like regular roasted and ground coffee. This strand is the most technologically sophisticated and capital-intensive way of processing coffee into final consumption form.

The fact that coffee is a tree crop has significant economic implications. Because coffee trees don't begin to produce for three to five years after planting, supply responds very slowly to price. In the absence of any intervention in the market, this tends to produce recurring tree crop price cycles. If world market coffee prices are high, growers will plant more coffee, but the coffee from this new planting will have no effect on the market for three to five years. Growers will tend to overplant as prices remain high, sowing the seeds of a glut on the market three to five years later. On this side of the market, if world market prices fall because of oversupply, the coffee trees continue to produce, and the grower has sunk capital in these new trees, and so continues to harvest it. Oversupply and low prices thus tend to persist for several years, until prices fall below the costs of production for growers in at least some countries. Growers stop maintaining their trees, and production declines. As the low prices continue, growers may lose their land because they are not able to pay back loans. Growers begin to abandon their farms, or to pull up the coffee and plant something else; and this eventually lowers supply and raises the price. But on this side of the market as well, supply tends to overshoot, because these decisions are being made by thousands of small growers in many different countries. More trees are taken out of production than necessary to balance supply and demand, and new shortages arise. This ushers in a new period of high prices and the cycle starts all over again (see Edwards and Parikh 1976; Ford 1978). Several price cycles like this have occurred during the period analyzed here; however, they were never this simple, because political factors intervened. The courses and the outcomes of the cycles were determined by the political strategies employed by the various participants in the coffee chain, most importantly, TNCs, producing country states, and consuming country states.

Tree crop price cycles often trigger a Polanyian "double movement." Karl Polanyi (1957) argued that the extension of the "self-regulating market," that is, a market free of any political regulation, depended on the assumption that three "fictitious commodities" could be treated exactly the same as any other commodity. These fictitious commodities are land, labor, and money. For the self-regulating market to function, these three must be freely exchanged on markets, with their prices determined solely by the unrestricted interplay of supply and demand. Polanyi argued that the extension of the self-regulating market on these terms created tendencies that were destructive of human society. Hence, the double movement: the extension of the self-regulating market inevitably creates a movement for social protection against its ravages.

In coffee growing regions, the local economy depends on coffee income. When coffee prices are very low, growers cannot afford to buy the necessities of life. This affects everyone in the local economy who sells those necessities, and impairs their abilities to buy their own necessities, setting off a downward economic spiral. In addition there is a high seasonal need for labor to harvest the coffee, and consequently, a large number of people who depend on the income they earn during the harvest season. During periods of very low prices, growers cannot afford to hire harvest workers, or cannot afford to pay them even a subsistence wage, and many people suffer severe economic hardship as a result. Periods of low coffee prices can thus disrupt the fabric of society in precisely the ways that Polanyi described.

The double movement is particularly important for the period analyzed here, because during part of this period, the world market was regulated by a series of international agreements that dampened the swings of the tree crop price cycle. When one of these agreements was suspended, and the self-regulating market was allowed to operate, the tree crop price cycle returned, leading to a prolonged period of low prices. The resulting economic devastation generated pressures on coffee producing states to do something to relieve the suffering. States in the coffee producing countries were forced to respond for two reasons. First, coffee is primarily a smallholder crop. Approximately twenty to twenty-five million people in the producing countries depend directly on coffee for their livelihoods. The economic impacts of low coffee prices are severe and are felt on a national scale. A state that fails to respond in some way may easily lose its legitimacy in the eyes of the people. Second, the states themselves are dependent on coffee earnings. Coffee is often a major source of export and foreign exchange earnings and thereby, of tariff revenues to the state. A state that fails to respond risks its ability to carry out its programs and ultimately to maintain control over its territory. During the period since World War II, the way states have typically responded to these pressures has been to attempt to regulate the world market to maintain prices.

The preceding discussion has laid out the material conditions of coffee production. These conditions set limits on the structure of the chain and on the ways in which it can be restructured as various participants struggle to improve their positions along it. The analysis of the structure of the chain and its evolution over time must be grounded in these material conditions. The analysis must also be situated in the context of the larger structure of the world economy, and the best way to do this is by situating coffee as the archetypal tropical commodity.

Material Grounds: The Tropical Commodities

The identification of the tropical commodities as a distinct class takes off from the work of Harriet Friedmann and Philip McMichael on food regimes. Friedmann (1991a) identified three major agri-food complexes that were reorganized during what she called the second food regime, between the end of World War II and about 1973, as described in the previous chapter: the wheat complex, the durable foods complex, and the livestock/feed complex. But as was noted there, her work overlooks the importance of a fourth agri-food complex, the tropical commodity complex. This is shown in table 2.1, which lists the leading primary commodities exported by Third World producers in 1970 and 1988, ranked in order of the total value of Third World exports in 1970.[2] For each commodity, the table shows the total percentage of world exports accounted for by Third World exporters, and the total percentage of world imports taken by core countries.

The three complexes that have been identified by Friedmann and McMichael can be seen in this table. The wheat complex is exemplified by wheat and wheat flour, which are produced mainly in the core and exported to the Third World. Core countries accounted for over 90 percent of total world exports, and over half of them went to the Third World; this pattern was already well established by 1970. The effect of the durable food complex can be seen in the case of palm oil. Palm oil is included with the tropical oils in 1970 in table 2.1, because its trading pattern matched those of the other members of this category. However, by 1988 the core share of world imports of palm oil had dropped from 75 percent to 28 percent, because it had been substituted for by temperate oils like canola, soy, and corn oils in core markets. Rice, although not part of the durable food complex, has a similar trading pattern—the Third World accounts for over half of world exports, but over 80 percent of those exports in 1970 and more than two-thirds of them in 1988 went to other Third World countries. The livestock/feed complex is visible in soybeans and soybean oil and coarse grains, two major constituents of feed, and in beef. These products are produced in and

Table 2.1 Export Earnings and Trading Patterns for Major Primary Commodity Exports of the Third World, 1970–1988

Commodity	1970 Total Third World Export Earnings[a]	1970 Third World Share of World Exports	1970 Core Share of World Imports	1988 Total Third World Export Earnings	1988 Third World Share of World Exports	1988 Core Share of World Imports
Crude oil	13,721	89.6	83.5	87,535	68.2	80.6
Coffee	3,006	97.2	95.8	9,394	88.3	92.3
Sugar[b]	1,899	74.8	81.6	7,924	68.2	70.2
Cotton[c]	1,686	66.6	78.2	7,012	54.9	64.4
Tropical timber[d]	1,346	100.0	87.7	8,488	100.0	76.1
Copper[e]	1,188	73.9	98.2	2,889	61.0	82.0
Nat. rubber	1,103	98.1	84.3	4,844	97.1	67.8
Iron ore	1,060	39.9	99.4	3,318	44.3	85.3
Tropical oil[f]	928	89.4	87.2	1,633	81.8	80.4
Palm oil				2,484	95.9	28.3
Cocoa	860	99.1	96.9	2,537	95.4	91.4
Rice	676	54.9	17.1	2,334	59.7	32.2
Tea	620	89.4	68.0	1,954	86.0	54.0
Beef	563	29.2	94.8	1,381	12.2	83.6
Coarse grains[g]	482	27.2	87.0	1,530	12.0	67.2
Bananas	459	92.2	94.8	1,906	94.4	94.2
Hides, skins	278	21.6	95.0	725	9.5	72.4
Bauxite	231	86.5	97.3	808	88.1	86.5
Phosphate	228	54.7	85.5	1,063	65.0	71.4
Wool	215	14.3	92.1	572	9.2	74.4
Jute[h]	208	95.5	77.5	622	87.2	67.8
Wheat, flour	177	5.0	47.7	1,060	6.3	42.2
Tin ore	161	89.1	71.5	1,142	80.7	73.0
Manganese	96	57.3	97.5	211	45.9	83.5
Soybeans/oil	88	5.5	82.3	2,753	31.5	65.0
Hard fibers[i]	88	97.8	91.0	244	69.5	90.9

Source: 1970 data are from UNCTAD, *Yearbook of International Commodity Statistics, 1984*, except for crude oil data, which are from UNCTAD, *Commodity Yearbook, 1988*. 1988 data are from UNCTAD, *Commodity Yearbook, 1990*. The core here includes USSR and Eastern Europe, except Yugoslavia. Other socialist countries (China, Vietnam, Cuba, etc.) are included in the Third World.
[a]Millions of U.S. dollars.
[b]1970 figure is for raw and refined sugar; 1980 figure for raw sugar only.
[c]1970 figure is for cotton linters only; 1988 includes cotton yarn.
[d]Nonconiferous timber exported from the Third World, including sawlogs, veneer logs, sawnwood veneer sheets, and plywood. Third World share of exports = 100 percent by definition. See note 3.
[e]Copper ore plus blister (unrefined) copper.
[f]Groundnuts and groundnut oil, copra and coconut oil, palm nuts and kernels, palm kernel oil, and palm oil. See note 3.
[g]1970 figure for maize only; 1988 figure includes barley, rye, oats, and other cereals, n.e.s.
[h]1970 figure for jute fiber only; 1988 figure includes jute products.
[i]1970 figure for sisal and abaca fibers only; 1988 figure includes henequen and coir, and manufactures of all these fibers.

traded primarily among core countries. Table 2.1 shows similar trading patterns for iron ore, hides and skins, and wool. The fall in the core share of world imports for these commodities between 1970 and 1988 reflects the extension of the livestock/feed complex, and of the intra-core trade more generally, to the NICs and the global upper class. In particular, the increase in the Third World share of exports of soybeans and soybean oil is due to the rapid expansion of exports from Brazil and Argentina, and reflects the integration of Latin America into the livestock/feed complex (Sanderson 1986). However, table 2.1 shows that even some commodities which are produced mainly in the North, and which are involved mainly in intra-core trade, are still major exports and important sources of foreign exchange earnings for some Third World countries.

The fourth complex, the tropical commodities, are produced in the Third World and consumed primarily in the core. Friedmann and McMichael see this pattern of production and trade as characteristic of the colonial period, and don't consider the role these commodities have played in the evolution of the world agricultural system since World War II. However, table 2.1 shows that these commodities remain very important sources of income for Third World producers; thus their role in the restructuring of the world economy since World War II needs to be taken into account. The class of tropical commodities shown in table 2.1 includes coffee, sugar, tropical timber, natural rubber, tropical oils and oilseeds, cocoa, tea, bananas, jute, and hard fibers. All of these commodities were included in UNCTAD's Integrated Program for Commodities.[3] These commodities have several characteristics in common. One of the most important characteristics of tropical commodity chains is the central role of ecology in the determination of their structures. First, this determines their South-North trading pattern and explains its durability. Since these crops can only be profitable produced in tropical climates, their production can not be relocated away from the Third World, and their major consumers continue to live in the core countries.[4] In addition, no suitable industrially or core-produced substitutes have been found for most of them (natural rubber was one of the earliest tropical products to be partially replaced by a synthetic substitute produced in the core, and sugar and tropical oils have been partially substituted for in the durable food complex, but these are still major Third World exports to the core).

A second characteristic common to the tropical commodity chains is that production of these crops has proved exceedingly difficult to mechanize, meaning that there is a large (and often seasonal) demand for labor associated with their production. Third, all of these crops need some kind of preliminary processing soon after they are harvested. Coffee cherries must be depulped or dried quickly, sugar cane must be crushed, and bananas packed and refrigerated to retard spoilage. So this initial processing stage must occur close to the point of production. Fourth, economies of scale vary at this early stage and influence who controls it. Some crops, such as coffee or cocoa, can be processed in small batches with rudimentary technology. They present few economies of scale and can be grown and initially processed by peasants and small farmers; control over the early stages of these chains tends to remain with the growers or with local

Table 2.2 Market Concentration and Export Dependence for the Top Eight Tropical Commodities, 1967 or 1970

COFFEE			SUGAR		
Exporter	Market Share	Dependence on Coffee	Exporter	Market Share	Dependence on Sugar
Brazil	33.2	44.3	Cuba	39.9	83.2
Colombia	14.6	63.2	Philippines	10.3	18.9
Angola	5.6	51.9	Dominican Rep.	6.1	57.7
Côte d'Ivoire	4.8	32.5	Mexico	5.9	8.5
El Salvador	4.5	47.7	Brazil	5.7	5.0
Uganda	4.4	53.3	Mauritius	4.1	94.5
Guatemala	3.2	35.2			
Total	70.3		Total	72.0	

TROPICAL TIMBER			NATURAL RUBBER		
Exporter	Market Share	Dependence on Timber	Exporter	Market Share	Dependence on Rubber
Malaysia	25.6	19.5	Malaysia	50.1	31.9
Philippines	21.5	23.6	Indonesia	22.0	23.4
Côte d'Ivoire	7.8	21.5	Thailand	9.5	15.1
Korea	7.7	11.1	Sri Lanka	6.6	22.3
Indonesia	6.5	8.3	Liberia	3.2	16.9
Total	69.1		Total	91.4	

TROPICAL OILS			COCOA		
Exporter	Market Share	Dependence on Trop. Oils	Exporter	Market Share	Dependence on Cocoa
Philippines	17.2	16.8	Ghana	31.6	73.5
Nigeria	13.2	11.1	Nigeria	24.5	23.1
Malaysia	10.3	6.4	Brazil	13.4	5.1
Indonesia	7.3	7.2	Côte d'Ivoire	10.5	20.4
Senegal	5.7	36.3	Cameroon	6.8	30.7
Zaire	3.9	5.6	Ecuador	3.9	12.6
Brazil	2.5	1.0			
Sri Lanka	2.2	7.2			
Papua N.G.	2.1	26.4			
Total	64.4		Total	90.7	

Continued on next page

Table 2.2 Market Concentration and Export Dependence for the Top Eight Tropical Commodities, 1967 or 1970 (continued)

	TEA			BANANAS	
	Market Share	Depen-dence on Tea		Market Share	Depen-dence on Bananas
Exporter			Exporter		
India	45.1	15.7	Ecuador	16.7	43.8
Sri Lanka	38.9	65.1	Honduras	14.5	42.5
Kenya	3.7	13.9	Costa Rica	13.6	29.3
Malawi	2.2	27.2	Panama	12.2	53.0
			Colombia	3.6	2.5
			Martinique	3.0	49.7
			Guatemala	2.9	5.0
Total	89.9		Total	66.5	

Source: Data for coffee, sugar, cocoa, and tea are for 1967, from UNCTAD, *Handbook of International Trade and Development Statistics*, 1976. Data for tropical timber, natural rubber, tropical oils, and bananas are for 1970; market shares from UNCTAD, *Yearbook of International Commodity Statistics*, 1984, and export dependence from UN, *Yearboook of International Trade Statistics*, 1972–1973 and 1974.

capitalists or the state. Crops such as sugar and bananas do have economies of scale at this early stage. Sugar mills need large volumes of cane in order to keep them operating continuously; large volumes of bananas must be packed and chilled in one place in order to ship them efficiently. These crops tend to be grown on large-scale plantations, and present opportunities for TNCs to invest in the growing and processing stages, integrating backward and exercising much more complete control over the chain than is feasible for coffee or cocoa.

For coffee, the fact that it is a labor-intensive crop with no economies of scale in production and early processing has important implications. It has been estimated that the growing and processing of coffee in the producing regions provides employment for as many as twenty million people. The level of the world market price for coffee, and the way that price is divided up amongst the various participants in the coffee chain within the producing countries, have a significant impact on these people's lives. In addition, since so many people depend on coffee for their livelihoods, the states in the producing regions cannot afford to be indifferent to the price of coffee. If it falls too low, and stays there too long, their countries experience economic crisis. And if the states can't act to influence the price of coffee, their legitimacy suffers.

If we focus on the exporters of tropical commodities, we can see two additional characteristics of their trading pattern: export dependence and resource power. Table 2.2 shows the export dependence of the major Third World exporters of tropical commodities in 1967 or 1970, near the end of the second food regime period. It also shows that a number of countries depended on more than one of these commodities, so that looking at only one commodity understates their dependence. Brazil appears four times in this table, for a total tropical commodity export dependence of 55 percent (coffee, cocoa, sugar, and tropical oils). Sri Lanka (95 percent), Côte d'Ivoire (74 percent), Philippines (59 percent), Malaysia (58 percent), and Indonesia (39 percent) are heavily dependent on combinations of three different tropical commodities. But even this table understates the total dependence of many of these countries. For example, Ecuador, which got 56 percent of its export earnings from bananas and cocoa, is not listed in table 2.2 as a coffee exporter because of its small market share, but an additional 20 percent of its export earnings came from coffee. Eight additional producers with smaller market shares also depended on coffee for at least 20 percent of their export earnings; an additional seven countries with small market shares depended on sugar for at least 20 percent of their export earnings.

At the same time, many of these major tropical commodity exporters had as their primary international trading partner their former colonial power.[5] Table 2.3 shows that the colonial trading pattern for coffee persisted even into the 1990s. Brazil and Colombia were the exceptions. They were the two largest exporters, and both had strong quasi-state coffee growers' federations with a great degree of control over state coffee policy, which led to aggressive state-capitalist initiatives to find new markets for their coffees. The destinations of their exports most closely matched the distribution of total world imports. The Central American producers tended to export disproportionately to the U.S. market, and the African producers exported disproportionately to the old colonial powers in the European Economic Community (EEC), and to other importers, mainly Asian NICs, the Middle East, and other African coffee importers (see note a, table 2.3). Indonesia, the major Asian producer, exported both to Europe, the old colonial power, and to Japan, the new regional capitalist power. This same pattern can be seen for other tropical commodities as well. For example, 52 percent of Brazil's cocoa exports in 1990 went to the United States, while 36 percent of Ghana's went to the U.K. Similarly, 31 percent of Nigeria's 1990 rubber exports went to the U.K., while 42 percent of Côte d'Ivoire's went to France. These patterns were even more pronounced during the 1960s and 1970s, heightening the sense in producing countries that low world market prices were a part of their colonial legacy, and increasing the pressure on their states for market intervention.

Table 2.2 also shows the concentrated nature of market shares in world markets for these commodities. For coffee, the seven largest exporters controlled 70 percent of world exports; six sugar exporters controlled over 70 percent of world exports. The five top exporters of tropical oils and natural rubber controlled almost 70 percent and over 90 percent of world exports respectively. Five exporters controlled over 80 percent of world cocoa exports; four tea exporters controlled almost 90 percent of world exports; and seven banana exporters accounted for over 65 percent of world exports. Market shares were somewhat more dispersed for tropical oils, where the top eight exporters accounted for over 60 percent of total world exports. Because of their heavy export dependence, the major producing states were thus forced to consider tropical commodity export policies as central elements of any economic development strategy,

Table 2.3 Destinations of Coffee Exports from Major Coffee Producers, 1990

	U.S. and Canada	EEC	Other Europe	Japan	Other[a]
			Importer		
Share of Total World Imports[b]	22.1%	46.5%	10.2%	6.9%	14.3%
Exporter		Importer's Share of Exporter's Exports			
Brazil[c]	28.8	35.0	13.3	8.0	14.9
Colombia[c]	21.2	50.5	9.3	7.9	11.1
Mexico[b]	85.3	8.0	2.8	1.4	2.5
Guatemala[b,d]	63.6	26.5	8.7	6.0	0.0
El Salvador[b]	30.6	38.4	1.8	1.7	27.5
Costa Rica[b]	21.8	43.5	18.6	3.8	12.3
Honduras[b]	31.2	32.7	14.0	17.5	4.6
Côte d'Ivoire[b]	3.5	39.0	1.1	0.8	55.6
Kenya[b]	5.6	43.9	14.6	0.4	35.5
Uganda[b]	7.7	49.6	0.9	2.1	39.7
Zaire[b]	0.7	51.4	2.6	0.0	45.3
Ethiopia[b]	11.6	31.4	3.8	12.8	40.4
Tanzania[b]	1.0	48.2	4.4	8.3	38.1
Indonesia[c]	11.2	47.6	1.2	18.4	21.6
Papua New Guinea[b]	2.9	52.0	2.5	1.9	40.7

Source: UN, *International Trade Statistics Yearbook 1990* (New York, 1992), Trade Matrix Tables. These figures are for SITC 071, which includes instant and other processed forms of coffee.
[a]This table includes only the eighteen largest coffee importers. Other large importers, which account for an additional 9.4 percent of imports, are (in order of total value of imports): Algeria, Australia, Korea, Portugal, Singapore, Argentina, Saudi Arabia, Israel, Andorra, Morocco, Hong Kong, Ireland, South Africa, Lebanon, Sudan, Malaysia, New Zealand, Jordan, Senegal, Kuwait, Turkey, and Egypt.
[b]As reported by the importing country.
[c]As reported by the exporting country.
[d]Due to different time periods used in reporting by the importing and exporting countries, figures add to more than 100 percent.

and their concentrated market power gave them the capacity for collective action to increase their export earnings from these commodities.

These tropical commodities became important items for mass consumption in the European core at a time when they were produced primarily under the direct control of colonial administrations. Thus they were initially incorporated into intra-national trade within colonial blocs. But as the system of nation-states was completed with the former colonies gaining their independence, and as the model of national economic regulation was extended within this system, tropical commodities increasingly entered into international trade. The geographic pattern of trade remained the same; only the form of its political regulation changed. The tropical commodities that had been produced in the colonies for metropolitan consumption became by default the major exportable products of the newly emerging nation-states, and export taxes on them became a major source of government revenues. The colonial legacy of these new nation-states was symbolized by their dependence on tropical commodity exports traded with former colonial powers, which earned low and decreasing prices on world markets. At the same time, the tropical nature of these commodities gave their producers a potentially high degree of market power. They reacted by organizing collectively, in a logical extension of their individual anticolonial movements, to exert their market power, restructure world markets, and improve their terms of trade. Thus it is clear why the tropical commodities became the central focus of the Integrated Program for Commodities (IPC) and the call for a New International Economic Order (NIEO).

In order to understand this process and the implications it had for the structure of the world economy and the development prospects of the Third World, this study focuses on coffee. Coffee is the most important of the tropical commodities, and the second-biggest revenue source for Third World countries among all of their primary commodity exports; only oil exports have earned them more.[6] In addition, although the top coffee exporters had somewhat less market power than the exporters of other tropical commodities such as rubber, cocoa, or tea, they were more successful in regulating the world market. This book analyzes the reasons for this anomaly.

Having placed the coffee commodity chain in the context of the larger world economy, we now need some historical grounds for the analysis, in order to understand how the coffee chain arrived at the situation it was in at the end of World War II.

Historical Grounds: A Brief History of the Coffee Trade

Arabica coffee is probably indigenous to the highlands of Ethiopia. The origins of coffee as a beverage are unclear, but it was being cultivated and used as a beverage by the Arabs in what is now Yemen (just across the Red Sea from Ethiopia) by the fifteenth century. From there, it spread through the Arab world to Constantinople, where European travelers got their first tastes of it. By the early 1600s, it had been introduced into Europe, and coffee houses spread rapidly through Italy, France, England, and the rest of the continent. But Arab traders controlled the cultivation of coffee, and, realizing that they had a monopoly on a highly desired product, strictly forbade the export of any seeds; they parboiled all beans before export to make sure they could not be germinated. According to legend, this monopoly was eventually broken by an Indian pilgrim to Mecca, who smuggled out a few seeds and planted them in Mysore. Later, the Dutch took a few seedlings from Southern India and planted them in Java. A

Dutch botanist carried several seeds from these trees in Java and grew a few coffee trees in a greenhouse in Amsterdam. One of these plants was later presented to Louis XIV as a gift. The Dutch then sent some seedlings from Amsterdam to their colony in Surinam, and the French sent some seedlings to their colony in Martinique. Most of these died, but one in Martinique and a few in Surinam survived. From trees propagated in Surinam, some seeds were later sent to Brazil, where the first coffee was planted in 1727.

From the one tree in Martinique, coffee gradually spread through the Caribbean and then to Guatemala, El Salvador, Colombia, and the rest of Latin America. Thus almost all of the coffee trees now growing in Latin America are direct descendants of a few seeds from Java, transported via Amsterdam and Paris. Catholic missionaries played a key role in this propagation. Coffee was also introduced to East Africa around 1900 by Catholic missionaries. And ironically, although it had probably originated there, the seeds for these plantings came from the Caribbean, completing a five-hundred-year journey around the world.

In part because all of these trees came from such a limited genetic stock, arabica is highly susceptible to a variety of diseases and pests. Over 330 separate fungi and bacteria that attack coffee plants have been cataloged. The most important clearly is coffee leaf rust, which killed off the original plantations in Ceylon and Java, and which is now spreading through Latin America. In addition, over 850 species of insects feed on coffee. Most of these are of very limited importance, but a few are major pests; in particular, the coffee berry borer worm (broca) that is now attacking coffee in Colombia and other Latin American countries (FAO 1947; Wrigley 1988).

Robusta coffee is indigenous to Central and West Africa, and there the cherry was picked unripe, boiled, dried, and chewed as a stimulant. French colonists found robusta growing wild there, and recognized its similarity to arabica coffee. They began to cultivate it, and spread it more widely through West and Central Africa. Seeds from the Congo were brought to Brussels and cultivated in a greenhouse there, and some seedlings from these plants were obtained by the Dutch and brought to Java in 1900. Although Java had been one of the original places where arabica was planted, and was the source of the highest quality arabicas in the mid-1800s, its plantations were attacked by coffee leaf rust, and were nearly wiped out by the end of the century. Robusta was resistant to leaf rust and was planted to replace the devastated arabica. Ceylon was the other major source of arabica coffee in the mid-1800s, and its plantations were also attacked by leaf rust; in this case, the coffee was replaced by tea. These developments left Latin America, and particularly Brazil, as the world's major supplier of arabica coffee by 1900 (Wrigley 1988).

The legacy of colonialism is clear in this early history. The reason that coffee spread around the world and the reason that it is grown in so many different countries today, is that it was carried by colonists looking all over the planet for ecological niches that would produce good coffee. As Mintz (1985) has shown, sugar, along with the bitter stimulants coffee, tea, and cocoa, became important sources of colonial power for Britain, as well as essential consumption items for the growing industrial working class. In Britain and other European powers, coffee and tea, sweetened with sugar, gradually replaced beer and wine as working-class beverages. This created a sober working class that was essential for the efficient operation of industrial machinery and for the attendant record-keeping needed to keep the system running. Tea won out as the preferred beverage in Britain, due in large part to the British East India Company monopoly and the fantastic revenues that the British colonial state was able to derive from the trade (Mintz 1985; Schivelbusch 1992). This in turn led to the United States becoming a coffee-drinking country, when the British attempt to extract revenues from the tea trade to its American colonies provoked the colonists to revolt.

The Latin American countries gained independence in the early 1800s, before they became the world's major suppliers of coffee. Coffee was established as a plantation crop in the Caribbean and Brazil. But, as Topik (1998, 61) states, "A colonial planter class created by sugar growing and extermination of the native population and a pre-existing thriving Atlantic slave trade explain this arrangement more than any inherent demands of coffee." In Brazil, he argues, the strength of the coffee planters and their influence on the state were the main reason that it was the last Western country to abolish slavery, in 1888. The slave labor system was replaced by the *colono* system. Almost a million Portuguese, Spanish, and Italian immigrants were attracted to Brazil to replace the slaves, "the only instance in history in which massive numbers of Europeans crossed the Atlantic to work on semitropical plantations" (1998, 45). However, these *colonos* were not coerced labor, and frequently moved from plantation to plantation, and many either returned to Europe or bought their own land in Brazil. The legacy of this system, along with a particular geographic quirk, determines the unique production system of Brazil today. Unlike other Latin American coffee producers, the coffee lands of Brazil are relatively flat and more suited to extensive, large-scale production. There was also ample land available for coffee cultivation, so production was increased by bringing more land into cultivation rather than by intensifying production on existing land. Thus most coffee in Brazil today is produced on large-scale, capitalist, diversified farms, and production is more mechanized than in any other producing country. Further, most coffee is produced by a low-cost method of stripping the branches of all cherries at once, and then dry processing them, rather than selectively picking only the ripe ones, and wet processing them. The system produces vast amounts of coffee at very low cost, but sacrifices quality for quantity.

The history of coffee in other Latin American countries, such as Colombia and Costa Rica, was different. Coffee did not become a major export crop until after independence. While large estates were established initially, large is a relative term—they were small by Brazilian standards. The terrain was much more rugged, and transportation systems were primitive. There was no way to produce massive amounts of coffee and get it easily to a port. They had to compete with Brazil by producing higher quality coffee, which required much more labor-intensive methods. The coffee had to be carefully maintained, selectively picked, and wet processed. Because there were no slaves available and labor was in short supply, peasant farmers using family labor were the most efficient producers. They could grow and process the coffee up to the parchment stage, and then transport it by mule to the nearest road or railroad. In addition, they practiced mixed agriculture. The coffee was grown under the shade of plantains, bananas, or other fruit trees, and interplanted with other food crops for the family's subsistence (Topik 1998).

According to Arrighi's (1994) periodization of systemic cycles in the world economy, the phase of material expansion under British hegemony began near the end of the 1700s, and ran until about 1870. Initially, the expansion of production occurred mainly in Britain (the "Industrial Revolution"), but by the 1840s, this had begun to yield diminishing returns. Capital goods were increasingly exported from Britain. Part of this larger trend was the export of railroad iron and steel and other machinery to Latin America. This improved the transportation infrastructure in Latin America, and tied it more closely to the European markets, setting the stage for what Topik and Wells (1998) have labeled the "export boom," 1850–1913, during which Latin American exports grew 1000 percent. These exports accounted for about one-third of total world exports of tropical products, and coffee was the most important of them. By the early 1900s, about 90 percent of the world's coffee came from Latin America. However, as would happen repeatedly during the twentieth century, the expansion of coffee production triggered the tree crop price cycle, as explained above. This led to an oversupply of coffee and falling world market prices around the beginning of the twentieth century. As the falling prices began to affect the coffee growers, they began to pressure their states to do something about it.

Brazil, by far the world's leading producer, accounting for about 70 percent of total world coffee exports, responded with the first state intervention into the coffee market. With this market share, Brazil had the market power to influence prices through unilateral intervention. At first, the Brazilian federal state refused to intervene, but the coffee planters controlled the Sao Paulo state government, and instituted the first "coffee valorization" plan in 1906. Fearing a bumper crop in that year that would have caused the already low price to collapse completely, the state government bought about eight million bags of coffee—over half of Brazil's production and about one-third of total world production—and held it off the market. This stabilized the price in 1906; however, the coffee still needed to be sold off over the next several years, in such a way as to not exert too strong a downward pressure on prices. This was facilitated somewhat by the two-year coffee cycle, since the 1907 crop was significantly smaller than that of 1906. But all of the coffee was not finally disposed of until 1916. The state needed a massive amount of financing to carry out the plan, to pay for the coffee purchases, storage, and insurance until the coffee was finally sold. Despite the fact that the world economy had by this time moved into the phase of financial expansion in the period of British hegemony, the European bankers were initially unwilling to get involved in this financial speculation. The London Rothschilds, the leading financial house of the time, publicly declined to participate in this interference with free trade, which made other European banks reluctant to advance funding. A consortium of coffee traders and banks was eventually put together by Herman Sielcken, head of one of the two largest coffee trading firms in the United States, to fund the plan. As the Paulistas continued to need additional funding to pay for the storage of the coffee while it was being liquidated, control over the coffee eventually passed into the hands of a valorization committee headed by Sielcken. He used his control over this coffee, which by then was stored in New York, to corner the New York market and raise prices there during 1909–1912 (Holloway 1975).

The 1906 valorization was generally regarded as a success in Brazil. It maintained coffee prices through the bumper crop of 1906, and planters eventually benefited from the higher prices caused by Sielcken's manipulation of the market. As the plan proceeded, the Rothschilds eventually became involved in some of the later financing of the stock-holding operation. And, as the financial obligations of the Sao Paulo state government mounted, the Brazilian federal state was eventually drawn into participation in guaranteeing the loans. Most importantly, this intervention changed the way Brazilian state officials thought about regulation of the market. "Before 1906, the fundamental question was whether or not the state should interfere with free market forces. After the first valorization, the problem was to find the most appropriate mechanisms for state action" (Holloway 1975, 84). Once the state had gotten involved in market intervention, there was pressure for it to continue; further valorizations were carried out in 1917, 1921, and 1925. These later interventions were carried out by the Brazilian federal state, and they ultimately got the state involved in regulating the coffee sector in Brazil. By buying coffee in Brazil, the state was indirectly influencing the internal price that coffee exporters had to pay to buy coffee for export. And by controlling stocks of coffee that would eventually need to be exported to recoup the money the state had laid out to purchase the coffee in the first place, the state became involved in coffee exporting. If not directly, by exporting the coffee itself, the involvement would have to be indirect, by deciding which exporters to sell the coffee to, and at what price. As the valorizations continued, therefore, the state began to play a regular role in managing the coffee sector, leading to the creation of the powerful state coffee agency, Instituto Brasileiro do Café (IBC).

These interventions were relatively successful in the short run in maintaining world prices, but they had two negative consequences for Brazil in the longer term. First, they encouraged continued expansion of coffee production in Brazil, leading to continual oversupply problems; and second, they provided a price umbrella under which other producers, particularly Colombia, could free ride and expand their coffee production and exports. Brazil couldn't continue to unilaterally intervene in the market without undercutting its ability to intervene in the future, and hurting its own coffee growers in the process. By the 1930s, Brazil's stockpiles of coffee had grown so large that the state abandoned hope of ever selling them, and began to destroy them. It has been estimated that enough coffee to supply two years' total world consumption was destroyed during the

1930s (although much of this coffee had been stored for so long that it might not have been usable anyway). Despite this, world market prices continued to decline as worldwide depression further lowered the demand for coffee. The low prices had begun to affect the other Latin American producers that had expanded their production under the Brazilian umbrella, and their coffee growers began to pressure their states to do something. In 1936 and 1937, the major Latin American producers met and decided to follow Brazil's policy of stockpiling some of their coffee to stop the price decline. But some of the other producers failed to follow through on their commitment, so in 1938 Brazil began to increase its exports, in order to avoid losing any more of its market share. This only exacerbated the oversupply situation (Fisher 1972, 13–14; Krasner 1973b; FAO 1947, 466–81; Bates 1997).

This was the situation when the outbreak of World War II cut Latin America off from the European market, and left the Latin American producers with potentially devastating overproduction. Prices in the U.S. market began to fall precipitously in 1940, as the producers competed for sales there. After the Vargas dictatorship in Brazil began to flirt with Hitler's Germany, the United States, which had previously been adamantly opposed to any market intervention, suddenly discovered the principle of "Pan-American solidarity among allies" and proposed an Inter-American Coffee Agreement. This Agreement, which was in effect 1940–1945, set import quotas for the U.S. market, restricting supplies and thereby guaranteeing Latin American producers higher prices for their coffee exports than they had obtained during the 1930s (Payer 1975; Fisher 1972, 15; FAO 1947, 495–504).

Notes

1. The descriptions in this section are based on material in FAO 1947; Singh et al. 1977; Marshall 1983; UNCTAD 1984; Mwandha, Nicholls, and Sargent 1985; de Graaf 1986; Economist Intelligence Unit 1987; Wrigley 1988; Finlayson and Zacher 1988; Pieterse and Silvis 1988; and Lucier 1988.

2. 1970 is the earliest date during the second food regime for which comparable data are available; 1988 is the last year before the coffee price crash. The 1988 data therefore show the typical position of coffee in Third World exports for most of the post–World War II period.

3. I have disaggregated the category of oils and oilseeds as defined in the IPC, because it contains commodities with different trading patterns; I have separated out soybeans and soybean oil, which are a key part of the livestock/feed complex. The main constituents of the new category of tropical oils and oilseeds are: groundnuts and groundnut oil; copra and coconut oil; and palm nuts and kernels, palm oil, and palm kernel oil. All of these are tropical products while soybeans and soybean oil are not. These oils and oilseeds have also been subjected to substitutionism in the production of durable foods, but they are still exported primarily to the core (except for palm oil by 1988) (cf. Friedmann 1991a, 77). The other problematic category included in the IPC is nonconiferous timber, as it includes tropical varieties as well as temperate hardwoods, but there is no

way to sort out the thousands of varieties of wood in this category in the UN trade statistics. Therefore I have defined the tropical timber exports in table 2.1 as all nonconiferous wood exported from the Third World. This includes some nontropical varieties, and overstates the importance of genuinely tropical varieties somewhat; it also means that the Third World share of tropical timber exports is 100 percent, by definition (but the actual share is very high in any case). The core share of world imports in table 2.1 is the share of all nonconiferous wood imports from all sources, and this probably understates the core share of imports of genuinely tropical varieties.

4. For purposes of this analysis, I have limited the tropical commodities to agricultural products. Table 2.1 shows that a few important minerals are also produced mainly by the Third World and consumed in the core—tin, bauxite, and to a lesser degree, copper. This similarity in trading patterns helps to explain why these minerals were included in the IPC, and why Third World producers have attempted to form cartels and negotiate international agreements for these commodities.

5. The United States, of course, is not the former colonial power in Latin America; however, at about the time of Latin American independence, the United States declared Latin America as its exclusive sphere of influence in the Monroe Doctrine. Despite a heavy British commercial presence in Latin America in the 1800s, most Latin American coffee exports went to New York rather than London. The United States also kept a rather tight reign on the important coffee-producing countries in Central America throughout the nineteenth and twentieth centuries.

6. It is worth emphasizing this point, because so many people who have written about coffee have gotten it wrong. Coffee is *not* the second most valuable primary commodity in world trade, as is often stated. Table 2.1 shows this clearly. It is *not* the second most traded commodity, a nebulous formulation that occurs repeatedly in the media. Coffee *is* the second most valuable primary commodity *exported by developing countries*.

Chapter 3

The Coffee Commodity Chain under U.S. Hegemony, 1945–1972

As the world emerged from World War II with the United States as the hegemonic power in the world system, the coffee commodity chain could be described as follows. In the United States, a national market was being consolidated out of what had been a number of smaller regional markets. Coffee roasting companies were still mainly regional, but that was beginning to change. There was one truly national brand, Maxwell House, owned by General Foods. Nestlé had a major share of the growing instant coffee market (see chapter 6). Other major coffee roasters, such as Folger's, Hills Bros., Chase and Sanborn, and Chock Full o' Nuts were strong in particular regions of the country, but did not have a national presence. In Europe, there were similar large coffee roasting companies that were beginning to dominate their national markets. In France, Jacob Suchard was the largest roaster; in Holland, it was Douwe Egberts. Two large companies, Tchibo and Eduscho, held dominant positions in the German market. Zoegas and Gevalia were the major Scandinavian roasters. For the most part, these companies did not yet have transnational coffee operations. General Foods had begun to go international, with operations in Canada, and a large share of the British market. There was one truly global coffee TNC, the Swiss-based Nestlé Corporation, with the leading market share in Britain, a major presence in France, and a dominant position in the U.S. market for instant coffee.

These national roasters developed distinctive national blends, based on the types of coffee the coffee drinkers in that country were used to getting from their former colonies or traditional suppliers. Thus, in France, coffee blends had a high proportion of robustas, the type grown in West Africa, while U.S. blends were based on Brazilian coffee.[1] The Germans consumed the highest quality Central and South American arabicas, obtained through contacts with German

51

immigrants who had gone into the coffee business in those countries. The large roasters obtained some of their supplies directly from exporters in the producing countries and the rest from national coffee importing companies. The use of blends enabled the roasters to substitute coffees within the four broad types to maintain the overall taste of the blend while purchasing the cheapest coffee available. For instance, U.S. roasters blended Brazils with some higher quality arabicas. If arabicas from El Salvador were unavailable or too high priced, they could substitute coffee from Guatemala or Costa Rica, and the blend would taste about the same. They could cheapen the blend somewhat by replacing a small proportion of the Colombian milds with other milds, or replacing a small proportion of the Brazils with robustas, but they depended on at least some Brazilian coffee as the basis for the blend.

These national roasters used extensive national advertising campaigns to establish their brand names, and engaged in oligopolistic competition with other major roasters in their national markets through brand name differentiation and cents-off promotions. Given the huge promotional efforts expended by roasters, supermarkets, particularly in the United States, often used coffee as a "loss leader," an item sold at or below cost in order to bring people into the store, where they would make other purchases. Once a company had established its brand as the dominant one in a particular market, it was hard for another brand, even one with heavy financial backing for advertising and promotion, to break into that market. This was shown most clearly by the ferocious battles that took place when Procter & Gamble attacked the eastern cities dominated by General Foods' Maxwell House in the 1970s. In 1963, P&G acquired the Folger Coffee Company, then a major regional roaster based in San Francisco. In the early 1970s, P&G took the Folger's brand name national, by going into the East Coast stronghold of Maxwell House and engaging in a series of brutal discount pricing wars, beginning in Cleveland in 1971. P&G eventually succeeded in establishing Folger's as a national brand, but it was a long and extremely costly battle (*New York Times*, January 28, 1979, section 3, p. 1; Hilke and Nelson 1989). While GF and P&G had the resources to engage in extended price wars in one or two regional markets at a time, the regional companies in those markets generally didn't, and they were the big losers in the price wars. This helped the three big national brands, Maxwell House, Folger's, and Nestlé, to consolidate their dominance in the emerging national market (Pendergrast 1999). By the end of this period, national markets had been established in the major consuming countries, and they were dominated by a few national roasting companies. Any new coffee manufacturer who wanted to break into one of the major consuming markets would need deep pockets, and a national strategy to challenge the dominant companies.

Therefore, one key characteristic of the coffee commodity chain during this period was the increasing control of a small number of national roasting companies over consumption end of the chain. In the U.S. market, the combined market share of the top four firms in sales of roasted coffee increased from 46 percent in 1958 to 69 percent in 1978; while the number of independent roasters decreased from 261 in 1963 to 162 in 1972 (UNCTAD 1984, table 11; UNCTC 1981, p. 84). Similar increases in concentration occurred in the major European markets (UNCTAD 1984, table 11). This trend was more dramatic for instant coffee, which involved a more highly industrialized final processing component. Because instant coffee was more capital intensive, its production was also more highly concentrated. The combined share of the top four firms in instant coffee sales in the U.S. market increased from 72 percent in 1958 to 91 percent in 1978, and similar increases also occurred in European markets (USFTC 1966, table 3; UNCTAD 1984, table 13). The share of instant coffee in total coffee consumption in core markets also increased during this period. For instance, in the United States, instant coffee represented about 10 percent of total coffee consumption in 1953, and this had increased to over 30 percent by 1975 (Mwandha et al. 1985, table 2.1).

As was the case with the coffee roasters, the coffee traders in this period were mainly national firms, and they specialized in importing coffee. The national coffee roasters themselves were major importers during this period, and what supplies they didn't obtain directly, they obtained through the national coffee traders. Many of these were family firms that had long histories in the coffee business. For instance, among the largest U.S. coffee traders were the A. C. Israel Company, and the Leon Israel Company, firms that could trace their family history in the coffee trade back to the late 1800s (these two firms later merged to form ACLI Coffee). Most of these trading firms imported coffee only into their national market. There were a few companies with international operations; for instance, Volkart Bros., a major German importer, was also one of the top importers in the U.S. market. Again, Nestlé stood out as the most global coffee company.

In the coffee producing countries, coffee was generally being produced by smallholders using rudimentary technology. The historical development of coffee production in Latin America was described briefly in the preceding chapter, and not much had changed through the 1960s. The wave of decolonization that swept through the African and Asian colonies in the postwar period increased the share of smallholder production in many countries. It did not significantly change the way that coffee was being produced in most countries, but it did change the management of the coffee sectors in these producing regions. Côte d'Ivoire serves as a good example of what happened in Francophone West and Central African countries. Here coffee production was expanded very late in the colonial period, beginning in the 1950s, by peasants bringing new land under cultivation in the central forest zone. These peasants were able to produce more efficiently than the French planters, once the latter's access to forced labor was ended by order of the French Constituent Assembly. Felix Houphet-Boigny, a coffee grower who went on to become the leader of independent Côte d'Ivoire, was instrumental in the campaign to end the forced labor system. In the 1950s, the colonial administration created the *Caisse de Stabilisation* to manage the coffee sector, and this agency was continued under Houphet-Boigny. The Caisse did not buy or sell coffee, but set the internal prices at which coffee was bought and sold by growers, traders, processors, and exporters. It used this power to create a large gap between the price exporters paid for coffee and the world market price, and used a high export tax to collect the rents thus created for the state (Rapley 1993).

In Kenya, in British East Africa, Africans had been prohibited from planting coffee by the colonial administration. Coffee was produced on large estates owned by colonists and worked by Africans. This gave the Africans some experience in coffee production, so that once the prohibition was lifted, just before independence, smallholder coffee production increased rapidly. The new independent government took over management of the coffee estates, and used legislation to subsidize inputs such as fertilizers, which were used by the estates but not the smallholders, in order to keep the estates competitive with the peasant producers. The colonial administration also created a state marketing board, the Kenya Coffee Board, that held a legal monopoly on coffee exporting, and this was continued under the newly independent state. The marketing board also had the power to set the price it paid for coffee considerably lower than the world market price, and to channel the rents it collected to the state to fund other projects (de Graaf 1986). Asian colonies followed roughly similar trajectories when they gained their independence. For instance, India, another British colony, emerged with a mix of smallholder and estate production and a coffee marketing board. Indonesia took over plantations that had been managed by the Dutch, but coffee production has increased mainly through the expansion of smallholder production since independence. Part of this expansion has been due to resettlement programs designed to move people off the overcrowded island of Java and onto less crowded islands such as Sulawesi (ICO EB2150/82).

Given the structures of the U.S. and European markets in the immediate postwar period, it was almost impossible for any coffee processors located in the coffee producing countries to break into the roasting, packing, and selling of coffee in the major consuming markets. For one thing, no single producing country could produce a blend comparable to those produced by the large national roasters. Each country grew one, or sometimes two, different types of coffee, and would have had to import coffee to produce comparable blends. For another, roasted coffee went stale quickly, and although the vacuum can did keep it fresher somewhat longer, it was an expensive technology. This put potential competitors in the producing countries at a further disadvantage, because they would have had to ship roasted coffee over long distances to the consuming markets. Further, few coffee processors in the producing countries had the market knowledge or the financial clout to compete with the national roasters' brand advertising and promotional strategies.

The colonial role of the peripheral and semiperipheral regions in the overall division of labor surrounding the production and processing of coffee was thus firmly locked in during the period of U.S. hegemony. These regions had originally been incorporated into the world economy as suppliers of a raw material, green coffee. In the newly emerging system of independent nation-states in the postwar world, the coffee producing countries continued to supply green coffee to the importers and roasters in the major consuming countries. The roasters processed this raw material into final form for consumption. There were two major developments in the structure of the commodity chain during this period. First, the national coffee companies increased their market power by consolidating control over the major consuming markets. Second, the coffee producing states increased their control over the production of green coffee within their territories, and began to look for ways to use coffee to stimulate economic development (Daviron 1996). With the strategy of forward integration nearly closed off by the structure of the chain,[2] the producers turned to the collective action strategy to try to increase their returns from their coffee-exporting role.

After the end of the war, the European market was reopened to coffee exports from Latin America, and as Europe was rebuilt, coffee consumption expanded rapidly. Price controls and rationing were lifted in the United States, and coffee consumption increased there also. Latin American exports had been limited by the Inter-American Coffee Agreement, so there had been little incentive to expand production. In addition, Indonesia, which had recovered from the leaf rust attack of the late 1800s to become one of the major non-Latin American producers before the war, had had its production destroyed again by the war. Thus in the late 1940s and early 1950s, demand for coffee was growing rapidly, while production had fallen below prewar levels. This sowed the seeds of a severe shortage on the world market, and marked the beginning of a new tree crop price cycle. Prices began to rise, but no new supplies were immediately forthcoming, and so they continued to rise.

Meanwhile, producers began to respond to the increasing prices in the early 1950s. Brazil, hoping to regain some of the market share it had lost while trying to get other producers to go along with its schemes to limit exports during the 1930s, expanded coffee planting south into the state of Paraná. This region was near the southern limit of coffee's ecological range, and was struck by occasional frosts; this would be the area hit hardest by the 1975 frost. Other Latin American producers also began to plant more coffee to take advantage of the high prices, in hopes of recovering from the economic downturn they had experienced when world demand for coffee began to fall during the 1930s. The European countries expanded planting in their African colonies, and independent African producers also planted more coffee. However, all of these new trees took several years to mature, and prices continued to increase while all of this new planting was underway. As this new coffee began to come onto the world market, supply caught up with and surpassed demand. Prices reached a peak in 1954, but began to fall steadily after that (Pan American Coffee Bureau 1966). Thus began the first Polanyian "double movement" in the postwar period. With the market freed of the restrictions of the Inter-American Coffee Agreement, and with demand expanding rapidly, the free market quickly resulted in overproduction, falling prices, and economic crisis for coffee growers throughout the producing regions, whose investments in planting and maintaining new coffee trees had just begun to bear fruit. They turned to their states for help, and this created the initial impetus for producers to begin to attempt collective action to limit their exports and stop the price decline. In order to understand these efforts, we need to see them in the context of the project to rebuild the world economy under U.S. hegemony that began immediately after the war.

As part of the effort to create international institutions in the aftermath of World War II, the Havana Charter was signed in 1948; however, it never went into effect because it was never ratified by most signatory governments. Nevertheless, it contained several important provisions that became guidelines for the management of the world economy. Chapter 4 of the Charter included principles of free trade and commitments to remove trade barriers; this was subsequently institutionalized in the GATT. Chapter 5 established an International Trade Organization; much later and in very different form, this would become the WTO. Chapter 6 allowed for exceptions to free-trade principles for agreements to regulate primary commodity markets, in cases where unstable prices or "burdensome surplus" might create "widespread unemployment or underemployment" in commodity exporting countries. Chapter 6 set out some principles for such agreements, which would later appear in the coffee agreements. First, the goal of such agreements would be to promote "stability of prices about a correct long-period trend," and "reasonably appropriate and stable incomes to producers." Second, the agreements would include both producing and consuming states, and each group would have an equal number of votes in determining regulatory policies (Brown 1980, 2–6; Finlayson and Zacher 1988, 17–31).

The basic principles of the postwar economic order are clear in these provisions. The commitment to remove trade barriers was a reaction to the conditions that had caused the decline of world trade in the 1930s. However, free trade was subordinated to national, and even international, economic management. The Charter implicitly recognized the dependence of peripheral and semiperipheral countries on primary commodity exports, and the impacts of commodity prices on economic development. If low or unstable commodity prices threatened economic development in producing countries, states were empowered to step in and regulate their trade by international agreement. This regulation was to be done under the watchful eye of the United States, by far the largest consumer of all primary commodities in the immediate postwar period, which would have a commanding position on the consumers' side of any such agreement.

Even though the Havana Charter never went into effect, study groups along the lines it had envisioned were established for a number of primary commodities, for which low and unstable prices were seen as potential problems. Two agreements, for tin and sugar, were signed in 1953. The United States played a major role in the conferences where these two agreements were negotiated, and both included major loopholes for the United States. The tin agreement set up an international buffer stock, which would buy up tin to support the price when world market prices were low, and sell it off when there was a shortage on the world market, to keep prices from going too high. However, the U.S. strategic tin stockpile was placed outside the control of the managers of the buffer stock. They thus were limited in the degree to which they could affect world market prices, because the United States could also buy and sell from its strategic stockpile to influence prices. The tin agreement lasted until 1985, making it the longest-lasting commodity agreement, but it collapsed spectacularly when the buffer stock went bankrupt.

The sugar agreement was an export quota agreement, in which each sugar exporting country was assigned a quota, or maximum amount it could export, in order to control the flow of sugar onto the world market. However, the U.S. market, which accounted for a quarter of world imports, and where the United States was already allocating quotas to exporting countries, was excluded from the agreement. The U.K.'s imports from its Commonwealth were also excluded. So the sugar agreement did not apply to two major consuming markets, and could only control world market prices to a limited degree. The sugar agreement fell apart in the early 1960s because of the Cuban Revolution. Cuba was the world's dominant sugar exporter, and had a large export quota to the U.S. market. After the Revolution, the United States cut off Cuba's access to the U.S. market and reallocated its quota to other Latin American producers. This stimulated other producers with access to the U.S. market to increase their production at the same time that it threw Cuba's entire production into the segment of the market that was regulated by the sugar agreement. The allocation of quotas to the different producing countries was thrown into disarray, and the producing states couldn't come to any agreement on how to adjust them. No other commodity agreements were concluded during the 1950s, and Third World impatience with the limited progress on the modest goals set out in the Havana Charter led to their demand for the creation of UNCTAD (Finlayson and Zacher 1988, 131–33, 81–106; Brown 1980, 5, 11–24).

This was the international context within which coffee producers began meeting after 1954 to discuss measures to stop the decline of coffee prices. The initial meetings and attempts at cooperation were organized through the Organization of American States. Brazil and Colombia, the two largest producers, took the lead, as they often would in future negotiations, but the five Central American producers (Mexico, Guatemala, El Salvador, Nicaragua, and Costa Rica) were also involved. These seven producers signed an agreement in 1957 to limit their exports, but it had little effect on prices. By 1958, while still opposed to market intervention, the United States had become concerned enough about declining coffee prices and their potential economic impact on Latin America that it sponsored the convening of a Coffee Study Group under UN auspices. The Coffee Study Group included not only Latin American producers, but also European colonial powers, who controlled coffee production in their African colonies. The Latin Americans were unable to come to agreement with the Europeans on limiting exports, but were able to negotiate a Latin American Coffee Agreement including fifteen producers (Fisher 1972, chapter 2).

By 1959, a few African producers, such as Cameroun and Togo, had gained independence and were able to participate in negotiations directly to protect their interests. In addition, some of the European colonial powers became more favorably disposed toward an international agreement as coffee prices continued to fall, causing economic problems in their African colonies at the same time that the decolonization movement was rapidly gaining momentum. An International Coffee Agreement among producers, including France and Portugal, was signed in 1959. It was extended in 1960, and by that time, it included producers (or their colonial representatives) accounting for 94 percent of world production.[3] Still, this ICA had two major problems: export quotas were set too high to maintain the world market price, and it lacked an enforcement mechanism to prevent producers from exceeding their quotas. Thus, this agreement slowed the price decline somewhat, but did not halt it (Finlayson and Zacher 1988, 153; Bilder 1963, 338, Fisher 1972, chapter 2).

At this point two major events intervened: the Cuban Revolution and the election of President Kennedy. The Cuban Revolution raised the specter of the spread of communism throughout Latin America and led to U.S. reexamination of its policies toward the region. Kennedy had a long-standing interest in Latin America and had expressed a willingness to explore price stabilization measures during his campaign. The result was the U.S. proposal of an "Alliance for Progress" to combat the spread of communism. One of its main components was economic aid, and Kennedy stated in his speech announcing the program that the United States was prepared to cooperate in resolving commodity problems. Coffee was clearly Latin America's most important commodity export; despite the expansion of production in other regions, Latin America still accounted for 70 percent of world exports. Kennedy stated that, "A drop of one cent a pound for green coffee costs Latin American producers $50 million in export proceeds, enough seriously to undermine what we are seeking to accomplish by the Alliance for Progress" (quoted in Greenstone 1981, 4). Thus, during 1961, the Coffee Study Group produced a draft coffee agreement, and in 1962 the UN convened a negotiating conference in New York. An International Coffee Agreement (ICA) including both producing and consuming countries, with full U.S. support and participation, was signed in August, 1962.[4]

The provisions of the ICA followed the outline of the Havana Charter closely. Its purpose was "to achieve a reasonable balance between supply and demand" and to assure "equitable prices" (Article 1). It established an export quota system that would be enforced by importing countries, who would monitor their imports and refuse to accept any over-quota exports from producers. Since almost all coffee producing countries and all major importers were members of the agreement, the export quota system could be an effective regulatory mechanism. The governing body of the agreement, which would set the quotas for each country, was the International Coffee Council, composed of all importing and exporting members. Importing and exporting members each had a total of 1000 votes in the Council, divided among them based on the sizes of their imports and exports. The United States, the largest importer, and Brazil, the largest exporter, each had 400 votes. Any decision on export quotas required a distributed two-thirds majority, that is, it had to be approved by two-thirds of importers and two-thirds of exporters. Thus the United States and Brazil had an effective veto over quota decisions (Fisher 1972, chapter 2; Finlayson and Zacher 1988, 151–56; Brown 1980, 25–29).

Previous authors have attempted to explain why the ICA was successfully negotiated at this time, and in particular, why the United States was such a strong supporter of it. They have only been partially successful, because they have not considered the larger context of the regulation of the world economy, and they have not seen how the coffee chain tied the national coffee companies to the producing countries. For Bates (1997), the ICA was primarily an agreement between Brazil, Colombia, and the United States. Brazil and Colombia sought to restrict their exports to raise world market prices. But they could not do this alone in the late 1950s and early 1960s, because the newer, smaller producers would have undersold them, driving down prices and cutting Brazil's and Colombia's market shares. For Brazil and Colombia, the ICA was a means of curbing free-riding by the other producers, and the export quotas served to limit the entry of new producers to the market. The smaller producers were forced to go along with Brazil and Colombia, once U.S. support for the agreement was secured, for fear of losing access to the huge U.S. market (40 percent of total world imports) if they did not join the agreement. Bates' explanation of Brazil's and Colombia's interests in pushing for an ICA are probably correct, but the implication that other producers were essentially coerced into joining is not completely convincing. Undoubtedly a desire to maintain access to the U.S. market played a role in their decisions. But the other producers also saw the value of restricting supplies in order to raise prices, or they would not have joined the earlier producers' agreements. They also continued to support the ICAs as consumption in Europe and Japan increased, eventually cutting the U.S. share of world imports to well below 30 percent. Further, this explanation overlooks the larger political context within which the agreement was negotiated, particularly the decolonization and antiimperialist movements which were influencing the views of Third World leaders. These movements provided an ideological rationale for collective action by commodity producers to organize against economic exploitation, manifested in low and declining prices for their major exports.

For the United States, Bates concurs that the primary motivation for supporting the ICA was geopolitical; however, he points out that this was the Kennedy administration's motivation, and it still had to secure the approval of Congress. Thus it took one year to get the agreement ratified and two more to get the implementing legislation passed, due to domestic political factors that had nothing to do with geopolitics. Mostly, this had to do with the strong public reaction against high coffee prices in 1954, and fear by members of Congress that the ICA could reignite this anger among their constituents. Nevertheless, geopolitics does explain why the United States joined; domestic political factors only explain why it took so long. Ultimately, the ICA was supported in Congress by Cold Warriors who were in agreement with the administration's view of the ICA, and by others who were convinced to vote for it because of support by the national coffee companies.

The national coffee companies that dominated the U.S. market were generally supportive of the ICA, even though it meant somewhat higher producer prices. Their interests were represented by the National Coffee Association (NCA), dominated by the national coffee companies and large coffee traders, which is described more fully in the next chapter. As early as 1958, a delegation from the NCA, representing some of the largest U.S. firms, had met with the Assistant Secretary of State for Economic Affairs to express their concern over the situation in the coffee market and in Latin America. They were worried that increasing economic instability could "wreak havoc on our lines of supply of green coffee" (John McKiernan, NCA president, quoted by Fisher 1972, 22). Many coffee traders traveled extensively in Latin America, and were very concerned by what they saw as increasing instability. The heads of the coffee companies also shared the prevalent anticommunist ideology of the time. They saw a political agreement that would prevent instability and communism in the producing countries, and thus assure their access to coffee at relatively stable prices, as being in their interests. On the other hand, they were concerned that a commodity agreement might lead to unreasonable price increases, and thus favored U.S. participation to defend their interests against unilateral actions by producers (Fisher 1972, chapter 2; Payer 1975).

Krasner (1973a, 1973b) argues that the coffee companies were hurt economically by the first ICA, and thus, while they made supportive public comments about the agreement, they only went along with it at the urging of the State Department, out of a sense of public duty. This argument seems implausible, given the difficulty that the U.S. administration had in getting the implementing legislation through Congress—this did not occur until 1965. John McKiernan, president of the NCA, appeared at all of the Congressional hearings on various drafts of this legislation during the 1962–1965 period, to voice the strong support of NCA members for the ICA. It seems unlikely that the legislation would have passed at all without this consistent support. Bates (1997) agrees that NCA support was crucial in getting the ICA through Congress. However, his explanation for NCA support centers on the fact that, once the ICA was signed, the national coffee companies were able to negotiate special deals with Brazil and Colombia to buy coffee at a discount, thereby giving them a competitive advantage over the smaller regional roasters. In return for these deals, they lobbied Congress in favor of ratification and of the implementing legislation. Once again, this probably played a role in their calculations. But this explanation overlooks the evidence that the heads of the companies supported an ICA as early as 1958, in part because they shared the geopolitical views of U.S. officials, and in part because they needed reliable supplies of coffee.

The politically regulated market was continued through the 1960s by a second ICA that went into effect in 1968, as the term of the first ICA expired. The second ICA included a number of modifications, most of them minor, but two were important. One, Article 44, is discussed below. The other was the Diversification Fund. This was intended to deal with the problems of oversupply and of excessive dependence on coffee exports by many producing countries. While the 1962 ICA had stabilized exports, total world production still exceeded demand, and some countries, most notably Brazil, were accumulating large stockpiles of coffee because their production exceeded their export quota. The fund was to be financed by contributions from exporting countries, with larger exporters paying a larger share, and used to provide loans to producing states to carry out diversification projects to replace some of their coffee with other exportable products (Brown 1980). It was an attempt to force producing states to develop national production goals in a coordinated fashion, in order to bring production, and not just exports, into balance with world demand. This would ultimately, if successful, put producers in a much stronger position to influence world market prices. It would also help countries most heavily dependent on coffee exports to lower their dependence, and thus mitigate the economic impacts of low world market prices on their economies. The Diversification Fund was not in operation long enough to have a major impact on production, and this would return to haunt the producing countries in the 1980s.

The second ICA was to be in effect until 1973, but negotiations to renew it broke down in 1972. The International Coffee Organization (ICO), which had been established by the ICA, was continued as a forum for producers and consumers to continue meeting to discuss problems in the world coffee market, and as an archive and data collection organization for information on the market. But the quotas, the economic teeth of the ICA, were discontinued. The breakdown of negotiations was due in part to the larger crisis of the world economy, as well as to factors specific to coffee. A major component of the multiple crises that struck the world economy around 1970 was the breakdown of the Bretton Woods system of fixed exchange rates. In addition, the United States abandoned the fixed exchange rate between the dollar and gold, and expanded the money supply, effectively devaluing the dollar. World coffee prices, as well as the prices of most other primary commodities, were denominated in U.S. dollars, and the devaluation meant an effective decrease in export earnings. Producers demanded that a new ICA include an upward revision of the target price range that quotas were meant to defend to compensate for this loss, but the United States refused to agree. Prices were already going up, following frosts in Paraná in 1969 and 1972, and the Nixon administration didn't want to be seen as contributing to inflation by further increasing coffee prices. The smaller producers, particularly the African countries, had the capacity to export more coffee at a higher price under these conditions than they could hope to obtain quotas for under a new ICA, and had little interest in agreeing to a new quota system. With neither producers nor consumers willing to compromise, there were no longer grounds for agreement on continuation of the quota system (Payer 1975; Brown 1980, 33–34; Marshall 1972).

The ICAs had also been partially undermined by increasing transnationalization during this period. This was most visible in instant coffee production, a struggle that is analyzed fully in chapter 6. The most significant move was made by Nestlé, which had pioneered the technology for spray-dried instant coffee in the 1930s. After the war, they began to establish subsidiaries to produce instant coffee in the Third World, first in Latin America, and then moving into Africa. By 1976, they had subsidiaries in twenty-one different Third World countries

(UNCTC 1981, 84). In the most aggressive response to the increasing dominance of the national coffee companies, ten regional coffee companies formed a joint venture called Tenco to produce instant coffee. They established several factories in Central America in order to produce it more cheaply than the national companies. In response to these trends, the major producing countries attempted to establish their own instant coffee industries. Brazil took this a step further and attempted to compete on the U.S. market. The state created incentives to encourage instant coffee production by local capitalists, including access to broken beans and non-export-quality coffee, and state purchase guarantees. Then it exempted instant coffee producers from the export taxes that all green coffee exporters had to pay. These incentives enabled Brazilian instant coffee firms to land instant coffee powder in the United States at a price significantly lower than the price at which it could be produced by factories in the United States buying green Brazilian coffee. Brazilian producers increased their share of the U.S. market from about 1 percent in 1965 to 14 percent in 1967.

This move by Brazil created a huge controversy in the United States. The national coffee companies, led by General Foods, felt their dominance in the U.S. instant coffee market threatened, and vigorously lobbied the U.S. state to stop this "unfair trading practice" by Brazil. The United States was unable to get Brazil to agree to "voluntary" restrictions on its exports of instant coffee to the United States, and so raised the issue in the negotiations to renew the ICA. As a result the 1968 ICA contained Article 44, which prohibited any ICA member from "discriminatory treatment in favor of processed coffee as opposed to green coffee" (Fisher 1972, 140). The United States, which at this same time was engaged in a massive subsidy operation to increase its wheat exports under the guise of "food aid" (Friedmann 1982), succeeded in imposing a regulation prohibiting Third World producers from doing exactly the same thing to increase their industrialized product exports. Further, most of the major European signatories to the ICA had escalating tariffs for coffee, in which a higher import tax was charged on instant coffee than on green coffee, a form of discriminatory treatment *against* processed coffee. However, the hypocrisy of the consuming countries' position was apparently recognized only in the Third World. As a result of this controversy, the national coffee companies began to see the producers not only as coffee suppliers, but also as potential competitors, and were therefore probably less willing to assist them by going along with a price increase in the 1972 negotiations.

The period considered in this chapter, of material expansion of the world economy under U.S. hegemony, as Arrighi has called it, or the second food regime, as Friedmann and McMichael have called it (see chapter 1), thus coincided with a Polanyian double movement. The period opened with the extension of the free market to coffee, which triggered the tree crop price cycle, leading to oversupply and declining prices. This created hardship for the coffee growers, who turned to their states for protection. The states, some newly freed former colonies, saw the declining coffee prices as symbolic of their continuing subordinate position in the world system, and organized collectively to stop the trend.

The consuming countries, particularly the United States, and their national coffee companies, saw the militance of the producers as a geopolitical threat, but also as a reminder of their dependence on the producers for a stable supply of coffee, which was important to millions of their consumers. In this situation, producing and consuming countries found grounds for an agreement to provide coffee growers social protection from the uncertainties of the free market, culminating in a ten-year period with a politically regulated world market. Market regulation brought supply and demand into balance and prevented the development of any new tree crop price cycles. Analysts have generally agreed that regulation of the market by the ICA between 1962 and 1972 also led to higher prices for coffee producing countries than they would have obtained under a free market (Geer 1971, 171–88; Galloway 1973). The ICA therefore came to be regarded by both consuming and producing states as a form of "disguised aid"; a means of transferring resources to Third World countries which did not require direct legislative approval.

The world coffee market during this period experienced the two contradictory tendencies identified by Friedmann and McMichael with the second food regime: the spread of the model of national regulation of economic production, and the increasing globalization of production. But because national regulation of the production of tropical commodities like coffee led logically to attempts at international regulation of their trade, these dynamics played out differently in the world coffee market than in the food regime. National regulation led to international regulation because, as Third World nation-states embarked on state-led industrialization and development strategies, the first obstacle they encountered was heavy dependence on tropical commodities and deteriorating terms of trade. The need for increased foreign exchange earnings made commodity export policies an essential part of development strategy; and the concentration of market shares and the colonial legacy provided the economic and political bases for collective action. As the world system of nation-states was completed during this period, international organizations were created to administer a variety of new international regimes. The Third World attempted to use the rules of these new regimes to improve their economic positions in the world economy; this is illustrated specifically by the negotiation of the ICAs, and more generally by the efforts of UNCTAD (Krasner 1985). In the ICAs, Third World states succeeded in replacing the private regulation of the world market organized primarily by coffee manufacturers and traders with a public regulatory regime, the rules of which were enforced by a multilateral institution, the International Coffee Organization (ICO).

The governance structure of the coffee chain at the beginning of this period most closely resembles Gereffi's producer-driven type. The national coffee companies, while consolidating their dominance in their national markets, were also consolidating their control over the governance of the chain. They manufactured coffee into its final consumption form and controlled the distribution of their products to the retail sellers. They globally sourced their raw material inputs from the suppliers, the coffee producing countries, and used the coffee traders as a way of adjusting to sudden changes in the market. If a certain coffee became unavailable from a direct supplier, the traders could find a reasonable substitute elsewhere. The traders were also best for handling imports from smaller producers, who sometimes dealt in lots of coffee too small for the national coffee companies to import profitably. The coffee companies, in their position of monopsonistic buyers in each major consuming market, were in a position to specify the quality criteria that producers had to meet in order to sell their coffee. They wanted large lots of coffee with consistent quality and taste characteristics, delivered reliably, at a reasonable (to them) price. However, this description of the governance structure treats the individual coffee producing countries as black boxes, unitary suppliers whose structure remains unexamined.

The governance structures of the production ends of the chain, that were located within the producing countries, varied enormously across countries. A complete analysis of them would require another book, but the broad outlines have been sketched above. All involved some state role in managing the coffee sector, because it was such an important export, a major source of state revenue, and an important source of domestic employment. They ranged from the system of state coffee agencies and private exporters in Latin America to the system of state marketing boards in Anglophone African countries to the more indirect management through a *Caisse* as in the Francophone African countries, and beyond.

A struggle over governance occurred at the point where this state-controlled governance structure at the production end intersected with the coffee companies' producer-driven structure at the consumption end. And the conflict quickly focused on the price at which the supplies would be delivered. For the producing states the world market price of coffee was a matter of national interest; it had major effects on the national economy and development prospects, and ultimately on the legitimacy of the government. Thus producing states could not be expected to act like normal suppliers in an economic model. They were prepared to engage in collective action to improve the prices they received, in a situation in which low coffee prices symbolized their subordinate and exploited position in the world economy, and in an atmosphere where anticolonialism and anti-imperialism were the reigning discourses.

The norms of the international economic regime worked in favor of the producers. They legitimated producing states' regulation of their coffee sectors, and they legitimated national development as a goal of the states' economic policies. The principles laid out in the Havana Charter also legitimated attempts to regulate world markets if they had adverse effects on Third World countries. Meanwhile, the geopolitics implicit in the U.S. anticommunist strategy also worked to their advantage. The United States was willing to participate in the political regulation of this key market, given the mix of Third World countries that were most directly affected: Brazil, Colombia, and the Central American producers. The Europeans were also motivated to participate by the growing presence of their former colonies in Africa and Asia in the coffee chain. They welcomed a multilateral mechanism through which to provide economic aid to their former colonies, to moderate their anticolonial confrontation with the core countries of the world economy.

The resolution of the governance struggle came through an agreement to set up a multilateral agency to manage this conflicted point where the two governance structures intersected, by negotiating the price. The ICAs did not do anything directly to change the governance structures of the two segments of the chain. They treated producing states and consuming states as sovereign entities who bought and sold coffee to one another, with the ICO as the forum for agreeing on the price. Governance of the production and consumption ends of the chain was left up to the respective states. At the production end of the chain, this was reasonably close to the reality of the situation; however, the reality was quite different at the consumption end. The ICAs ignored the roles of the national coffee companies, soon to become transnationals, in the world market. The fiction of the consuming states as coffee buyers worked reasonably well as long as state leaders and heads of the coffee companies shared an interest in containing communism and insuring stable supplies of coffee. It would become problematic when the interests of these two groups began to diverge.

Even though the ICAs were not intended to change the governance structures of the two segments of the chain, they did have implications for governance at both ends. In the consuming countries, the ICAs provided stability of supply, which changed the way the coffee companies did business. They had used the coffee futures markets to hedge their purchases of green coffee, but the stability provided by the ICAs made this increasingly unnecessary, and the New York coffee futures exchange closed down briefly in the late 1960s because of this (see the next chapter for a fuller discussion). In the producing countries, the ICA helped to consolidate state control over the production end of the chain (Daviron 1996). It mandated the producing states to control their exports, and this necessitated tighter control over exporters. If there was already a state marketing board, this required little change. However, in other types of governance structures, it usually required closer control over private exporters. In addition, the states needed a mechanism to store coffee that was produced in excess of the export quota. Either the state had to adopt a mechanism to acquire the excess coffee and store it, or it had to compel the private exporters to store the excess coffee themselves. For states such as Brazil, which had long been engaged in this practice, it didn't require much adjustment, but for many other producers it did.

The existence of the first two ICAs for a ten-year period, as well as the creation of the ICO, left an important legacy of their own. The producers had engaged in collective action and had succeeded in stabilizing and raising world market prices for coffee. They had learned a great deal about the coffee commodity chain, about the way the world market functioned, and about the way the coffee companies operated in the consuming markets. The crisis of the world economy in the early 1970s had ended the period of the politically regulated market and opened a new period in which the self-regulating market would once again be extended to coffee. This would eventually trigger a new tree crop price cycle and start a new Polanyian double movement. All of this would occur under very different conditions in the world economy, since the United States would abandon the model of national economic regulation in response to the crisis. However, the legacy of the first ICAs would give the producers the capacity to swim against the tide and reestablish a politically regulated market.

Notes

1. See the discussion of the different types of coffee and their export niches in the preceding chapter.

2. A few coffee producing countries did have some success integrating forward into instant coffee production, but not until the 1970s, and not enough to dissuade them from collective action. See chapter 6.

3. Brazil, Colombia, Costa Rica, Cuba, Dominican Republic, Ecuador, El Salvador, Guatemala, Haiti, Honduras, Mexico, Nicaragua, Panama, Peru, and Venezuela were the signatories to the 1959 ICA; they were joined in 1960 by the newly independent "franc zone" countries of Cameroun, Central African Republic, Congo (Brazzaville), Côte d'Ivoire, Dahomey, Gabon, Malagasy Republic, and Togo, along with Portugal (for Angola) and the United Kingdom (for Kenya, Tanganyika, and Uganda) (Fisher 1972, 19–27).

4. Members of the 1962 ICA were, as exporting members: Brazil, Burundi, Cameroun, Central African Republic, Colombia, Congo-Brazzaville, Congo-Leopoldville, Costa Rica, Côte d'Ivoire, Cuba, Dahomey, Dominican Republic, Ecuador, El Salvador, Ethiopia, Gabon, Ghana, Guatemala, India, Indonesia, Madagascar, Mexico, Nicaragua, Nigeria, Panama, Peru, Portugal (Angola), Rwanda, Sierra Leone, Tanzania, Togo, Trinidad and Tobago, Uganda, and Venezuela; and as importing members: Argentina, Australia, Austria, Belgium, Canada, Denmark, West Germany, Finland, France, Japan, Luxembourg, Netherlands, New Zealand, Norway, Spain, Sweden, Tunisia, United Kingdom, United States, and the Soviet Union.

Chapter 4

Struggles over Regulation of the Chain, 1973–1989

The crises of the world economy in the late 1960s and early 1970s touched off a struggle between North and South over the rules of the international economy. Although the South's attempts to institute a New International Economic Order (NIEO) had been largely defeated by the early 1980s, the struggle over control of the coffee commodity chain, which was a part of this larger struggle, continued through the 1980s. This was due in part to the collective strength that coffee producing countries had built during the 1950s, 1960s, and 1970s. Ultimately, however, some of the same factors that caused the defeat of the NIEO led to the defeat of coffee producers' collective action: the debt crisis, structural adjustment, and competition between southern countries. But the way the struggle developed was determined by the structure of the coffee chain. Beginning in the early 1970s, the self-regulating market was once again extended to coffee, starting a new Polanyian double movement. The "free" market went into a new tree crop price cycle following a killer frost in Brazil in 1975. As this cycle reached its declining price phase in the late 1970s, coffee growers pressured their states for protection from the market. The result was a return to a regulated market in 1980, under the third and fourth ICAs. Meanwhile, a combination of coffee growers' responses to the high prices of the mid-1970s, USAID funding of coffee intensification programs, and pressures from the World Bank to expand exports, caused a chronic oversupply of coffee on the world market during the 1980s. Oversupply, changes in world demand, and the provisions of the ICA itself combined to weaken support for continued regulation, and the defeat of producers' collective action was signaled by the breakdown of negotiations to renew the ICA in 1989. This chapter analyzes this struggle, beginning with an account of the 1975 Brazilian frost.

The 1975 Frost

On the night of July 17, 1975, a killer frost struck the coffee growing regions of Brazil, hitting hardest in the southern areas of Paraná, Minas Gerais, and Sao Paulo states. Most of the frosts that strike this area are called "white frosts," which kill the leaves of the coffee trees and the flowers that will become the next year's coffee crop. But this was a "black frost," one that turns the sap black and kills the entire tree. Even so, Brazil's 1975/76 crop was not severely damaged; the main harvest had begun in April and was about two-thirds completed, and many of the coffee cherries remaining on the trees were mature enough to survive the frost. But the dead trees would produce no crop in the 1976/77 harvest year, and even if new trees were planted immediately, they wouldn't begin to bear for another four years. Brazil at this time accounted for about a third of total world coffee production; its production in the 1974/75 season had been about twenty-six million bags of sixty kilograms each. The frost struck at a particularly bad time. There were civil wars raging in Ethiopia, another producer of arabica coffees of a similar quality to Brazil's, and in Angola, the second-largest producer of robusta coffee. Uganda, another large robusta producer, was also in chaos under Idi Amin. Thus the supply situation was already uncertain. However, traders and roasters in the United States had been betting on a bumper crop from Brazil that would lower prices, and they had held off buying, so had relatively low stocks on hand.[1]

The *Instituto Brasileiro do Café* (IBC), the state agency that regulated the coffee industry, temporarily suspended exports immediately after the frost. The IBC regulated exports by setting a minimum registration price—all exporters had to register their exports, and the IBC would refuse registration for any coffee to be exported at less than its minimum price. In the wake of the frost, prices would obviously be higher, and the IBC needed time to assess the situation before raising the registration price. On July 23, a week after the frost, the IBC announced that more than 50 percent of Brazil's 1976/77 crop had been wiped out by the frost. It also announced that it had fifteen million bags of coffee in stocks, and that growers and exporters held an additional six million bags. These stocks could be used to replace some of the output lost to the frost. On August 1, the IBC lifted the temporary ban, and raised the minimum export price from fifty to eighty cents a pound. Other coffee exporting countries had already posted similar large increases.[2]

The main independent U.S. source for information on crop damage and stock levels was the U.S. Department of Agriculture's Foreign Agricultural Service (FAS). They produced regular crop forecasts for a variety of tropical crops produced in Third World countries, including coffee. There was an agricultural officer stationed in the U.S. Embassy in each of the major producing countries to keep tabs on the agricultural situation. Immediately after the frost, an official from the FAS flew to Brazil, and with the agricultural officer stationed there, began a field survey to assess the damage. On August 21, the FAS reported that the 1976/77 crop had been more than 50 percent damaged. Their preliminary forecast for the crop was between eight and eleven million bags. The IBC's forecast was for a maximum of eight million bags.[3] There were also questions about the amount of stocks held in Brazil. While the export quotas under the first two ICAs were in effect, from 1962 to 1972, Brazil had built up massive stocks, probably amounting to well over seventy million bags, more than one year's total world consumption of coffee. But after a series of minor frosts in the late 1960s and early 1970s affected production, Brazil had drawn down those stocks dramatically. Coffee can be stored for up to six or seven years under optimal conditions, but after that, its quality has deteriorated to the point where it is no longer usable. So even if the total of twenty-one million bags in stocks that the IBC had announced was accurate, it was unclear how much of it was of exportable quality.[4]

Meanwhile, the situation set off a buying frenzy that some traders labeled "frost panic," as traders and roasters bought up whatever coffee became available, even though the real supply shortage was not likely to be felt for another year. Everyone expected the price to go higher, and wanted to buy as much as they could before it did. Roasters also began to raise their prices. The upper line in figure 4.1 shows the average retail price of coffee, which followed the wholesale price closely, because retailers' margins on coffee tended to be very small. The first to announce an increase was General Foods (Maxwell House), the largest roaster. It increased its wholesale price by twenty cents a pound on July

Figure 4.1: ICO Indicator Price for Green Coffee and Average Retail Price of Roasted and Ground Coffee, Monthly Average, January 1974 – December 1980

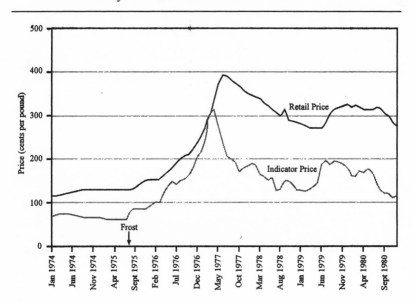

Table 4.1 Brazilian and Total World Production and Exports of Green Coffee around the 1975 Frost

	Production		Exports	
Year	Brazil	World	Brazil	World
1973/74	16,240	75,455	15,273	57,425
1974/75	26,290	74,770	14,808	56,643
1975/76	22,444	56,226	13,014	56,868
1976/77	6,663	68,997	14,741	52,382
1977/78	16,048	74,371	9,268	50,882
1978/79	20,853	81,140	13,217	63,372
1979/80	21,296	76,601	14,192	60,335

Sources: International Coffee Organization, *Quarterly Statistical Bulletin on Coffee*, no. 19, July–September 1981. Brazilian production is for crop years, April 1–March 30; world production and both export figures are for coffee years, October 1–September 30. All figures are in thousands of bags of coffee, each weighing 60 kg.

28, and the other major roasters soon followed suit.[5] As prices continued to rise through 1976, retailers and consumers began to hoard coffee, following the same logic as the traders and roasters—buy it now, before it gets more expensive. Coffee roastings in the United States were up 15.6 percent in the first half of 1976, compared with the same period a year before. By October 1976, the national average retail price of a pound of coffee had risen to $2.12, up from $1.27 in June 1975, before the frost, and there appeared to be no end in sight. By the end of 1976, Folger's had broken the previously unimaginable $3.00 barrier, raising its wholesale price to $3.08.[6] By early 1977, consumers were fed up after almost a year and a half of steadily increasing prices, and there was talk of a coffee boycott. One of the most prominent organizers was Elinor Guggenheimer, New York City Consumer Affairs Commissioner, a self-proclaimed fourteen-cup per day addict. There were also calls for a Congressional investigation into the soaring prices.[7]

Table 4.1 shows the effect of the frost on Brazilian production and exports. If 1974/75 is taken as a baseline, the frost wiped out about three-fourths of Brazilian production in 1976/77. This production shortfall in Brazil's 1976/77 crop year began to be manifested in world production for the 1975/76 coffee year (which overlapped the Brazilian crop year for the six months of April–September 1976), causing a decrease of about 25 percent. Brazil maintained its export level by drawing down stocks, but by the 1977/78 coffee year, that was no longer possible, and its exports fell below ten million bags, leading to a world export shortage of about 10 percent.[8] The response of the prices of both physical coffee and coffee futures to this situation followed a similar trajectory; the lower line in figure 4.1 shows the trend of the ICO indicator price, an average of the prices of different grades of physical coffee in major importing ports. Before the frost, for the first half of 1975, the ICO indicator price had been hovering in the low 60-cent range, and the "C" futures contract in New York was trading in the 40–50 cent range. The ICO indicator jumped to the mid-80s and the futures price to around 80 cents immediately after the frost, and prices stayed there through 1975. Both rose steadily through 1976, the ICO indicator from 95 cents in January to $2.05 in December, and the "C" contract from around 90 cents at the start of the year up to about $2.20 by the end. Both prices continued to rise in early 1977, with the ICO indicator price peaking at $3.15 in April, and the futures price topping out at $3.40 on April 14. From that point, it was all downhill. Ironically, world market prices began to fall as total exports reached their lowest point. This was probably due to declining demand in response to the huge price increases, which slowed panic buying and hoarding, as well as to anticipation of increased production in the following year. Folger's was the first to respond, dropping its wholesale price on May 12 from $4.43 to $4.18 per pound. General Foods followed with a 25-cent cut the next day. Physical and futures prices continued to fall until hitting a low of about $1.25 in February 1979.[9]

The 1975 frost was arguably the most important event to happen in the coffee commodity chain in the post–World War II period. As described below, its effects reverberated through the chain for the rest of the period considered in this chapter. With this account of the events surrounding the frost as backdrop, the remainder of the chapter analyzes how the struggle over control of the chain between producing states on the one hand, and TNCs and their home states on the other, developed following the end of the second ICA in 1972.

Collective Action by Producers

The response of coffee producing states to the breakdown of the ICA negotiations in 1972 was swift; if the consuming states wouldn't cooperate in regulating the market, the producers decided to try to impose their own forms of regulation. This collective action began in April 1972, even before the ICA negotiations had formally ended. By that time it had become clear to the producers that the negotiations were not going to succeed, and fourteen producers, led by Brazil, Colombia, Côte d'Ivoire and Portugal (for Angola), formed the Geneva Group. These countries pledged to maintain exports at the 1972 quota levels, in order to hold prices at the relatively high levels that had prevailed through the 1960s. As a complement to this strategy, Brazil, Colombia, and Côte d'Ivoire formed a corporation called Café Mundial in 1973, to operate a multinational buffer stock for coffee. Café Mundial would buy coffee on the world market if the price became too low, and sell off its stocks as the price improved. African robusta producers and Central American milds producers also announced minimum export prices for their coffees, and pledged to hold their coffees off the market unless they obtained this price. Since these arrangements were all private agreements between producing states, not much is publicly known about the details and the scale of their operations. But various shifts in world market prices during 1973–1974 came to be attributed to these operations. The coincidence of these efforts with UNCTAD's IPC proposals worried the core states; it seemed as if Third World states, anticipating a core refusal to go along with the IPC, might attempt to implement it unilaterally. This was the situation when the frost struck Brazil in 1975, further heightening the concerns of the large national coffee companies over the stability of their supplies (Finlayson and Zacher 1988, 158–59; Economist Intelligence Unit 1987, 18; Wasserman 1972; Yorgason 1976).

Under these conditions, the United States and other core consuming states decided that a renewed ICA might be in their best interests. But under these conditions, it is harder to explain why the producing states would have had any interest in a new ICA. It seems likely that most of them realized that the shortage of supplies would only be temporary, and that quotas would probably be necessary to stem the fall in price which would happen as Brazilian production began to recover. Previous experiences in the late 1950s and early 1960s had taught them that efforts to limit exports were more effective when the consuming states agreed to enforce the limits. At the same time, it was easier for producers to agree on how export quotas would be divided up among them when it was just an academic exercise. They all knew that any quotas would be immediately suspended as soon as a new ICA went into effect, because of the impending shortages of coffee after the frost. For the moment, the producers could have their cake and eat it, too; they could agree to quotas but continue to export as much coffee as they could produce. In any case, a third ICA was negotiated, and went into effect in 1976, with the quotas suspended.

The rapid price increases following the Brazilian frost made further collective action by producers unnecessary. For about two years, coffee producers enjoyed a boom. But prices began to fall after April 1977, and producers quickly sought ways to stop them from declining too rapidly and to establish a floor under them. During 1977 and 1978, they pulled off a temporarily successful manipulation of the coffee futures market, by executing a series of "short squeezes."[10] The first occurred in July 1977 and worked as follows. The main players were the IBC and the *Compania Salvadorena de Café*. They bought July futures contracts on the New York Coffee, Sugar, and Cocoa Exchange (CSCE) during June, 1977 (in market parlance, they "went long"). This entitled them, if they so chose, to take delivery of specific grades of Central American or Colombian coffee in New York at the end of July, from the "shorts," traders who had sold July futures contracts. But they knew that there was very little coffee available in New York of the quality certified by the CSCE as deliverable against the New York "C" contract, and they prevented any more from arriving, by buying it and shipping it to Europe. The "shorts" had sold futures contracts for hedging or speculative purposes, and had no intention of actually delivering coffee. They had intended to liquidate their positions, by buying futures contracts back from the "longs." But the "longs" weren't selling. The only other option the "shorts" had was to find suitable coffee somewhere and somehow get it to New York, to fulfill their obligations under the futures contracts. But the "longs" already held this coffee. In this situation, the "longs" could practically name their price for allowing the "shorts" to liquidate their positions, and make a handsome profit on the deal. A similar operation was carried out on the London exchange (where robusta coffee futures were traded), and the operation was repeated for the December 1977 futures contract. At that point, the Commodity Futures Trading Commission (CFTC) stepped in and ordered the "longs" to liquidate their positions in an orderly fashion (*New York Times*, December 30, 1977, p. 1).

The 1976 ICA provided for the automatic reintroduction of quotas if the ICO indicator price reached 78 cents per pound, but after the price levels reached during the coffee boom, producers were in no mood to wait for prices to fall that far. By mid-1978, the price had fallen to about $1.50, and producers sought a reintroduction of quotas at the September ICO meetings. But consumers generally felt that prices were still too high, and were upset over the producer manipulations, and would not agree to an upward revision of the 78-cent trigger price. Following that meeting, eight Latin American producers formed the Bogota Group (Brazil, Colombia, El Salvador, Costa Rica, Guatemala, Honduras, Mexico, and Venezuela), and established a fund of $140 million to carry out similar futures market operations during 1978. In 1979, they made a killing on the July futures contract because of an early frost in Brazil. The Group coordinated its buying of the futures contract with the IBC's announcement of its estimate of the damage caused by the frost, which was probably artificially inflated. They were holding futures contracts bought at low prices before the announcement, and when the market reacted to the news, futures prices jumped. They reportedly made over $300 million on this operation. In May 1980, the group incorporated as Pancafé, but by this time, there was too much surplus coffee floating around, and such manipulations were no longer feasible. Brazilian production had recovered, and new trees planted in other countries as prices began to increase in 1975–1976 were beginning to produce. Pancafé lost money and was disbanded later in the year, as part of an agreement to reinstate export quotas under the ICA. The ICO indicator price was still in the range of $1.20 per pound at this point, well above the 78-cent trigger (Finlayson and Zacher 1988; Marshall 1979, 1980).

There were several important similarities between the situations in 1962, when producers and consumers came to an agreement on the first ICA, and in 1980, when they again agreed to impose regulation on the market. In 1962, as in 1980, geopolitical concerns were important in motivating participation in market regulation by the core states. In 1962, it had been the Cuban Revolution, the threat of spreading revolution in Latin America, and the decolonization movement in Africa, which caused core states, led by the United States, to suddenly become interested in promoting the economic development of the Third World. In 1980, it was the Sandinista revolution in Nicaragua, the civil wars in El Salvador, Guatemala, and Angola, and escalating guerrilla warfare in Colombia, which caused similar concerns. In this geopolitical context, a mechanism for the provision of disguised aid to specific Third World states by the United States and other core states became an important instrument of foreign policy. In 1980, as in 1962, core states' geopolitical concerns became linked to the concerns of the national coffee companies over the stability and prices of their coffee supplies. In both cases, the actual disruption of coffee supplies because of political upheavals was compounded by fears that future supplies might also be cut off by U.S. import bans, as had been applied against Cuba in the early 1960s, or against Uganda under Idi Amin, in the late 1970s. The coffee companies thus supported market regulation to stabilize the market, and approved of the use of the regulation mechanism to transfer aid to the coffee producing countries to stabilize their political situations, because these measures also stabilized their coffee supply lines. Finally, in 1962 and in 1980, core states and coffee companies alike were concerned about the possible effects of collective action by Third World producers, who were attempting to impose their own forms of regulation, under their control, on the world market. Thus a form of regulation over which the core states could exercise some degree of control seemed to them to be a preferable alternative. However, in 1962, collective action by producers was limited to efforts to cut their exports, and was not very effective. By the 1970s, the producers had moved into the coffee spot and futures markets in the heart of the core, and their actions were reputedly very effective, at least during several short periods. Further, these actions were more difficult to detect than export limits, and therefore created even greater uncertainty and anxiety on the part of core traders.

These similarities show that grounds for agreement among producing and consuming states and TNCs existed in both 1962 and 1980, and help to explain why market regulation was imposed at these two points in time. However, the 1980 agreement is still remarkable because it occurred in a very different international context. In 1962, with the development project (McMichael 2000) in full swing, national management of coffee sectors by the producing states in the interest of national development was internationally seen as legitimate. During this period, the established and newly emerging Third World states were engaged in collective action to change the terms of trade, in what was still a largely colonial pattern of trade. This collective action resulted in a wide variety of international agreements to regulate trade, and the ICA was just one of these. By 1980, the United States was moving to abandon this model of national economic regulation, which included integrated agricultural and industrial sectors within a national economy. A new "Washington consensus" was emerging, in which liberalization and global economic integration were seen as the legitimate means through which to pursue economic development. However, coffee was a primary commodity which was still produced and traded on the old colonial pattern, its production remained firmly under the control of the producing states, and it still provided a livelihood for millions of small farmers. Producers had demonstrated an ability to collectively control their own exports, and a remarkable ability to coordinate market interventions that moved up the chain and into the markets of the core consuming countries. Through 20 years of experience, the producers had developed the state capacity and the institutional framework that made effective collective action possible, and this is the main reason why the coffee market remained regulated through the 1980s, as many other economic sectors were liberalized.

The Roots of Overproduction

However, even as regulation was reimposed in 1980, forces were already at work that would lead to increased coffee production during the 1980s, despite the fact that world production was already in excess of what was needed to meet world demand. The direct impact of this chronic overproduction was minimized in the short run by the operation of the ICA, which controlled the flow of coffee into the major ICO-member consuming markets, allowing the overproduction to continue through the 1980s. But in the long run it undermined the grounds for agreement on continuation of the ICA.

The first factor was the tree crop price cycle triggered by the Brazilian frost. As coffee prices remained at record levels through 1976 and 1977, growers planted more coffee to try to take advantage of the high prices. However, the fact that these new trees took several years to mature and start producing meant that this new planting had no immediate effect on the market, causing over-planting. It was only in 1979 and 1980 that the first of this coffee began to hit the market, causing the rapid price decline that put Pancafé out of business and brought the reintroduction of controls through the ICA. The reimposition of export quotas cut off the tree crop price cycle in the middle of its price decline phase. On the one hand, this prevented a slide to disastrously low price levels and the attendant economic and social consequences in the producing countries; on the other, it allowed production to remain at a level somewhat higher than needed to meet worldwide demand.

The second factor was the technification[11] of coffee production in Colombia and Central America. The state coffee agencies in these countries provided agricultural extension services to coffee growers and also funded research into the improvement of coffee. One impetus for this R&D was the desire to increase production. Increased coffee production meant increased export revenues. The "green revolution" that had greatly expanded the productivity of basic grains—corn, wheat, and rice—served as a model, and coffee research agencies in several coffee producing countries developed new "dwarf" coffee varieties that produced substantially greater volumes of coffee.

This development was an initiative of local capitalist classes seeking to modernize coffee production through the application of science and technology, as London (1997) convincingly argues for the case of Colombia. But it also meshed nicely with the consolidation of the coffee traders and manufacturers in the core consuming markets during the 1980s (discussed in the next chapter). The coffee manufacturers blended coffees from different origins to achieve a consistent taste. As they began to manufacture in larger and larger volumes, they began to demand from the producing countries larger and larger volumes of coffee of consistent quality and taste. The new technified varieties were able to supply this more efficiently than were a large number of smaller growers using somewhat different varieties and production methods. This development was also partially funded by the United States. Coffee technification was a local

Table 4.2 Technification of Coffee Production, Early 1990s, and Increases in Production, Early 1970s to Early 1990s

Country	% Technification	Total Coffee Production		
		1974/76	1992/94	% Increase
Colombia	69	8750	13,475	54
Costa Rica	40	1348	2548	89
Honduras	35	829	1991	140
Nicaragua	29	757	623	-18
Dominican Rep.	25	960	734	-24
Guatemala	20	2345	3192	36
Mexico	17	4050	4165	3

Sources: Technification figures are from Rice and Ward (1996). % Technification is the percentage of total coffee area that is under technified production. Coffee production is in thousands of 60-kg bags. Production 1974/76 is an average of crop years 1974/75 and 1975/76, from USDA, Foreign Agricultural Service, *Foreign Agricultural Circular—Coffee, FCOF 1–78*, (USGPO, June 1978). Production 1992/94 is an average of crop years 1992/93 and 1993/94, from USDA, Foreign Agricultural Service, *Tropical Products: World Markets and Trade, FTROP 2–94*, (USGPO, June 1994). Production is averaged over two crop years because of the two-year coffee cycle in which a particularly large crop is usually followed by a much smaller one.

project, and in countries like Colombia and Mexico it was funded by the state coffee agencies, but USAID provided considerable funding for other projects in Central America and the Caribbean (Rice 1999; Rice and Ward 1996).

Table 4.2 shows how the technification of production translated into production increases through the 1980s and into the 1990s, using data from the seven most highly technified countries. Production in 1974/76 indicates the level of production before technification programs had begun. Although Colombia's program began in the early 1970s, it initially had little effect on production. USAID's funding programs began in 1978. Production in 1992/94 indicates these countries' production at roughly the same time as their percent of technification was measured. It probably underestimates the increase in production due to technification during the 1980s, because production had already begun to decline after the ICA collapsed and coffee prices crashed in 1989. The three most technified countries, Colombia, Costa Rica, and Honduras, had the largest production increases. Nicaragua's decrease in production can be attributed primarily to the contra war in the 1980s. The apparent decline of the Dominican Republic's production is mainly a statistical artifact, due to a bumper crop in 1975/76. When annual production figures are examined, Dominican production in the late 1980s was at about the same level as it was in the early 1970s; so technification had little impact on its total production. Nevertheless, it is clear that technification had a significant impact on total production in a number of countries.

The third factor leading to overproduction was the debt crisis of the 1980s and the World Bank and International Monetary Fund (IMF) structural adjustment programs. This had an indirect effect on coffee production, as mounting debt and structural adjustment created pressures for Third World countries to expand and diversify their exports in order to earn more foreign exchange to repay debts. The global recession of the early 1980s, which had touched off the debt crisis, made coffee look like an attractive alternative. The demand in developed countries for the primary commodity exports of the developing world slumped during the recession, as did their prices. However, world market prices for coffee were maintained at reasonable levels by the ICA. While these prices were considerably lower than they had been during the coffee boom of the mid-1970s, they were relatively better than the prices of most other commodities. Countries that had been minor coffee exporters, such as Thailand and the Philippines, greatly expanded their production during the 1980s.

Fourth, the rules governing export quotas under the ICA created an incentive for exporting member countries that were producing coffee in excess of their export quotas to maintain this level of production. The division of the total export quota into individual shares for each exporting member was always one of the most politically contentious issues in ICA negotiations. The formula used resulted from a compromise between established members such as Brazil and Colombia, who wanted to maintain their market shares, and newer members who were expanding their production and wanted larger quotas. The formula combined a country's "historic" world market share with its "demonstrated capacity" to produce and export coffee to arrive at a quota. Countries that consistently overproduced their quota and had stored coffee on hand thus had ammunition to argue for a larger share because of their "demonstrated capacity" every time the quotas were reallocated. The regulatory regime attempted to limit total coffee exports while simultaneously creating conditions under which producers would tend to produce coffee in excess of the amount needed to fill the global quota (F. O. Licht March 22, 1988). The contradictory nature of the quota system might not have been a major problem if there hadn't been additional forces pushing in the direction of increasing production. But as the oversupply situation continued through the 1980s, it began to create problems for the ICA.

The Fruits of Overproduction

The convergence of these tendencies toward increasing production, under a regime that provided incentives for excess production, led to a situation of chronic oversupply during the 1980s. When the ICA quotas went back into effect in 1980, coffee-importing states once again began to cooperate in regulating the market. They agreed not to accept any over-quota imports from exporting members, and they agreed to limit the amount of coffee they could import from non-member exporting countries. However, there was one major flaw in the system. There was a strong incentive for new coffee producing countries to join the agreement, because that was the only way to obtain access to the major consuming markets, but there was no similar incentive for new consuming countries to join. During the 1970s and 1980s, there was a globalization of coffee consumption, as Western patterns of coffee drinking spread to Eastern Europe and the more affluent Third World countries.[12] These new coffee-consuming countries generally remained outside the ICA. The first ICA had been signed by twenty-five consuming countries accounting for 94 percent of world coffee imports; the fourth ICA of 1983 was signed by twenty-seven consuming members, but by 1989 they accounted for only about 80 percent of world imports. Meanwhile, the producing membership of the ICO grew from thirty-seven in 1962 to forty-eight in 1983, and in 1989 producing members still accounted for about 98 percent of world exports of green coffee.[13]

These new consuming markets became outlets for the excess coffee stored in some of the producing countries. These producers began to compete for sales to the new non-quota markets by offering discounts from the prices that were being paid by ICO-member importers. For the producing countries, it was preferable to sell the coffee that they were producing in excess of their quotas, even at a discount, rather than paying the costs of stockpiling it, or simply letting it deteriorate in storage and getting nothing in return for it. As production continued to exceed demand in the quota markets, the stocks in exporting countries grew, and so did the discounts, reaching 50 percent by the mid-1980s according to some estimates. This two-tier market, in which ICO-member consuming countries in effect subsidized exports to non-member importing countries, began to turn consuming states and coffee companies against the ICA (Akiyama and Varangis 1990).

The coffee companies complained vociferously about this unfair subsidy they were providing to the new consumers, but at the same time, they were also attempting to take advantage of the existence of the two-tier market to buy some of their coffee at a discount. Some of the exports shipped to the non-quota markets were reexported to the quota markets in ways that were difficult for the ICO to trace. This so-called "tourist coffee" (because it visited several countries on its journey) had been a problem in the first two ICAs, but the increased importance of the non-member market, the growing surpluses of coffee, and the large price differential which opened in the 1980s made it an increasingly significant problem. One of the most common methods for accomplishing this diversion was for an exporting country to transship coffee ostensibly destined for a non-member market through one of the world's major coffee ports, such as Hamburg or Singapore. While the coffee was in port, high-quality coffee destined for a non-member market could easily be switched with low-quality coffee destined for a member market, thus providing an effective discount. The coffee could also be supplied with forged ICO export stamps, or authentic stamps could be purchased from another exporting member that did not have sufficient coffee to meet its quota for that year. Another method was to ship for "inward processing"—the coffee would be imported into a member market, supposedly to be processed into roasted or instant coffee to be sold in a non-member market. In this way, it did not count against the exporting country's quota. But once it had entered the member market, its final destination was impossible to trace. Such transactions generally required the complicity of both exporters and importers, and there was a high degree of creativity on both sides of the market.

Table 4.3 Exports to Member and Non-Member Markets and the "Tourist Coffee" Trade, Early 1980s

	Avg. 1975– 80	1980/ 81	1981/ 82	1982/ 83	1983/ 84	1984/ 85	1985/ 86
Member markets							
Export volume	51960	51251	54352	54878	59750	57173	61567
Export unit value	144.9	106.6	106.8	110.4	124.1	119.4	159.0
Non-member markets							
Export volume	5719	7988	8882	10853	9979	11439	6926
Export unit value	148.5	104.5	85.3	71.6	73.0	81.6	145.1
"Tourist" trade							
Excess volume[a]		988	1882	3853	2979	4439	
Discount	–2%	2%	20%	35%	41%	32%	9%

Source: International Coffee Organization, WP Agreement No. 13/88 Rev. 2. Data are for coffee years, October 1–September 30. Volumes are in thousands of bags (60 kg) of green bean equivalents; unit values are in U.S. cents per pound.
[a]Based on the assumption of average annual consumption of seven million bags in non-member countries while quotas were in effect. See text for details.

By the 1980s, what had been large national coffee companies had begun to go transnational (this is discussed more fully in the next chapter). These TNCs, with offices and warehouses in a number of the major coffee ports were obviously in the best position to take advantage of this tourist trade. Some TNCs, particularly Nestlé, already had a presence in the new consuming markets and had direct access to this discounted coffee. The large U.S.-based coffee companies, led by General Foods, were thus the ones that objected most strenuously.

Because this was a clandestine trade, it is very difficult to get any data on the volume of the trade or the size of the discounts. The evidence is largely anecdotal and mainly supplied by major participants in the market, whose interests were sometimes served by dissemination of misleading information on the extent of this trade. That discounts were at times as high as 50 percent seems to be generally accepted, and estimates of the volume range from about 1.5–2 million bags per year, or about 2.5–3.5 percent of the global quota, by the mid-1980s.[14]

Table 4.3 presents some imperfect data on this trade, derived from ICO statistics. It shows the volume and unit value of exports to ICO-member and non-member markets, before and after the imposition of quotas in 1980. The data are imperfect because they are based on reports by exporting states. Some states had an interest in disguising the extent of the tourist trade; others may have been deceived by their export firms. The data show that the volume of exports to non-member markets increased sharply after 1980, and their unit value also fell dramatically. Consumption in non-member countries was increasing during this period, but not as fast as imports; if we assume an average annual consumption of seven million bags in these countries after 1980, then these data indicate a tourist trade of over 2.5 million bags per year. The quality and price of coffee exported to non-member markets is generally lower than that sent to the core member markets, but this can't account for the huge differential of twenty to forty percent between member and non-member prices during 1981–1985. Events of 1985–1986 confirmed that these changes in volumes and value of exports were due to the quotas. In the middle of the 1985/86 coffee year, quotas were again suspended, because of a severe drought in Brazil that cut its production. Exports to the non-member markets quickly fell from over eleven million bags to just under seven million, and the price difference fell to less than 10 percent. These figures indicate that the two-tier market had become a significant problem by the mid-1980s.

While U.S.-based coffee companies may have benefited less from this trade than the European companies in the first half of the 1980s, they did get an opportunity to take advantage of it. For almost a year after quotas were reinstated in 1987, the United States had no customs regulations in place to allow it to refuse entry of any coffee. It is estimated that about 2 million "illegal" bags of coffee entered the United States during that year, probably also at hefty discounts (F. O. Licht February 8, 1989). Despite the complaints of the U.S.-based companies, therefore, it is quite likely that they also benefited from the tourist trade.

The other problem that emerged from the oversupply situation during the 1980s was "selectivity." As world coffee consumption increased, demand began to shift away from the low-quality robusta coffees produced mainly in Africa and Asia, and toward high-quality arabicas produced mainly in Central America and Colombia (also Kenya, Indonesia, and several other countries). Because the different types of coffee were produced in different countries, an unintended consequence of the quota system was a set of global limits on the availability of the different types of coffee.[15] The quotas thus limited the ability of importers to meet the shifting demand in consuming member countries by increasing their imports of higher quality arabicas, a further annoyance for the large coffee companies. But it also deepened the divisions among producers. In particular, the Central American "other milds" producers felt that they were in a position to significantly increase their world market shares because of the shift in demand, but were being prevented from taking advantage of the opportunity by the quota system. The evidence suggests that the Central American producers responded to this situation through aggressive discounting in sales to the non-member markets.[16] Other producers such as Colombia consistently accused them of undermining the ICA in this fashion during the 1980s. Through these sales and the "tourist" trade, additional "other mild" coffee undoubtedly found its way into the quota markets, the protests of the large coffee companies notwithstanding.

This was the situation when producing and consuming ICO member states began to meet in late 1988 to negotiate a new ICA (the fourth ICA, signed in

1983, was set to expire in September 1989). The two-tier market and the selectivity problem had convinced consumers that major revisions would have to be made in any new ICA. And by 1989, with the Soviet Bloc crumbling, the United States and other consumers had fewer geopolitical reasons for using the ICA as a means to provide aid to the producing countries, the rationale behind the original 1962 ICA and the reimposition of quotas in 1980. In addition, there was increased distrust among producers, as structural adjustment forced them to compete against one another for niches in the world economy, and this was exacerbated by conflicts over the tourist trade and the selectivity problem. The stage was set for the demise of regulation.

The Demise of the ICA

In order to understand the details of the demise of the ICA, a brief description of its voting structure is necessary. Formally, the governing body of the ICO is the International Coffee Council (ICC), consisting of all member countries. Importing countries and exporting countries each have 1000 votes in the Council. Each member has a small number of "basic" votes, three for exporters and five for importers (because there are more exporting than importing members), to insure that small members have some voting power. The remaining votes are distributed proportionally to members on the basis of their shares of total exports or total imports, with the limitation that no member can have more than 400 votes (ICO 1982, Articles 9 and 13). Most decisions of the ICC require a distributed simple majority vote (Article 15). That is, they must be supported by a group of importers who have at least 501 votes, and a group of exporters who have at least 501 votes. However, all decisions regarding quotas (allocation, revision, suspension, or reintroduction) require a distributed two-thirds majority vote (Article 28). While the distribution of votes proportional to shares of total imports or exports gives the large importers and exporters voting power to influence all decisions of the ICC, this latter provision gives the largest importers and exporters virtual veto power over quota decisions. In 1989, the United States, with 279 votes, was 55 votes short of absolute veto power. Germany, France, Japan, and Italy, the next four largest importers, each had more than 55 votes. Brazil and Colombia, with 212 and 144 votes respectively, could combine to veto any quota proposal. Finally, any decision to extend or renegotiate the agreement required the support of 58 percent of the members having not less than a distributed majority of 70 percent of the votes (Article 68). This provision insured the support of a majority of the member countries (with one member, one vote), as well as supermajorities of importers and exporters (with votes weighted by import and export shares), for this most important decision on the life or death of the agreement.

The 1983 ICA was set to expire on September 30, 1989. In order to keep the quota regime in effect, the members of the ICO had to either agree to extend the Agreement as it was for a period of time, or negotiate a new Agreement, and, given the dissatisfaction among consumers, a simple extension was unlikely. The negotiations formally started in the spring of 1988 with the appointment of a Technical Preparatory Group "to identify the problems of the Agreement and to examine proposals submitted by members to solve these problems" (ICC 49-3). This Group met twice in mid-1988, and accumulated a sizable collection of statements and proposals from members, as well as numerous statistical reports from ICO staff, all of which were presented to the ICC in Fall 1988. At that time, a Negotiating Group was established, and directed to prepare a draft for a new Agreement (ICC 50-10). More proposals and counterproposals were circulated, and this group met in November 1988 and February 1989, but was unable to agree on any language for a new Agreement that would resolve the major problems of selectivity and the two-tier market.

The next Council session, in April 1989, became crucial. Any new ICA had to be ratified by a sufficient number of member states in order to go into effect by October 1, 1989, and the states had to deposit formal instruments of ratification with the UN Secretary General before then. Many member countries needed a lead time of at least six months in order to complete their formal ratification processes, so that, if the text of a new Agreement was not agreed on at the April session, continuation of the quota regime was thrown into question. Yet disagreements between producers and consumers persisted, as well as disagreements among producers and among consumers. The Colombian delegation tried hard to forge a compromise, but failed, finally settling for convincing the Council to call a special session for June to make one final attempt at agreement (F. O. Licht April 25, 1989).

At the June meeting, the positions of the disparate factions finally coalesced into two blocs, which presented alternative proposals for a new ICA. The "majority" group included Brazil and Colombia, all African producers, the Philippines, and the EEC. Their proposal was for a one-year extension of the 1983 ICA, with a separate set of quotas imposed on sales to non-members. This one-year extension would serve as a transitional period during which a "universal" quota that would apply to all sales by exporting members, to both member and non-member markets, could be negotiated. A redistribution of quota shares would also be a part of the negotiation of this new universal quota. The "dissident" group consisted of the "other milds" group (Costa Rica, Dominican Republic, Ecuador, El Salvador, Guatemala, Honduras, India, Mexico, Nicaragua, Papua New Guinea, and Peru), Indonesia, and the United States. They demanded that a redistribution of quota shares be a part of any initial agreement; they felt that putting off the issue for a year was unlikely to result in agreement on the changes they demanded. They proposed an extension with an immediate increase to a 48 percent share for all mild arabicas (the "other milds" plus Colombian milds, produced by Colombia, Kenya, and Tanzania). This was an increase of 4.6 percent in the mild arabica share, or a shift of about three million bags of coffee (worth about $415 million at June 1989 prices), away from the share held by Brazilian milds and robustas. This would have given the "other milds" the increase they wanted, and was also an attempt to split Colombia off from the majority group, as it also would have gotten a significant increase in its quota share. The Colombian delegation denounced this attempt to buy its support and continued its efforts to find a compromise that at least some of the "other milds" producers would agree to. But despite three one-day extensions of the session and a final effort in which the clocks were turned off at midnight on the last day and negotiation continued until daybreak, the dissident group refused to compromise. No vote was taken on either proposal at this session, since no fallback position had been prepared, and the legal status of the ICO would have been in question if both proposals had been voted down. Thus another session was scheduled for July 3 to vote on the two proposals, but everyone realized that it was merely a formality. The intervening time allowed the ICO staff to prepare a resolution for an extension of the 1983 ICA with all economic clauses suspended. This would keep the ICO in existence, but end the quota regime (F. O. Licht June 22, 1989).

The votes on the two resolutions at the July 3 session are shown in table 4.4. The "majority" resolution had gotten a majority of the votes of both the producers and consumers, but only 52 percent of the members had voted for it (short of the required 58 percent), and it had not achieved the required 70 percent majority on either side. The major obstacle was clearly the United States; with U.S. support it would have gotten virtually 100 percent consumer support. Further, without U.S. support for their position, it is likely that some of the "other milds" producers could have been persuaded to vote for it as well, and this would have given it the 70 percent distributed majority needed.[17] The "dissident" resolution clearly had the support of only a minority of producers and consumers, primarily the United States and the "other milds" group. The EEC voted as a bloc for the "majority" proposal and abstained on the "dissident" proposal, probably in deference to the United States. Brazil, Colombia, and all African producers voted for the "majority" proposal and against the dissidents; Brazil and especially the African producers would have been the biggest losers under the dissident proposal. Immediately following these votes, members voted unanimously to continue the existence of the ICO, but to suspend the "economic clauses" (the quotas) indefinitely.

By April, it was already becoming clear that the ICA was in serious trouble, and importers held off purchasing because they expected prices to go down. Thus prices began to slide in April, and by October, over a period of only six months, they had fallen by 50 percent. Once the quotas were suspended, producers released the stocks they had been holding and increased their exports to try to make up some of the lost revenue, but this only exacerbated the situation. El Salvador, for example, increased its export volume by 53 percent in 1989, and earned 8 percent less than it had in 1988.

Given the importance of this vote, several different explanations of it have been offered, none entirely satisfactory. Perhaps the most influential of these explanations was actually issued before the final impasse was reached, and may have played a role in it. A World Bank Working Paper by Takamasa Akiyama and Panayotis Varangis was published in February 1989, and was circulating

84   *Chapter 4*

Table 4.4 The Votes That Ended the ICA Quota System, July 1989

	For	Against	Absent/Abstain	Total
"Majority" Resolution				
Exporting Members	675	218	107	1000
Importing Members	520	297	183	1000
"Dissident" Resolution				
Exporting Members	251	595	154	1000
Importing Members	372	0	628	1000

Votes against the "Majority" Resolution: Exporters: Mexico, Honduras, Peru, Costa Rica, Guatemala, Panama, Haiti, Indonesia, Papua New Guinea, and India (i.e., the Other Milds group minus the Dominican Republic, El Salvador, and Ecuador, plus Haiti and Panama). Only the United States and Singapore among the importers voted against it.

Absent/Abstain on the "Majority" Resolution: Exporters: Thailand, Sri Lanka, Ecuador, El Salvador, Dominican Republic, Bolivia, Paraguay, Guinea, Nigeria, Malawi, and Zambia. Importers: Australia, Fiji, Switzerland, Austria, Finland, Cyprus, Japan, and Canada.

Votes in favor of the "Dissident" Resolution: Exporters: Mexico, Ecuador, Honduras, El Salvador, Peru, Costa Rica, Guatemala, Nicaragua, Panama, Haiti, Paraguay, India, and Papua New Guinea (i.e., the Other Milds group minus the Dominican Republic, plus Panama, Paraguay, and Haiti). Importers: United States, Canada, Finland, Norway, and Sweden.

Sources: ICC 53-7; F. O. Licht July 7, 1989; Montenegro, Aparicio, and Langebaek (1989), Anexos 1 and 2, pp. 9–10.

among the delegations as the negotiations reached their critical stage (Gilbert 1996). It opens with the statement that "there is a fairly high degree of uncertainty about whether a new Agreement will come into force in October 1989" (1). The cover of the paper carries the following summary: "The new global coffee model shows which producing countries have gained and which have lost from the operation of the International Coffee Agreement—and what would happen if the Agreement were discontinued." The econometric model of the world coffee economy developed in the paper is run for the period 1981–1985 with quotas in effect, and then run for the same period to simulate the operation of the market during this period if there had been no quotas. The results are compared to see which producing countries would have earned more for their coffee exports without quotas than they did with quotas. A key, and somewhat dubious, assumption necessary to make this comparison is that producing state policies would have been the same under the non-quota situation as they were with quotas. The model also ignores the high degree of concentration among the coffee importing and roasting firms that had occurred by 1989 (discussed in the next chapter).

The results showed three of the largest producers, Brazil, Colombia, and Côte d'Ivoire, benefiting from the quotas. A number of African producers also benefited: Uganda, Ethiopia, Cameroun, Kenya, and Zaire. The main losers, according to Akiyama and Varangis, were Indonesia and some of the "other milds" producers: Mexico, Costa Rica, Guatemala, Honduras, Nicaragua, Ecuador, Peru, India, and Papua New Guinea. El Salvador was an exception; the simulation showed it benefiting from the quota system. It is easy to understand these results given the situation prevailing in the early 1980s. The "other milds" group had increased production, in response to the high prices of the late 1970s or the debt pressures of the 1980s, and/or because of technification. The quotas limited their sales to the ICO-member importers, and drove up the prices of their coffees in these markets. They responded by selling heavily to the non-member markets, driving those prices down, and setting up the conditions under which the "tourist coffee" problem grew. Under the non-quota simulation, they would have been able to sell more coffee to the member markets, earning higher incomes, and this is why they looked like losers from the quotas. The price crash that followed the end of quotas in 1989 devastated all producers, including the "other milds," and cast serious doubts on these results. The model seems to have underestimated the extent to which increased sales to the member markets in the absence of quotas would have driven down all prices, so that all producers lost, no matter how much they were able to increase the volumes of their exports. But it is also easy to understand how the results of this simulation strengthened the resolve of the "other milds" to stick to their demand for a higher quota share.

Akiyama and Varangis also ran projections to the year 2000 under the assumptions of continued quotas and no quotas. The results showed that prices would be higher over most of the period with continuation of the quotas, but by the year 2000, the total export earnings of producers would actually be slightly higher if the quotas were discontinued in 1989. A few countries would even earn more over the entire period under the non-quota condition: Costa Rica, Cameroun, Zaire, Rwanda, Indonesia, Philippines, and Papua New Guinea. These countries were among a group of low-cost producers that would be able to increase production even with low world market prices. Also included in this group were Brazil, Mexico, Peru, Burundi, and Tanzania. The biggest losers in the non-quota scenario were high-cost producers who would be most hurt by the low prices: El Salvador, Angola, Côte d'Ivoire, Ethiopia, and India. However, the non-quota simulation showed a much smaller price decrease and a much quicker price recovery than actually happened in 1989 and the early 1990s. This may have been due to its failure to incorporate the market power of the coffee TNCs, which enabled them to drive prices down after the quotas ended, and to keep them there for an extended period. But again, this result may have strengthened the resolve of Indonesia and the "other milds" group—they may have felt that they could ride out the temporary price decline with few harmful effects.

Another interesting analysis was published in the Colombian coffee journal *Ensayos sobre Economia Cafetera* in late 1989 (Montenegro, Aparicio, and Langebaek 1989). These analysts conducted a quantitative analysis of the vote on the majority proposal.[18] For producers, they used two economic explanatory variables. The ratio of a country's exportable production to its quota was used to indicate the strength of a country's desire for a larger export share. Two measures indicated a country's ability and willingness to comply with ICA rules on shipments to non-members. The first was a ratio of inventories to the size of the quota and the second was the ratio of volume of sales to the non-member market to the total coffee available for export. As a political factor, they attempted to capture the effect of a country's commitment to collective action; they did this by including a dummy variable for membership in the Non-Aligned Movement (G77). Thirty-six of the fifty producers included in the analysis were members. Their regression analysis showed that all of these variables had significant effects on a country's vote—those countries that had high desire for a larger quota and high willingness to break ICA rules by large shipments to non-quota markets were more likely to vote against the proposal. Those who built up inventories, thereby complying with ICA rules, and those who were members of the G77 were more likely to vote for it. Further, membership in the G77 appeared to partially explain a country's willingness to restrict sales to the non-quota markets. It should be pointed out that this explanation closely followed the official Colombian position. Colombia had significant overproduction and large stockpiles, but refrained from selling to non-members, and repeatedly criticized those countries that did, for breaking solidarity and undermining the agreement. The Colombian delegation was also the one that worked hardest to forge some kind of compromise as the time ran out.

For consumers, Montenegro et al. used one economic explanatory variable, the excess demand for "other milds" coffee. This was measured by the proportion of "other milds" in a country's imports in 1986 (without quotas) versus 1988 (with quotas). Consuming countries with high excess demand for "other milds" that couldn't be met under the quotas tended to vote against the proposal. Their one political explanatory factor is desire to support a particular group of producers, assuming that consumers took a position on the agreement based on the position taken by a favored group of producers. Statistically, this part of the analysis leaves much to be desired, because there were only two consuming countries voting against the proposal: the United States and Singapore. Empirically, it does capture the essence of the impasse, that the major opposition came from the United States and the "other milds" group, prominent among which were most of the Central American producers. The United States was still trying to stem the tide of revolution in this region, and so favored what they saw as the Central Americans' interests.

Robert Bates (1997) has also offered an explanation of the demise of the ICA that brings in another crucial factor: domestic political considerations. He focuses on the structure of policy making in the United States. First, he argues, the Reagan administration, particularly Secretary of State George Schultz, was strongly committed to free markets. They therefore structured the U.S. delegation to the negotiations "precisely to prevent it from reaching an agreement that would violate the principle of free markets" (174). In addition, the State Department saw Brazil as the biggest beneficiary of the ICA, and as an economic rival rather than a developing country needing economic assistance. Second, the large roasting firms withdrew their support for the agreement because of two developments during the 1980s: the European roasters opened plants in Berlin, where they could easily take advantage of "tourist" coffee coming through Eastern Europe, and Nestlé, a European firm, entered the U.S. market. This explanation is partial at best, since it only explains the U.S. position, and does not do an adequate job of that. To be fair to Bates, his main purpose is to explain why the ICA came into existence, not why it collapsed, and this explanation of the collapse is only sketched in the last five pages of a 175-page book. To see why his explanation is inadequate, we need to consider the domestic roots of U.S. coffee policy.

The U.S. coffee industry's interests are represented by the National Coffee Association (NCA), to which most roasters and importers belong. NCA members account for about 90 percent of the total volume of coffee imported into and processed within the United States.[19] The NCA was founded in 1911.[20] It has about two hundred member firms, roughly evenly divided between roasters, importers, and "allied firms." The allied firms include manufacturers of coffee equipment, shipping lines, and other firms that provide services to the coffee industry. They are NCA members because of their interest in the coffee business, but it is the roasters and importers who have the major interest in lobbying the U.S. government over coffee policies. The NCA is run by a Board of Directors elected annually by the member firms. The Directors are usually senior executives of these firms, and usually come from the larger firms; Board members are usually roughly equally divided between importer and roaster representatives. The Directors are volunteers and service on the Board can take a significant amount of time; it is mainly the larger firms that can afford to have their senior executives devoting a major share of their time to the organization. Smaller firms have fewer senior executives, and they need to spend most of their time running their firms. The NCA also has a number of appointed standing committees, which advise the Board on various issues; the most important of these for international coffee policy is the Foreign Affairs Committee. Committee members are also volunteers, and therefore also tend to represent the largest firms. In the case of the Foreign Affairs Committee this is even more pronounced, because the committee members also need extensive international experience in order to advise the Board and the government on international policy. Committee members are also roughly equally divided between roaster and importer representatives.

There are sometimes severe differences of opinion between members, not only between roasters and importers, but sometimes also between large and small firms or between firms with differing political philosophies. In general, importers tended to be more supportive of ICAs than roasters. The importers have personal contacts with exporters in the producing countries and understand the role of coffee in their economies. Roasters are more sensitive to price levels, since green coffee is their main raw material input. Importers, on the other hand, work on percentage margins, and when the world market price increases, so does the size of their fee. But some importers may also have been more opposed to the political "fixing" of prices as occurred under the ICAs, because the price at which they would be able to buy and sell coffee depended every year on the decision by the ICC on the size of the global quota. Therefore, for several weeks every year, they were left in limbo, uncertain whether it was wise to conclude long-term contracts before the decision was made, or to wait until after it was made. At the same time, some of the largest roasters may have been more favorably inclined toward the ICA, because they were conglomerates with many products besides coffee to sell, and some of them were sold in the coffee-growing countries. Public support for the ICA in the United States could thus buy them favor with states that controlled their access to foreign markets. Out of these divergent opinions, the NCA committees and Board had to forge a position which could be supported by most of the larger importers and roasters as well as by a significant number of the smaller firms, in order to have any influence on U.S. government policy. Most of the time, they have been able to do this, but there have been a number of times when opinions were so divided that the NCA has been unable to take a position on an issue.

This has not usually happened in the Foreign Affairs Committee with respect to the ICA. But differences of opinion have led to very diplomatically phrased NCA resolutions over the years. Members of the NCA Foreign Affairs Committee have served as advisors to U.S. delegations to the ICA negotiations since the beginning of negotiations on the formation of an ICA in the late 1950s. They also regularly met with U.S. government representatives to inform them of U.S. industry concerns and help to work out the details of U.S. positions (Fisher 1972; *New York Times*, November 11, 1977). Lobbying by the NCA was instrumental in getting the first ICA ratified by the U.S. Senate and the enabling legislation passed by Congress. Through the 1980s, the NCA continued to support the ICA, but its 1988 resolution on the renewal negotiations reflected compromises between pro- and anti-ICA factions within the organization:

NOW THEREFORE BE IT RESOLVED THAT:

The National Coffee Association advise the appropriate United States Government officials of its views that:
1. The interests of the United States Coffee Consumer and industry are best accommodated by a free and unrestricted trade in coffee; and
2. If nevertheless the United States Government decides to continue U.S. participation in an extended or renegotiated agreement such agreement should embody solutions to the following serious weaknesses in the operation of the current agreement:
a. The sale of coffee to non-members of the Agreement, outside the export quotas, at prices substantially below the price at which coffee is offered to members of the agreement; and
b. The inflexibility of the quota system in making coffee of the origin types required by consumers available to the market. (NCA document, 1988)

Thus at least some NCA members were prepared to support an ICA that resolved, in some way, the problems of selectivity and the two-tier market.

U.S. coffee policy had been the responsibility of the State Department from the beginning of the coffee negotiations in the late 1950s, but in 1980 there was a change in the organization of trade policy which signaled the beginning of a shift in U.S. positions on the ICA. In 1980, President Carter centralized coordination of trade policy under the office of the United States Trade Representative (USTR), and created a Trade Policy Committee (TPC) chaired by the USTR and including representatives from the Departments of State, Commerce, Treasury, and Agriculture (*New York Times*, January 3, 1980). This meant that the Assistant Trade Representative was now the head of the U.S. delegation to the ICC meetings; previously the delegation had been headed by the Deputy Assistant Secretary of State for Economic Affairs. The State Department continued to have two representatives on the U.S. delegation and continued to be influential in the formulation of U.S. positions, and Commerce, Treasury, and Agriculture, which had also been represented on earlier delegations, continued to influence U.S. policy through the TPC. The U.S. contribution to the funding of the ICO also continued to come out of the State Department budget, and it was the fourth largest item in State's budget allocation for international organizations (*Tea and Coffee Trade Journal*, October 1986, 38–39; Boecklin interview).

This change in the organization of coffee policy decision making subtly shifted the orientation of U.S. policy, in a way that was not immediately apparent, but became decisive by the time of the 1988–1989 negotiations. The State Department saw the ICA as primarily a geopolitical agreement designed to provide aid to Third World countries; the USTR's primary mission was to fight trade barriers in various countries that disadvantaged U.S. exports. Therefore, while State had evaluated the ICAs on mainly political grounds, the USTR was more likely to evaluate them on purely economic grounds, grounds which held free and unrestricted trade as the ideal. State and the USTR continued to support the ICAs on Capitol Hill through the mid-1980s, testifying in support of ratification of the 1983 ICA and its implementing legislation, but the USTR's support was clearly lukewarm, as evidenced by the following exchange from the September 19, 1983 hearing of the Subcommittee on Trade of the House Ways and Means Committee on the implementing legislation:

> *Rep. Bill Frenzel (R-MN):* . . . is this coffee agreement on pure economic terms hard to justify for the consumer countries?
> *Michael B. Smith, Deputy USTR:* Well, sir, I am no lover of commodity agreements . . .
> It has a long tradition and appears to have worked reasonably well as far as commodity agreements go.
> *Rep. Frenzel:* What we call damning with faint praise.
> *Mr. Smith:* . . . I think this is, if you will, a least objectionable sort of situation, or less objectionable. (U.S. House of Representatives 1983, p. 9)

There was also very little interest in Congress in the ICA legislation; a few Senators and Representatives who were ideologically committed to free trade raised questions, but the majorities in both Chambers were inclined to pass the legislation as long as it was supported by the administration.

However, by the late 1980s, the USTR was involved in a number of trade disputes with Brazil, over computer software and pharmaceuticals, among other things. In a 1986 report on trade barriers, the USTR had ranked Brazil as the country with the most restrictive trade policies against U.S. exports. Given the widely held view that Brazil was the main beneficiary of the ICAs, the USTR was much less inclined to make any concessions which might benefit Brazil when the ICA negotiations began in 1988. Concessions might be seen as rewarding Brazil, or at least failing to punish it, for its restrictive practices (*New York Times*, November 18, 1986). In addition, the State Department was less inclined to support the ICA for its own geopolitical reasons. First, the Eastern European countries, part of the Soviet bloc through the 1980s, had been major beneficiaries of the two-tier market. Second, the ICA was seen as benefiting two producing countries that State had no desire to aid directly or indirectly: Cuba and Nicaragua. For all of these reasons, the U.S. delegation took a hard line at the negotiations, hardened their position even further as the talks went along, and encouraged the other milds group to hold out for a quota reallocation, thereby effectively scuttling the agreement.

Bates' (1997) explanation of the shift in U.S. position on the ICA is therefore partially correct. He is right to focus on the organization of policy making in the administration, and in particular on the declining support of State for the ICA. But equally important was the reorganization that increased the importance of the USTR—this reflected the general ascendance of neoliberalism within U.S. government circles. And it is noteworthy that it took place under Carter, before the Reagan administration shifted the U.S. policy orientation even further in this direction.

However, Bates' contention that the large roasters withdrew their support from the ICA is not convincing. As we have seen, the NCA was divided; support for the ICA was probably declining over time, as it was within the administration, but it still had its supporters in both places. Bates argues that one factor in this shift was the move of European roasters to Berlin, where they had easy access to tourist coffee. But as shown in chapter 3, they already had access through one of the major free ports which was involved, in Hamburg, and to a lesser extent, also in Trieste. In addition, the U.S. industry had gotten about two million "illegal" bags during 1987–1988, while implementing legislation was held up because of a dispute between Congress and the administration over trade legislation. And coffee-importing firms were globalizing; European importers were operating in the United States, and U.S. importers in Europe. Bates further argues that Nestlé, a European roaster, presumably with better access to tourist coffee, entered the U.S. market in 1986. But Nestlé had been manufacturing instant in the United States since the 1940s. If Nestlé's access to tourist coffee posed a threat to other major U.S. firms, it would have become apparent by the time of the signing of the fourth ICA in 1983; yet the NCA supported that agreement. Nestlé had also been active in the NCA for a long time, and had supported the ICA in the past. As we will see in chapter 6, it declined to oppose Brazil's exports of instant coffee to the U.S. market, in part to protect its investments in Brazil. Nestlé did enter the U.S. R&G market in the mid-1980s, with its purchases of Hills Bros. and MJB. But by this time, its largest U.S. competitor, Philip Morris/General Foods, was already operating in Europe; GF had been manufacturing instant coffee there since the 1950s. Finally, implicit in Bates' arguments is the view, expressed by some in the U.S. industry, that European support for the agreement was based solely on their easy access to tourist coffee; that is an oversimplification.

The coffee sectors of the European countries are very similar to that of the United States. The two main groups are importers and roasters, and both are fairly highly concentrated and dominated by a few large firms. Most European countries also have national coffee associations that are similar in structure and purpose to the NCA. In addition, there are Community-wide associations of roasters (EUCA) and importers (CECA), linked together to form the European Coffee Federation (ECF). The national coffee associations advise their governments on coffee policy in much the same way as the NCA, and are usually included in the national delegations to the ICC. At the same time, the EEC is an organizational member of the ICO, its member states often act as a bloc in the ICO, and representatives of the ECF play a similar advisory role to the EEC bloc. As in the United States, there are differences of opinion on the ICA between roasters and importers and between large and small firms. However, the European firms seem to be generally less committed to a free-trade ideology and more willing to accept political intervention in the market in order to stabilize supplies and provide aid to Third World countries (*Tea and Coffee Trade Journal*, May 1988, 6–8; August 1988, 44–47).

In addition to this difference in philosophy between the U.S. and European coffee firms, there was also a more important difference between U.S. and European negotiators. While the United States had shifted primary responsibility for coffee negotiations to the USTR, the European countries had generally left this responsibility to the agencies that had always had it, and they were more committed to using the ICA as a means of providing indirect foreign aid. These same agencies generally managed EEC participation in the Lomé Agreement, which sought to stabilize the export earnings of their former colonies in Africa, the Caribbean, and the Pacific. One U.S. representative described the orientation of the European negotiators by saying, "it would be as if we put USAID in charge of our delegation."[21] In other words, the European negotiators were still committed to the development of the coffee producing countries; the U.S. delegation was committed to "free" trade. The European negotiators also did not have major objections to providing aid to Nicaragua or Cuba. For all of these reasons, the EEC was willing to support the continuation of an agreement which was not in its best interests in narrow economic terms, but which was seen as having a variety of desirable political benefits (F. O. Licht June 22, 1989).

Thus far, we have explained why the United States was opposed to a new ICA while the EEC supported it. But why did the dissident group of producers, the "other milds" group and Indonesia, break from the other producers and join the United States? The answer involves excess production, domestic politics,

Table 4.5 Production Increases and Excesses of Exportable Production over Quotas, for the Five Largest Producers and the "Other Milds" Group

| | Production Increases | | | Quotas versus Production | | |
	Avg. Prod. 1972/74	Avg. Prod. 1981/83	% Change	Avg. Quota 1981/83	Avg. Exportable[a] Production 1981/83	Ratio of Prod. to Quota
Five Largest						
Brazil	21564	23973	11.2	15738	16173	1.03
Colombia	8150	14010	71.9	8554	12158	1.42
Indonesia	2953	4900	65.9	2329	3670	1.58
Côte d'Ivoire	3624	4580	26.4	4102	4363	1.06
Other Milds						
Mexico[b]	3634	4348	19.6	1900	2698	1.42
El Salvador	2304	2762	19.6	2323	2608	1.12
Guatemala	2279	2610	14.5	1841	2301	1.25
India	1489	2362	58.6	801	1512	1.89
Costa Rica	1408	1960	39.2	1216	1724	1.42
Ecuador	1198	1976	39.2	1129	1630	1.44
Honduras	814	1415	73.8	866	1227	1.42
Dominican Republic	842	1050	24.7	534	750	1.40
Peru	993	1012	1.9	732	906	1.24
Nicaragua	610	986	61.6	680	868	1.28
Papa New Guinea	602	792	31.6	606	787	1.30
All members	71654	89266	24.6	56000	69718	1.24

Sources: ICO, *Quarterly Statistical Bulletin*, various years; ICC 36-16; ICC 38-7. All quantities are in thousand bags of 60 kg. of green beans. Production is averaged over two crop years because of the two-year coffee cycle in which a particularly large crop is usually followed by a much smaller one. Quotas and exportable production are for coffee years (October 1–September 30). Crop years and coffee years are the same for most of these producers except Brazil, Indonesia, Peru, and Ecuador, whose crop years begin April 1.
[a]Exportable production is equal to total production minus domestic consumption.
[b]Mexico is one of the five largest producers and is also a member of the "other milds" group.

and a bad misreading of the world market situation, no doubt encouraged by the World Bank and the United States. Table 4.5 shows that most of these countries were saddled with significant excess production; they were producing more coffee than they were allowed to export under the ICA quotas. The reasons for this were varied. As we have seen, many countries responded to the coffee boom of the late 1970s by planting coffee, which was just beginning to come into production in 1980 when the quotas were reimposed. In addition, several Central American countries had significantly increased production through technification programs. The World Bank was encouraging a general expansion of primary commodity exports, and the provisions of the ICA provided incentives for coffee producing countries to maintain some surplus production. In addition, Indonesia in the early 1970s was engaged in a program of settling people off the crowded island of Java onto Sumatra, which was much less densely populated. The state gave people land on Sumatra and encouraged them to plant coffee as a cash crop. Between 1970 and 1978 the land area of Sumatra planted with coffee increased by 50 percent (ICO EB 2150/82). Due to the combination of all of these factors, by the early 1980s, the total exportable production of all members was about 25 percent above the global quota, which was set to be approximately equal to projected demand in the ICO-member importing countries. Indonesia and most of the other milds group had even larger excesses. But many of the African robusta producers had not increased their production as rapidly and faced a much smaller imbalance between exportable production and their quota. Côte d'Ivoire's coffee production was declining, as state incentives for cocoa production were more favorable than for coffee production. Brazil's production had been decreased drastically by the 1975 frost, and it suffered another minor frost in 1981, and a severe drought in 1985/86, so it had virtually no excess production.[22]

Once quotas went back into effect in 1980, they were renegotiated every year and approved by the Council. Every year, the "other milds" and Indonesia lobbied for increased shares because of their high excess of production over quota. But they could not bring about a redistribution as long as Brazil, Colombia, and the African producers opposed it, which they did. The "other milds" producers were a diverse group with varying degrees of regulation of their coffee sectors, and various policy-making apparatuses. India and Papua New Guinea both had state marketing boards that bought and exported some or all of their coffee. The Latin American producers all had state agencies which regulated their coffee sectors to some degree, usually including setting minimum purchase prices for growers, regulation of exports, and tax-collection powers. None of these boards or agencies had the autonomy or power of the Colombian FNC or the Brazilian IBC. For all of these countries, coffee was a major export crop, on which tens of thousands of small farmers, as well as local capitalists involved in trading and processing, and large exporting firms, depended for their existence. The political legitimacy of the state thus depended in part on being able to maintain a profitable internal price for coffee. During the period of the first two ICAs and into the early 1980s, the best way to do this was clearly to cooperate with other producers in regulating the market. However, by the late 1980s, the situation had begun to change. Most of the coffee agencies had only limited capacity to buy and store coffee. Thus, when faced with large surpluses of production over their quotas in the early 1980s, many of these marketing boards and agencies either assisted with or condoned increased sales to the non-member markets. The discounted sales cut into their coffee revenues, and they began to view the ICA more as a constraint on their ability to maximize their coffee revenues than as a mechanism to help them achieve this.

However, not all of these countries had huge surpluses or large non-member

sales. The fact that they acted as a bloc in the 1988–1989 negotiations was ultimately due to the fact that they had worked together as a bloc in the ICO for
over ten years. They felt that they had common interests, opposed to those of
Brazil and the African producers. Even those without large surpluses of production over their quotas were certain that they would benefit from an increased
quota share for the "other milds" group. If they supported the group position and
achieved a redistribution of quotas, then it would be divided among all of them.
They probably believed that the high world demand for their coffees would insulate them from any price falls that might result from the end of quotas. This
belief was probably strengthened by the World Bank analysis that was circulating in early 1989, and further encouraged by the United States. The high demand for other milds would minimize the declines of their prices—even the
European analysts believed this (*Tea and Coffee Trade Journal*, August 1988,
44–47). Thus their position was that a suspension of the quotas was preferable to
a continuation of quotas without redistribution.

Further, some members of this group, such as Mexico, the largest member,
had embraced openness and free markets under U.S. tutelage, and this provided
further rationale for their willingness to break with other producers and abandon
the ICA. Costa Rica exemplifies the other milds countries that had embraced the
free market. In the early 1980s, it had an exportable production 42 percent above
its quota, because of technification and expanded production during the coffee
boom. It was also one of those countries that had been making large non-
member sales. At the same time, it was desperate for foreign exchange to pay its
ballooning debt; this economic situation forced it into the non-member market.
By 1989, Costa Rica was staging a mild recovery. It had embraced structural
adjustment, increased its nontraditional and manufactured exports, and received
large amounts of aid from the United States. All of this tended to promote and
reinforce state support for free markets. At the same time, the rhetoric of the
consumers, who were complaining about the selectivity problem, as well as the
World Bank analysis, probably convinced Costa Rica that there was high demand for their coffee. If any prices fell once the quotas were lifted, they thought,
it would be the prices of Brazils and robustas. This sentiment was captured in a
statement by the Costa Rican delegate, Luis Escalante, to the Council's June
session:

> The current Agreement . . . should be revised to achieve a balance in the market
> by providing a fairer distribution of quotas. Costa Rica was not in favor of a
> simple extension. Any extension should correct current distortions. An exten-
> sion of the Agreement without economic provisions would be preferable if it
> were not possible to establish satisfactory terms and conditions. A free market
> would show the real situation of supply and demand. (Remarks paraphrased in
> ICC 52-m-15, "Summary Record of the Third Plenary Meeting")

By the end of 1989, he may have been regretting those words.

The period considered in this chapter spans the transition from developmentalism to globalization. Although the end of the period of material expansion under U.S. hegemony, in Arrighi's terms, the end of the second food regime, in Friedmann's terms, or the end of the development project, in McMichael's terms, all occurred in the early 1970s, it took some time for the full effects of these changes to be felt in the world economy. The 1970s were a decade of collective revolt by the Third World. In response to the failure of developmentalism and the shocks that had disorganized the world economy, Third World states banded together and attempted to set new rules for a global economic system (McMichael 2000). The most far-reaching aspect of this attempt was the program for a NIEO presented by the G77 countries at the Special Session of the UN General Assembly in 1974. Collective action by groups of commodity-producing Third World countries attempting to use their "resource power" was also a major part of this effort. While the actions of OPEC, which precipitated oil crises in 1973 and 1979, received the most attention, a number of other groups were active. The Council of Copper Exporting Countries (CIPEC), and the International Bauxite Association (IBA) tried to emulate OPEC's success. Cocoa producers, united in the CPA (Cocoa Producers Alliance) began taking unilateral actions to control the world market in the 1960s. Banana exporters formed UPEB (Union de Paises Expotadores de Banana) in 1974, and rubber producers formed ANRPC (Association of Natural Rubber Producing Countries) in 1970. As a result of these efforts, two additional international commodity agreements were concluded under UN auspices, for cocoa in 1972, and natural rubber in 1979 (Finlayson and Zacher 1988).

Seen in this context, the struggles of coffee producing countries to control the market for their commodity were not all that unusual. Bananas, rubber, and cocoa are all tropical commodities, while copper and bauxite were still being traded in the old colonial mode—produced in the Third World and consumed in the First World (see table 2.1). These commodities were still extremely important to the economies of the countries where they were produced, and this sparked collective action. What was unusual about the efforts of coffee producers was their method. While the other groups were attempting to control production and exports in order to influence the level of world market prices, coffee producers were intervening directly in the markets of the consuming countries. The reinstatement of coffee export quotas in 1980 was a move against the tide toward liberalization and free markets, but it was not unique. Three other commodity agreements, for tin, cocoa, and rubber, functioned through the first half of the 1980s. The coffee agreement was arguably the strongest and most successful of these, and that was due to the collective strength of the coffee producers.

One measure of this success was the ability of the ICA to dampen the wild price swings caused by the tree crop price cycle. This can be seen by comparing the effects of the 1975 frost on the world market with those of the severe Brazilian drought of 1985/86. We have seen that the 1975 frost, which occurred when ICA quotas were not in effect, precipitated a prolonged increase in world market prices, followed by a steep drop that was only halted by the reintroduction of quotas in 1980. Part of the reason that the price increase was so large and lasted for such a long time was that no one outside of Brazil had any significant stocks of coffee on hand when the frost struck. In 1985, a severe drought in Brazil caused another sharp price increase, leading to the suspension of quotas in February 1986. However, because the quotas were in effect, a number of producing countries (those that were less active in the non-quota market) had coffee on hand that could be immediately exported once the quotas were suspended. Because of this, it has been estimated that prices would have gone 24 percent higher if quotas had not been in effect at the time (Akiyama and Varangis 1990). Prices returned to predrought levels by late 1987, leading to a reintroduction of the quotas. While the drought did not have as much impact on Brazilian production as did the frost, part of the reason that the 1986–1987 price spike was much less severe than the one in 1976–1979 was the existence of the ICA quotas. They mitigated the price increase in 1985–1986, as well as stopping the price decline in 1987.

However, by the end of the 1980s, globalization had begun to take its toll on Third World solidarity. Many of their economies had been opened and their states restructured in the neoliberal mode, often under pressure of debt and structural adjustment. Many states had begun to openly embrace the neoliberal doctrine, and one component of this new view of the world was that they saw themselves as atomized competitors within a world economy. The pressures of competing to find a set of profitable niches for their nations in this new global economy created an apparent divergence of interest with former allies, and undermined the possibilities of collective action. In addition, as a few of these countries emerged as NICs, while others stagnated or even went into economic decline, their interests in restructuring the rules for the world economy also began to diverge. Brazil and Mexico were two major coffee producers that became NICs, while most African producers faced severe economic problems. The Central American producers (except Nicaragua), key players in the "other milds" group, were drawn even more tightly into the U.S. orbit by the civil wars of the 1980s. They were probably among the most active participants in the non-quota market that undermined the ICA. Thus the split between Brazil, Colombia, and the African producers on one side, and the other milds producers on the other, which led to the demise of the ICA, was simply a manifestation of this atomization of the Third World. Yet the legacy of over thirty years of cooperation, and the state capacities that had been built up over that time, did not simply wither and disappear. Further attempts at collective action would continue through the 1990s, although they would never achieve the success seen in the ICAs.

Finally, it is important to understand the role of the United States in the demise of regulation of the world coffee market. This analysis makes it clear that the United States played the key role. It was virtually the only dissident consumer, and its support of the dissident "other milds" group was an important factor in their rejection of the ICA. The analysis also establishes that the most important domestic political factor in the U.S. turn against the ICA was the ideological reorientation of U.S. foreign policy toward support of unrestrained neoliberalism. This was symbolized by the reorganization of trade policy that put the USTR in charge of the U.S. delegation to the coffee negotiations. Although the support of the coffee TNCs, as represented by the NCA, for the ICA was declining, it was not the decisive factor in U.S. policy. Great pains have been taken to establish this conclusion, in part because of the revisionist history that has been written about the collapse of the ICA since 1989. It has generally sought to deny any U.S. government responsibility and to place the blame on the coffee industry or the producers. For instance, Akiyama (2001), in a World Bank review of commodity market liberalization since the 1980s, attributes the demise of the ICA solely to Brazil's decision to abandon the agreement, despite the fact that Brazil voted with the majority to extend the ICA. In light of the facts, such revisionist explanations do not hold water. As we will see in the next chapter, the U.S. government bears a major responsibility for the suffering of millions of coffee growers around the world since 1989.

The governance structures of the coffee commodity chain continued through this period in more or less the same form that had been established with the first ICA in 1962. Producing states governed the segments of the chain that occurred within their borders and the national coffee importing and manufacturing companies controlled the rest. The breakdown of the regulatory regime in 1972 led to struggles over governance between the producers and the coffee companies. These struggles still focused primarily on the point at which the two governance structures intersected—the world market—and the issue was still who would control that price. But this time, the producers attempted to exercise control over the world market price by influencing the coffee markets within the consuming countries. They recognized the linked nature of the price chain and reasoned that they could control the world market price by extending their control forward along the chain to the other side of the world market. If the consuming states would not cooperate in negotiating a price, then the producing states would have to take on the coffee companies directly, in their own markets. It is not clear whether this strategy could have been successful in the long run, but it was successful enough to persuade the consuming states to reinstate the ICA quotas. However, the demise of the ICA in 1989 would prove to be a decisive defeat for coffee producers. Power was beginning to shift to the transnationalizing coffee companies, and during the 1990s, they would begin to attempt to extend their control backward along the chain, into the producing countries.

Notes

1. *Tea and Coffee Trade Journal* September 1975, pp. 20–24; *World Coffee and Tea* September 1975, pp. 14–16, 31, 39; October 1975, pp. 18, 50.

2. *Tea and Coffee Trade Journal* September 1975, pp. 20–24; *World Coffee and Tea* September 1975, pp. 14–16, 31, 39; October 1975, pp. 18, 50; *Business Week* September 8, 1975, p. 21; *New York Times* July 24, 1975, p. 10; August 4, 1975, p. 29; August 7, 1975, p. 46; August 22, 1975, p. 43.

3. *Tea and Coffee Trade Journal* September 1975, pp. 20–24; *World Coffee and Tea* September 1975, pp. 14–16, 31, 39; October 1975, pp. 18, 50; *New York Times* August 22, 1975, p. 43; *Business Week* November 15, 1976, p. 154.

4. *New York Times* August 4, 1975, p. 29; November 23, 1975, Section 3, p. 7.

5. *New York Times* July 29, 1975, p. 35; September 30, 1975, p. 56; January 17, 1976, p. 37; January 24, 1976, p. 43; February 3, 1976, p. 33.

6. *New York Times* August 18, 1976, p. 55; October 13, 1976, p. 63; November 2, 1976, p. 39; December 9, 1976, p. 70; December 21, 1976, p. 57; December 24, 1976, p. D5; January 7, 1977, p. D1.

7. *New York Times* December 28, 1976, p. 31; December 29, 176, p. 55; January 4, 1977, p. 12; January 5, 1977, p. D1.

8. Brazil is also a major coffee consuming country, with annual consumption esti-mated at around seven million bags at this time. For the first time in history following the frost, Brazil actually imported lower quality robustas from Angola and other African countries, for internal consumption and for use in its instant coffee industry. This allowed it to export a higher percentage of the coffee it produced and benefit from the higher prices.

9. Commodity Research Bureau (1983), p. 97; International Coffee Organization; *New York Times* May 13, 1977, p. D7; May 14, 1977, p. 27.

10. Information on this manipulation comes primarily from Greenstone (1981) and Edmunds (1982).

11. "Technification" is a word borrowed from Spanish. It is widely used in Latin America to describe the development being discussed here, but is not easily translatable into English.

12. This was part of a larger "standardization of class diets" identified by Friedmann (1991a) as one of the major trends which undermined the second food regime.

13. Members of the 1962 ICA were, as exporting members: Brazil, Burundi, Camer-oun, Central African Republic, Colombia, Congo-Brazzaville, Congo-Leopoldville (Za-ire), Costa Rica, Côte d'Ivoire, Cuba, Dahomey (Benin), Dominican Republic, Ecuador, El Salvador, Ethiopia, Gabon, Guatemala, Haiti, Honduras, India, Indonesia, Kenya, Malagasy Republic (Madagascar), Mexico, Nicaragua, Nigeria, Panama, Peru, Portugal (Angola), Rwanda, Sierra Leone, Tanganyika (Tanzania), Togo, Trinidad and Tobago, Uganda, Venezuela, and Yemen; and as importing members: Argentina, Australia, Aus-tria, Belgium, Canada, Cyprus, Czechoslovakia, Denmark, Finland, France, West Ger-many, Israel, Italy, Japan, Luxembourg, Netherlands, New Zealand, Norway, Spain, Sweden, Switzerland, Tunisia, United Kingdom, United States, and USSR.

By 1983, Bolivia, Ghana, Guinea, Jamaica, Liberia, Malawi, Papua New Guinea, Paraguay, Philippines, Sri Lanka, Thailand, and Zimbabwe had joined as exporting members, while Yemen dropped out. In the late 1980s, Equatorial Guinea, Vietnam, and Zambia also joined as exporting members. There was more turnover among importing members, as Argentina, Czechoslovakia, Tunisia, and USSR had dropped out by 1983, while Greece, Hungary, Ireland, Portugal, Singapore, and Yugoslavia were added (Fisher 1972; Akiyama and Varangis 1990; Bohman and Jarvis 1990; Mwandha et al. 1985; ICO documents).

14. F. O. Licht November 3, 1987; May 25, 1988; Landell Mills December 1986; January 1987; ICO documents EB3159/89 and EB3196/90.

15. See the discussion of the four basic types of coffee in chapter 2.

16. F. O. Licht November 24, 1988; April 25, 1989.

17. For instance, if El Salvador, with 37 votes, had switched from abstention to sup-port, it would have surpassed 70 percent of exporters' votes. El Salvador, though a mem-

ber of the "other milds" group, abstained because it would have gotten only a negligible increase in its quota under the dissident proposal.

18. The vote on the dissident proposal is more difficult to analyze because of the high number of abstentions. Their data on the vote on the majority proposal are a bit problematic, since their vote totals are slightly different than those reported by the ICA (1 more in favor, 3 more against, 4 fewer abstentions), and they misclassify Netherlands as voting against it, rather than for it. Nonetheless, the results are suggestive.

19. Another association, the Specialty Coffee Association of America (SCAA), represents specialty coffee roasters and importers accounting for about 30 percent of total U.S. coffee volume. But many of them, particularly the larger specialty roasters, such as Starbucks, belong to both associations. The NCA is clearly the dominant industry association in terms of its influence on U.S. government coffee policies.

20. Some of the following information on the NCA comes from an interview with Executive Director George Boecklin, July 1994; see also Bates 1997; *Tea and Coffee Trade Journal* August 1988, pp. 34–37.

21. Personal interview; source wished to remain anonymous.

22. However, Brazil has always maintained large stockpiles of coffee, amounting to almost ten million bags even after the frost.

Chapter 5

Globalization and Coffee Crises, 1990–?

The previous chapter focused on struggles over the governance structure of the coffee commodity chain. While these struggles were going on, there were important changes happening in the other two dimensions of the chain: the input-output structure, and the distribution of production among different sizes of firms. These changes would change the terms under which further struggles over governance would be conducted. Once the ICA regulatory regime had met its demise, the way was cleared for the self-regulating market to be extended to coffee once more. The collapse of prices that accompanied the end of the ICA set off another tree crop price cycle, but because of the ways in which the structure of the chain had been changed, producers were unsuccessful in their attempts to reimpose control on the world market. The results were devastating for millions of small coffee growers around the world.

Globalization and the Coffee Commodity Chain

The changes in the structure of the world economy that occurred in the 1980s and 1990s are generally understood to be the products of globalization. However, the term "globalization" has been so widely and indiscriminately applied that it has begun to lose its analytical power. Using Giovanni Arrighi's (1994) theory of systemic cycles of accumulation, as outlined in chapter 1, we can see that the current period of "globalization" is actually the most recent instance of a period of financial expansion. According to Arrighi, periods of financial expansion are driven by over-accumulation crises. A hegemonic cycle begins with a period of material expansion, during which capital accumulation is driven by investments in increasing production and expanding trade. This period lasted from the end of World War II through the multiple crises around 1970. After a period of material expansion, there comes a point at which there is an excess of capital in search of profitable investments in the further expansion of material production and trade, driving down rates of profit. In response to this develop-ment, capital is increasingly invested in various kinds of financial deals and speculation, which yield higher profits than investments in production, as well as preserving the liquidity of capital, so that it can be shifted quickly to more profitable opportunities. The multiple crises around 1970 touched off a period of uncertainty and struggle over the rules for the world economy, but by the 1980s, the "globalization project," in McMichael's (2000) terms, was being consoli-dated, and the financial expansion was underway.

One result of this financial expansion was a concentration of capital, but another was increasing instability. Arrighi argues that the U.S. government re-sponse to the 1970 crises was to abandon the ideal of state management of the national economy and to put its faith in the "self-regulating market." The hope was that this would preserve the competitive advantage of U.S.-based TNCs on the world market, and maintain U.S. hegemony. But rather than just benefiting U.S.-based TNCs, the new ideology of the self-regulating market has enabled all core-based TNCs to tighten their control over production located in the periph-eral and semiperipheral regions of the world, through their control over financial capital. This has enabled them to squeeze additional profits out of those regions to fuel their capital accumulation. This newest form of international inequality has been superimposed on the old forms—the old colonial division of labor that was exemplified by coffee and other tropical commodities, as well as the newer international division of labor established during the development project, or the period of material expansion. This new form of inequality just increases the overall degree of inequality in the world. But it is also fundamentally different from the old inequalities. The old inequalities were based on control over pro-duction processes, while the new inequality is based on control over financial capital and closely related flows of information.

The financial expansion fundamentally changed the economic conditions under which the coffee trade operated. The changed conditions led to five inter-related changes in the structure of the coffee commodity chain between the mid-1970s and the mid-1990s. First, the concentration of capital took the form of a major consolidation of both coffee trading and coffee manufacturing TNCs. Companies shifted from growth through investment in expanding production to growth by acquisition. Second, producing states' abilities to regulate the seg-ments of the commodity chain within their own borders were weakened, also hampering their abilities to intervene in the world market. Third, there was an explosion of speculative trading in financial derivatives based on coffee: futures and options contracts. This growing speculative interest loosened the connection between changes in the supply of, and demand for, coffee and movements of coffee futures prices, and increased instability in the futures market. Fourth, prices of physical coffee became increasingly linked to futures prices, thereby increasing the uncertainty in the prices at which coffee producers would be able to sell their coffee. Fifth, these changes increased the need for detailed, instantaneous information about coffee supplies and futures markets movements, creating a situation where a decisive advantage accrued to the giant, consolidated coffee TNCs. Each of these changes is described in detail below.

Consolidation of Capital

The flurry of mergers and acquisitions that was part of the financial expansion, and that was given further impetus by the Reagan deregulation of the early 1980s, was also felt in the coffee trade. By the early 1990s, four major manufacturers and about eight major trading companies controlled a majority of the coffee flowing into, being processed, and being consumed in the major consuming markets in North America, Europe, Japan, and Australia.

Four TNCs now account for well over 60 percent of total coffee sales across all major consuming markets.[1] The largest is Nestlé, the world's largest food processing company. Nestlé pioneered the manufacture of instant coffee for the mass market, and began opening plants around the world in the late 1930s. Nestlé has been the world leader in instant coffee for virtually the entire postwar period, with the top-selling brand in almost every major consuming market. In the 1980s, it further consolidated its position by moving aggressively into the R&G (roasted and ground) segment of the market. In the United States, Nestlé bought Hills Bros. in 1983, and Hills in turn acquired Chase and Sanborn in 1984. In 1985, Nestlé added MJB to its U.S. acquisitions, and in 1987 it bought Sark's Gourmet Coffees. In Europe, it acquired Zoegas, a Swedish roaster with large market shares in Northern European markets, in 1986. But in 1999, Nestlé changed strategy, selling Hills, MJB, and Chase and Sanborn to Sara Lee and discontinuing the Sark's brand. Instead, it introduced a new line of gourmet and whole bean coffees in the U.S. market, under the old Nescafé brand name. Nestlé has also been the leader in the Japanese instant coffee market since the 1960s, and has used this position to move into the rapidly expanding East Asian market.

Close behind Nestlé is Philip Morris, which began to diversify out of tobacco and into food processing in the 1980s. It had a huge amount of cash on hand from tobacco profits, but saw that it was no longer profitable to invest most of that capital in tobacco. Philip Morris is now the largest food processing company in the United States, and second in the world to Nestlé. In 1985, Philip Morris acquired General Foods; GF's Maxwell House division had been the largest U.S. coffee company for most of the postwar period, and number one in the market for R&G coffee, until Folger's passed it in the late 1980s. GF also already had significant market shares in many of the major European markets, and Philip Morris further consolidated its position there in 1990, by acquiring Jacob Suchard, one of the largest roasters in France, with a large share of the EEC market; and Gevalia, a major Swedish roaster with large shares of Northern European markets. General Foods, in a joint venture with food processing giant

Ajinomoto, is also the largest coffee company in Japan.[2]

The world's third largest coffee manufacturer is Sara Lee, the U.S. clothing and food processing giant, which owns Superior Coffee in the United States. In 1989, it acquired Douwe Egberts, a Dutch roaster with large market shares throughout Northern Europe, which itself had previously merged with Van Nelle, another major Dutch roaster and food processing conglomerate. Sara Lee also has significant shares of the French and Spanish markets, and is the largest coffee roaster in Brazil. In 1999, Sara Lee moved into third position overall in the U.S. market, by acquiring Chock Full o' Nuts, the fourth largest coffee company in the United States, including Tenco, the largest supplier of private label instant coffee in the country. It also purchased Hills Bros., MJB, and Chase and Sanborn from Nestlé.

The fourth coffee TNC is Procter & Gamble. In 1963, P&G acquired the Folger Coffee Company, then a major regional roaster based in San Francisco. In the early 1970s, P&G took the Folger's brand name national by going into the East Coast stronghold of Maxwell House and engaging in a series of brutal dis-count pricing wars, beginning in Cleveland in 1971 (Hilke and Nelson 1989). By the late 1980s, Folger's passed Maxwell House to become the best-selling brand of R&G in the country. In 1989, P&G bought Maryland Club Foods, producer of the Butter-Nut brand, with large market shares on the East Coast. In 1995 it ac-quired Millstone Coffee, and in 1999, it bought the bankrupt Brothers Gourmet Coffee, to gain a foothold in the growing specialty coffee market. Procter & Gamble does not have large coffee sales outside North America, but is still the world's fourth largest coffee company by virtue of being the largest overall in the United States, by far the largest consuming market.

All four of these TNCs are multiproduct conglomerates, and despite the fact that they are the largest coffee manufacturers in the world, coffee is not their main product. These four companies control over 60 percent of coffee sales in the major consuming markets, but this statistic actually underestimates the de-gree of TNC control. In some of the major markets, coffee and food-processing TNCs of only slightly smaller scale also have significant market shares, for in-stance Tchibo-Eduscho in Germany (these two large roasters merged in 1996), Lavazza in Italy, Paulig in Finland, and Ueshima and Key Coffee in Japan. All of the second-tier European TNCs have expanded their operations and consoli-dated their market shares since the unification of the European market. All of them plus the four major TNCs have moved rapidly into, and are competing vigorously for, the newly-opened Eastern European markets, particularly the more stable ones, such as Poland, Hungary, and the Czech Republic.[3]

Through the 1980s, the increasing concentration of coffee manufacturers in consuming markets began to lead to concentration of coffee importing firms. At the beginning of the 1970s, most commodity trading firms specialized in a sin-gle commodity, but during the 1970s, the largest ones began to expand into other commodities related to their main specialization. Tropical commodities were prominent in this movement; thus Gill and Duffus, the largest cocoa trader, moved into coffee and later into sugar, while Sucres et Denrees, the large French sugar trader, moved into cocoa and later coffee. In the late 1970s and early 1980s, the largest manufacturing TNCs, which had been directly importing some of their own coffee, particularly from the large suppliers like Brazil and Colombia, began to turn all of their importing operations over to the trading companies. High interest rates, fluctuating exchange rates, fluctuating prices in the world coffee market, and political instability in some of the producing countries, all combined to increase the risks involved in importing, and the manufacturing TNCs preferred to transfer these risks to the importers. In addition, under pressure of high interest rates in the late 1970s, manufacturers significantly reduced the stocks of green coffee they carried, relying on the importers and on improved transportation and communication systems to supply green coffee for more flexible, just-in-time production. As the TNCs acquired significant market shares in a number of consuming markets, they began to rationalize their operations, closing roasting or instant coffee plants with small capacity or outdated equipment, and expanding their more modern plants or building new state-of-the-art facilities. These new plants were strategically located near major coffee ports (e.g., New Orleans, Hamburg, and Marseilles) and were often designed to produce for major markets in several different consuming countries. The manufacturers were thus bringing in larger volumes of coffee through a smaller number of ports, and preferred to deal with the largest importers, who could handle the volumes of coffee they required. All of these developments favored the larger trading firms, particularly those that had established multi-commodity operations. As the manufacturing TNCs consolidated, they were also able to use their oligopsony positions to demand better deals from the importers, driving down their profits. Due to all of these added pressures on the importers, when there were sharp downward price movements, as happened in 1979–1980 and again in 1986–1987, some traders, even some of the largest ones, were driven out of business.[4]

In 1989, the world market price of coffee crashed, following the suspension of export quotas under the ICA, and this drove many more importers, both large and small, out of business. Some of them were already in precarious positions after the 1986–1987 coffee price decline and the October 1987 stock market crash (F. O. Licht, November 3, 1987). Some were holding large stockpiles of coffee purchased at high quota prices, which declined precipitously in value after the end of the quotas, and had to be sold at a loss. Others were holding large speculative positions in the futures markets, and also took large losses. But most importers worked on percentage commissions, and when the price fell by 50 percent, so did their commissions. Thus by the early 1990s, the five largest coffee importers (Neumann Gruppe, Volcafe, ED&F Man, ECOM Agroindustrial, and Goldman, Sachs) controlled over 40 percent of total world imports (*Boletín Cafetera*, May 15, 1993; UNCTAD 1995; Fitter and Kaplinsky 2001). Since all five of these companies are privately owned, it is much more difficult to get good information on the companies and their operations than it is for the publicly traded manufacturing TNCs.

Neumann, already a large coffee trader, became the world's largest coffee importer after taking over Europe's largest coffee importer, Bernhard Rothfos, in 1988. The combined company was reorganized in 1989–1990 into the Neumann Kaffee Gruppe, and now comprises over fifty companies that deal in coffee exporting from producing countries, importing into consuming countries, futures trading, shipping, insurance, and coffee processing. It reportedly handles about 15 percent of total world coffee imports, and is unique among the largest traders because its focus is solely on coffee.[5] Volcafe is the former coffee trading operation of Volkart Brothers, a large European multi-commodity trader and financial company. In 1989, the coffee operation was spun off to a management group as a separate company, and was then acquired by the ERB Gruppe, a Swiss conglomerate that deals in everything from commodity trading to banking to auto importing and distribution.[6] ED&F Man, already a major sugar and coffee importer, became the world's largest cocoa trader when it acquired Gill and Duffus. In 1994, the company went public, but in 2000, its futures trading business became a separate, publicly traded company, while the commodity trading business returned to being privately held.[7] J. Aron, one of the top two U.S. coffee importers, as well as a major diversified commodities trading firm, was taken over by Goldman, Sachs in 1981.[8] Cargill, the giant grain trader, instantly became one of the world's largest coffee importers when it purchased the other top U.S. importer, ACLI Coffee, in 1984. In 2000, Cargill sold its coffee business to ECOM Agroindustrial Corporation of Geneva, which was already a major European coffee importer, as well as a major trader of cocoa, cotton, and rubber.[9] In addition to the more than 40 percent share held by these five majors, the largest *sogo shosha*, C. Itoh, Marubeni, and Mitsubishi, control most coffee imports into Japan, the third largest consuming market, and also import some coffee into the U.S. and European markets. All of these importers are large, multi-commodity TNC traders, and most of them specialize in a range of tropical commodities. As is true for the major coffee manufacturing TNCs, although these firms are the world's largest coffee importers, coffee is generally not their most important commodity.[10]

By the mid-1990s, these major trading houses had established their own exporting subsidiaries in the major producing countries. Two important developments created the opportunity for this to happen. The first was the wave of structural adjustment and market liberalization programs forced on developing countries, beginning during the debt crisis of the 1980s and continuing into the 1990s. This scaled back or eliminated many restrictions on foreign ownership and control of trading firms within the producing countries. It also led to the ending of the coffee export monopolies of many state marketing boards in African countries. This opened up coffee exporting opportunities to privately owned firms for the first time, and in some of these countries, there were few capitalists or private firms with the capital and expertise to move in and take advantage of this opening. The second development was the price crash following the lifting of export quotas in 1989. In addition to driving many green coffee importers in the consuming countries out of business, this crash also put many large exporting companies in the producing countries into financial difficulties, leaving them ripe for takeover by the major importers. For example, Neumann now has export companies in Brazil, Colombia, Peru, Costa Rica, El Salvador, Guatemala, Honduras, Mexico, Burundi, Cameroon, Ivory Coast, Kenya, Rwanda, Tanzania, Uganda, Indonesia, Papua New Guinea, and Vietnam. Volcafe has export companies in Brazil, Colombia, Peru, Costa Rica, Guatemala, Honduras, Nicaragua, Mexico, Kenya, Tanzania, Uganda, Indonesia, and Papua New Guinea.[11]

This concentration of coffee importing and processing TNCs has gone hand-in-hand with an increasing role for financial capital. For the manufacturing TNCs, access to large amounts of capital is crucial, both for pursuit of their merger and acquisition strategies, and for financing the purchases of the huge volumes of coffee with which they deal. Because they are large multiproduct conglomerates, they are better able to generate this capital in-house, and have more clout with the largest banks to be able to borrow what they need on the most favorable terms. For the trading TNCs, the line between banks and commodity traders became increasingly blurred as a result of the U.S. banking deregulation of the 1980s. On the one hand, the large traders were increasingly participating on the commodity futures markets, both to protect themselves against losses on their purchases and sales of physical commodities, and also as part of an integrated trading strategy designed to maximize their profits. They added financial services to their range of commodity trading activities. On the other hand, while some banks got out of commodity financing altogether, other banks began developing specialized commodity divisions to handle this aspect of their business, as it got more risky and complex. As banking was deregulated, some banks also began to trade in financial instruments, including commodity futures, to protect their loans, and also to increase their profits. And some financial services companies, such as Goldman, Sachs, became importers of physical commodities as well. The end result was a set of giant trading and financial companies that had three important advantages in the world market conditions of the 1980s and 1990s. They had the ability to shift funds from one commodity to another in response to price changes and profit opportunities. Second, they had access to large amounts of capital, both in-house and from major banks. This not only allowed them to purchase the huge lots of coffee demanded by the consolidated giant roasting TNCs, but also to be able to take quick advantage of opportunities to take over other coffee traders who might find themselves in financial difficulties. Finally, they also had the capital and the expertise to play the commodity futures markets, not only to hedge their coffee purchases, but also to increase their profits. For some, the trading of financial instruments became almost as important to their bottom lines as the trading of physical commodities.[12]

Weakening of Producing States

As we have seen, most states in the coffee producing countries exerted some control over coffee growing, processing, and exporting that occurred within their own borders. In Latin America, most producing countries had state coffee agencies that performed a variety of functions. Typically they had agricultural extension and research services for growers, but they also attempted to protect growers by setting minimum prices at which processors and exporters could buy coffee from the growers. Most of these agencies also regulated exports by issuing export licenses to exporters and setting minimum export prices. African countries typically had state marketing boards that held a monopoly over coffee exporting, in addition to providing agricultural extension and regulating the internal market. Brazil's state coffee agency, the *Instituto Brasileiro do Café* (IBC) was a typical Latin American agency, but it also performed several additional important functions. It regulated the coffee roasting industry that produced for Brazil's large internal coffee market. It maintained the massive Brazilian coffee stockpiles, using them to regulate the internal price of roasted coffee and also to promote the Brazilian instant coffee industry that produced for export, by selling coffee from the stockpile cheaply to these industries. The Colombian agency, the *Federación Nacional de Cafeteros* (FNC), was unique. It was an independent organization, jointly controlled by the state and the large coffee growers, with broad responsibilities for regulating the coffee sector. In addition, it also exported coffee, in competition with the private exporters, and aggressively sought new markets for its coffee. It is probably best known for its invention of Juan Valdez, used to promote the image of Colombian coffee in the consuming countries.

The state agencies used their regulatory power to extract revenues from the coffee sector, so that coffee growers usually only received a percentage of the world market price. In Latin American countries this percentage was usually fairly high, but in the African and some Asian countries, the marketing boards extracted significant revenues from the coffee sector, and this percentage was often less than half. However, there were advantages to this arrangement for the growers. The coffee agencies and marketing boards used some of these funds for research and agricultural extension. They also extended low cost loans to coffee growers, and subsidized inputs such as fertilizers and pesticides. In a world market where prices tended to fluctuate wildly, the state agencies could cushion the growers from these price swings by adjusting the percentage of the world market price that was returned to growers. When world market prices were high, they could return a lower percentage to the growers and retain the additional revenue to allow them to maintain a steady price to growers even when the world market price dropped.

After the crisis of the 1970s, the U.S. government decided to abandon the ideal of national regulation of nationally based economies that had governed its international economic policies in the postwar period. In its place, the United States began a push to "free" markets, in order to open them up to U.S.-based TNCs (Arrighi 1994). This new "Washington consensus" was forced on many peripheral and semiperipheral countries through structural adjustment programs during the debt crisis of the 1980s (McMichael 2000). The effects of structural adjustment on the state coffee agencies were delayed by the existence of the

ICA, because the agencies needed to regulate their coffee sectors in order to comply with the export quotas. But after the ICA quotas ended in 1989, the World Bank began to pressure coffee producing countries to reduce the roles of their state agencies in the coffee sector. In particular, many of the state marketing boards were forced to end their monopolies on coffee exporting, and open the trade up to private exporters.

After the world market price crashed in 1989, following the lifting of export quotas, the United States and the international financial institutions gained an unlikely ally in some countries: coffee growers. World market coffee prices remained at historically low levels for several years, and the coffee agencies and marketing boards were forced to significantly lower the prices paid to growers. Many growers then seized on the fact that they had only been receiving a percentage (sometimes very low) of the world market price, and began to actively campaign for reducing the power of the coffee agencies and abolishing the marketing boards (Akiyama 2001). There is no doubt that there was a need for reform in many cases. Some of the marketing boards took more than half of the world market price, leaving very little for the growers. Some were just inefficient and others were corrupt. In addition, payments to farmers were often delayed substantially. Typically, the grower would get a partial payment when they delivered their coffee to the marketing board, and an additional payment after the coffee had been exported and the marketing board had taken its share. Often, these second payments were delayed by six months or more, leaving the growers perennially short of cash. There were thus sufficient grounds for grievances against the marketing boards, but many growers also mistakenly believed that they would receive much higher prices if the marketing boards were abolished. In some cases, they found that private exporters could be equally predatory.

Thus, at the same time that the coffee TNCs were consolidating their control over the coffee markets in the major consuming countries, the abilities of states in the producing countries to manage their own coffee sectors were being weakened. This weakening facilitated the penetration of the coffee trading TNCs into the export sectors of the producing countries. The overall balance of power was shifted decisively in favor of the coffee TNCs, and they began to extend their control backward along the chain into segments that had previously been under the control of producing states. The presence of TNC subsidiaries in the producing countries enabled them to exert influence on producing states' coffee policies. In particular, it allowed the subsidiaries to lobby against cooperation among producing states to control exports, and it put them in a position to subvert any export restrictions that the producing states tried to impose.

Increased Financial Speculation

The third way in which the period of financial expansion was manifested in the coffee trade was in the expansion of trading in financial derivatives based on coffee. Coffee futures have been traded in New York since the founding of the New York Coffee Exchange in 1882. Sugar futures were added in 1916, and in 1970 it merged with the New York Cocoa Exchange to assume its present identity as the New York Coffee, Sugar, and Cocoa Exchange (CSCE) (*World Coffee and Tea*, March 1982, pp. 22–24). The coffee futures contract traded on the New York exchange is called the "C" contract, based on Central American arabica coffees. A futures contract for robusta coffee futures began to be traded on the London Commodity Exchange in the 1970s; this exchange has been reorganized several times and is now the London International Financial Futures Exchange (LIFFE).

Until the 1980s, the major participants in coffee futures trading were importers and roasters, who used it mainly for hedging, or protecting themselves against sudden price changes.[13] This is clearly shown by the relationship between the trading volume on the CSCE and the status of the ICA quotas; when quotas were in effect and prices were relatively predictable, trading volume went down. Trading volume began falling in the early 1960s, as the first ICA was being negotiated. By 1966, after the ICA had been in effect long enough to stabilize prices, the exchange was forced to close trading on the "C" contract because the trading volume was so low. Just as some members of the trade were beginning to suggest that the futures market might be unnecessary because of the stabilizing effects of the ICA, a frost hit Brazil in 1969. This destabilized prices, despite the fact that quotas were still in effect, and trading picked up again. By 1971, strains within the membership of the Agreement were making its renewal uncertain (see chapter 3), and trading volume kept increasing, spurred on again by the suspension of the quotas in 1972. By 1973, trading volume had surpassed its late-1950s peak, and the 1975 Brazilian frost drove it to record highs. Trading volume fell off again as quotas were reinstated in 1980.[14]

Trading was stimulated again in 1985–1986, when the Brazilian drought began to drive up prices and introduce instability into the market once more. But by this time, a number of other changes had occurred, which increased the centrality of the futures markets. The first change was part of the general proliferation of financial instruments and derivatives in the mid-1980s: the introduction of trading in options on coffee futures contracts by the CSCE in 1986. Since these options contracts were considerably cheaper than the futures contracts themselves, they allowed smaller traders and roasters (and speculators) to participate in the market.[15] But they also gave the TNCs (roasters, importers, and financiers) another instrument to juggle into their integrated trading strategies. The second change in the market in the mid-1980s was the rise of the commodity funds, huge conglomerations of financial capital seeking the highest and most rapid profits available, by trading in financial, oil, metals, and agricultural futures markets. The funds were another way in which smaller speculators, who found trading in coffee futures and options alone too risky, but who could not afford to invest in a diversified portfolio of commodity futures, were drawn into the financial markets. Due to these changes, futures trading remained heavy

Table 5.1 Total Volume of Coffee Futures Trading, New York and London, and Total World Imports of Green Coffee, 1980–1995

Year	Exchange New York	London	Total Futures Contracts	Gross World Imports
1980	15.2	5.5	20.7	4.1
1985	11.1	5.1	16.2	4.5
1990	30.2	5.8	36.0	5.3
1991	30.2	6.5	36.7	5.1
1992	36.6	4.8	41.4	5.5
1993	44.1	4.4	48.5	5.3
1994	45.2	6.2	51.4	5.4

Source: ITC (1996), table 14, p. 72. All figures are in millions of tons of coffee.

through the late 1980s, despite the reinstatement of quotas in 1987–1989. And since the end of quotas in 1989, the volume of futures and options trading has taken off, posting new record highs each year.[16]

These developments decisively shifted the balance of trading on the coffee futures exchanges, from hedgers who were involved in the coffee trade to speculators who were in it only to make a profit.[17] This is demonstrated in table 5.1, which compares the volume of futures contracts traded on the New York and London exchanges to the volume of physical coffee traded on the world market. If futures contracts were being traded simply to hedge purchases of physical coffee, then total futures volume would be expected to be about two times the volume of physical coffee traded, assuming that the buyer and the seller in each purchase fully hedged their positions. Table 5.1 shows that the total volume of futures traded exploded from five times the volume of physical coffee in 1980, to nearly 10 times the volume in 1994. If options contracts, which were not traded in 1980, are added in, the total volume of futures and options traded in 1994 was the equivalent of 73.0 million tons of coffee, or almost 15 times the volume of physical coffee (ITC 1992, 1996). Thus, by the mid-1990s, the vast majority of trades made on the coffee futures markets were made for purely speculative purposes, and were not connected to sales of physical coffee.[18]

The shift from hedging to speculation was also accompanied by a shift in the type of speculation, from that based on fundamental analysis to that based on technical analysis. Speculators who play the coffee futures market based on fundamental analysis rely on projections of future supply and demand to forecast whether coffee prices are likely to rise or fall in the coming months, and buy or sell futures accordingly, hoping to profit when the futures prices rise or fall. Technical analysis, in contrast, attempts to predict market movements in the future solely on the basis of past market movements, independent of supply and demand conditions. Technical analysts look at the combination of moving averages of prices, trends in total volume, and trends in open interest (the total number of outstanding futures contracts at a given time), to predict whether the market is likely to move up or down. Since they rely on charts of these indicators to make their forecasts, they are often referred to as "chart" traders. The development and refinement of chart trading during the 1980s meant that many small speculators could engage in commodity speculation without knowing a great deal about the commodities they were speculating in. And while the commodity funds use both kinds of analysis, they tend to rely more heavily on charting. Since the funds are also invested in many different financial instruments, they may sometimes move capital into or out of the coffee futures markets because of their judgements of the profitably of coffee futures relative to other instruments. All of these developments meant that large amounts of money were being shifted into and out of the coffee futures markets, for reasons that were often only marginally related to the actual global situation of supplies of, and demand for, coffee.[19]

Finally, the increased volume of trading on the futures exchanges, and the changing nature of the trading, also increased the volatility of futures prices. Speculators followed developments in the coffee market hour-by-hour, if not minute-by-minute. A forecast of cold weather in the coffee growing regions of Brazil, possibly portending a damaging frost, might set off a wave of buying by fundamental analysts, raising the price. The surge in volume and price could trigger a wave of buy orders from the technical analysts, who often had their computers set up to issue an automatic buy or sell order if market trends met certain conditions. Then, a couple of large speculators who decided to sell their contracts to take a quick profit might trigger a wave of sell orders, driving the price back down. A market movement like this could easily take place in the course of one trading day, a four hour and forty-five minute period on the New York exchange, without any change at all occurring in the overall world supply and demand for coffee, simply in response to speculation that there *might be* a frost in Brazil.

Linking of Physical Coffee Prices to the Futures Market

Another major development linked to the expansion of trading in financial derivatives was the computerization of trading, and this ultimately revolutionized the business. First, reporting of futures trading was completely computerized, so that the details of each transaction made on the trading floor could be flashed to computer screens around the world almost instantaneously. All of the major roasters and importers were linked into this system and kept continuous watch on the movements of the market. Second, physical coffee transactions were increasingly being carried out by computer. In the early 1970s, offers to sell coffee were made by exporters through cables sent to the offices of importing companies, with replies expected by the end of the day or by the next morning. By the mid-1980s, these offers were mostly made by computer messages, with replies expected within the hour.[20]

Third, since the current futures prices were immediately available to the traders on their computer screens, and they received offers to buy coffee in the same way, they began to use futures prices to set the prices for their sales and purchases of physical green coffee. Since the "C" contract specified a generally accepted quality standard, prices would be set at a differential to the "C" contract, depending on whether the coffee was of higher or lower quality than the standard Central American coffees on which the "C" contract was based. This linkage made it easier for traders to agree on green coffee contract terms and then immediately hedge the transaction, by buying or selling the appropriate futures contracts. But it also increased the uncertainty involved in the transaction. Exporters could agree to sell a certain amount of coffee at a fixed differential, and then watch the futures price, waiting for what they thought was a peak in the futures price to contact the importer and fix the actual price for the coffee. Of course, neither party to the deal knew whether the futures price would go up or down after the price of the physical coffee was fixed. But the importer didn't really care, as long as he had hedged his purchase. Usually, he had already contracted to sell this coffee to a roaster, with price also to be fixed against the exchange, and made his profit by charging the roaster a higher (or lower) differential that he was paying the exporter.[21] In the mid-1970s, almost all coffee was sold at prices fixed when the sale was made; by the mid-1990s, as much as 90 percent of coffee was sold at a fixed differential to the futures exchanges, with the actual price to be fixed later, by either the buyer or the seller.[22]

This development made the futures market the key price determination mechanism for the entire industry. In the mid-1970s, when hedgers dominated speculators on the futures exchanges, the price of physical coffee drove the price of futures contracts. By the mid-1990s, when speculators dominated on the exchanges, the price of paper contracts drove the price of physical coffee. Of course, the price of futures contracts was constrained by the fact that they were contracts for the actual delivery of physical coffee at some time in the future. Therefore, a speculator holding a futures contract had to either liquidate it before the start of the delivery month, or be faced with the prospect of having to take delivery of 37,500 pounds of green coffee. This insured that the price of a futures contract always converged on the price of physical coffee as the delivery month approached, and kept a linkage between futures and physicals prices. But the developments over this period significantly weakened the linkage of futures prices to the underlying supply and demand conditions for coffee. The combination of pegging the price of coffee to the futures markets and the increased weight of the commodity funds in these markets has probably increased the overall instability of world market prices for coffee.[23]

Increased Need for Information

By the mid-1990s, anyone who was trading in physical coffee needed to have access to up-to-the-minute information from all over the world. On any day that the futures exchanges were open, they needed to keep an eye on market movements, so that they would not be surprised by sudden price movements that could affect their business. They needed information about weather conditions in several major producing countries, where severe weather that damaged the crop could shift overall world supply conditions. They needed crop forecasts from these countries, because even in the absence of severe weather, an unusually large or small crop could change conditions (see chapter 2 regarding the two-year bearing cycles). They needed information about political conditions and government policies in producing and consuming countries that could change tariffs or interrupt the flow of coffee. They needed information about economic conditions in consuming countries and exchange rate fluctuations that could change the demand for coffee or its import price. Many of these information needs were also present in the mid-1970s. But under the market conditions of the mid-1990s, they were much more pressing. The market was more unstable; it was moving much faster in response to news as well as to rumor. It had a tendency to overreact in one direction, and then overcompensate in the other. Because coffee trading firms were operating under integrated strategies involving buying physical coffee, hedging, and speculating, anyone missing out on a major market move stood to potentially lose a lot of money.

Under these conditions, information itself has become a commodity in the coffee trade, as it has in most other sectors of the economy. News services and wire services provide a wide variety of political and economic news from around the world, as well as weather reports. One daily publication, *Complete Coffee Coverage*, provides news specifically related to the coffee trade. Other newsletters giving more in-depth analysis are produced by the largest trading houses, such as ED&F Man in the U.K., or by firms specializing in commodity analysis, such as F. O. Licht in Germany. All of these services are available on a subscription basis, and most subscriptions are quite expensive. The business of providing statistical data, market analysis, and charting programs for commodity market speculation has itself become a growth industry. There are several different statistical packages for performing chart analysis available on the market, and other services providing the raw data from commodity futures markets to input into these packages. Keeping on top of all of this information requires money and time—money to buy access to it, and time to digest it. In this situation, the largest trading houses that dealt in multiple commodities and combined physical purchases with financial speculation were clearly in the most advantageous position. They had the capital to access the information, the manpower and expertise to analyze it, and the capacity to develop their own in-house fundamental and statistical analyses of the market (ITC 1992).

But the most important advantage held by the largest trading houses was the capacity to develop their own in-house information systems. They had offices in most of the major consuming markets, and subsidiaries in many of the producing countries. They could get up-to-the-minute information from their own operatives inside these countries, who were familiar with the situation on the ground there, without having it filtered through some external service. And they could centralize and integrate these huge volumes of information from all over the world to develop their integrated trading strategies.

All of these changes in the structure of the commodity chain, and in the rules governing its transactions, influenced the ways in which struggles over governance of the chain unfolded after the end of the ICA quotas in 1989. The extension of the self-regulating market in coffee unleashed new tree crop price cycles that led to two deep crises. The trading and manufacturing TNCs were positioned to protect themselves from the effects of these crises; indeed, they were positioned to benefit from them. Meanwhile, the producing states were increasingly unable to react to these crises. They attempted to reimpose some control over the flow of coffee onto the world market, but ultimately failed. And they proved unable to protect their coffee growers from the ravages of the self-regulating market.

The First Coffee Crisis, 1989–1993

As the world coffee market entered the new free market period in July 1989, prices immediately crashed. Producing countries were anxious to unload the stocks which had been accumulating under the quota system, and TNCs demanded prices closer to those which had prevailed in the non-quota markets. At these low prices, the TNCs were eager to stock up on coffee; and within the first few months of the free market, there was a massive transfer of coffee stockpiles from producing to consuming countries, at bargain prices. These massive stocks held by the TNC traders, combined with their dominant positions in the consuming markets, enabled them to squeeze the lowest possible prices out of coffee producers. If the producers refused to sell at the prices demanded by traders, the traders could afford to wait them out; eventually, the producers would need cash, and would agree to the traders' prices. At the same time, the manufacturing TNCs that dominated the consuming markets were able to use their market power to maintain the level of the retail prices that they charged for their final processed coffee products. This opened a massive gap between the cost of green coffee to the TNCs, and the prices they received for their finished products. The overall average level of retail prices in ICO consuming member markets declined by only 1 percent in the two years following the end of quotas, despite the decline of over 50 percent in green coffee prices.[24]

Producing states were able to partially offset the impact of the price crash in the short run. By exporting their accumulated stockpiles of coffee, they cut the costs of maintaining these stocks, and earned some additional income through the increased volume of exports. Still, the total coffee earnings of all producing countries fell from $9.2 billion in coffee year 1988/89 to $6.7 billion in coffee year 1989/90, a 27 percent decline in earnings despite a 13 percent increase in the volume of exports.[25] Prices recovered somewhat in 1990, after the selling frenzy by producers had subsided, with the ICO Indicator price averaging just over 71 cents for the year. But beginning in April 1991, and continuing through 1992, prices resumed their slide, reaching historically low levels by the summer of 1992, when the ICO Indicator price fell below 50 cents per pound for the first time since 1972. In real terms, the price of coffee was lower than it had been since the 1930s. In the three years following the price crash, it has been estimated that the producing countries lost a total of $10–12 billion in export earnings because of the low prices. Meanwhile, the TNCs continued to maintain their retail prices near their pre-1989 levels, reaping windfall profits of $2–3 billion per year.[26]

This prolonged period of low prices, combined with protests from coffee growers, gave an impetus to the efforts of the World Bank to weaken producing state control over the early stages of the coffee chain. After the 1989 price crash, coffee growers began to protest the low prices they were receiving for their coffee, and states became increasingly concerned about the economic impacts that prolonged low prices would have in the coffee growing regions. Pressured from above by the Bank and from below by the growers, states lowered or eliminated export taxes, abolished marketing boards or ended their monopolies on coffee exporting, and generally withdrew from regulating their coffee sectors. These changes allowed growers to receive a larger share of the export price than they had before 1989, and somewhat cushioned the blow of the price crash. But these changes also meant that the states could no longer afford to provide the range of services that many growers had come to expect. As the period of low prices dragged on, the effects began to "trickle down" to the coffee growers.

The growers responded by cutting back on their variable costs: labor, fertilizers, and pesticides used to maintain their coffee trees, but these decisions had little immediate effect on output. By the time the first effects of the low prices began to be felt among growers, the 1989/90 crop was already on the trees, and the flowering of the 1990/91 crop was beginning. And because of producing states' responses to the price crash, growers in many countries did not feel the full effects of the low world prices until 1991, when the 1991/92 crop was already on the trees. Reduced maintenance could have had a minor effect on the output for 1990/91 and a somewhat larger effect for 1991/92, but wouldn't produce a serious effect on world supply until at least 1993. However, with the vast systems of information gathering that were in place, reports of reduced maintenance began to reach the major players in the consuming markets by early 1992. Some began to warn that continued low prices threatened the quality, and eventually the quantity, of coffee that would be available.[27] But in the short run, this wasn't happening, and TNCs were quite content with the low world market prices, so no actions were taken to change the situation.

On the ground in the producing countries, the effects of the prolonged low world market prices were devastating. Consider this example from one of the major producing countries—Colombia.[28] The municipality of Líbano in the department of Tolima lies in the Central Cordillera of the Andes, in the largest coffee producing region of Colombia. Líbano was once the fifth-largest producing municipality, in terms of total volume, in the country, with most of this coffee grown on small peasant holdings and family farms. As the prices they were paid for their coffee began to decline, especially after 1990, many were forced to sell their mules to pay old debts and supplement their subsistence production. Then, in April 1992, the coffee berry borer worm invaded. This is a parasite that burrows into the coffee cherry to lay its eggs on the coffee beans, thereby destroying them. By this time most of the growers had no money for the pesticides needed to fight the coffee borer, and it rapidly spread to all farms in the area. Already in debt, with no way to repay it, and with their coffee trees dying, many began to abandon their farms. Some went to the towns to try to scratch out a living in the informal sector; others left for the jungle to go to work in the drug trade. The repercussions from this migration drove many other small businesses in the municipality out of business. The community organized to demand assistance from the government, but the government officials had few resources with which to provide assistance, and were faced with similar demands from all sides. To the leaders of the community movement, the officials seemed as sensitive as marble statues to their plight. The guerrillas of the Ejercito de Liberación Nacional began to move in, and took control of most of the rural zones surrounding Líbano. None of Colombia's various guerrilla groups, some of which date back to the early 1960s, had ever had a very significant presence in the coffee growing zones of Colombia, because they had always been among the more affluent rural areas of the country. But the guerrillas were the only force capable of stopping the banks from confiscating peasants' farms when their debts were declared in default. Some of the youths from the area went to join the guerrillas, because they at least offered a steady salary.

Colombia is the best example of a country with state coffee policies controlled by large growers and exporters, which has always had the capacity to respond effectively to such situations. Its quasi-state coffee agency, the FNC, has consistently followed a countercyclical policy, collecting heavy taxes while world prices were high, which enabled it to maintain high internal prices for coffee, and in effect provide subsidies to growers when world prices were low. It has combined this with consistent support for political regulation of the world market to increase and stabilize prices (Cardenas 1991). The FNC has used its income to invest in infrastructure in coffee growing zones, and to fund major research efforts and extension services. In the 1970s, it developed high-yielding varieties of coffee and provided credit to growers so that they could replace their older varieties. In the 1980s, when coffee leaf rust struck in Colombia, it developed new rust-resistant strains, and again provided loans to support conversion to the new variety. It has maintained an impressive extension effort to educate growers about proper cultivation techniques. Through 1990 and 1991, the FNC cut export taxes and used its accumulated reserves to subsidize growers. But as the period of low prices dragged on and its reserves dwindled, it was forced to lower prices to growers and cut back on its services. By 1993, it was in such desperate straights that it was forced to begin selling its interests in the *Banco Cafetero* and the Colombian shipping line, *Flota Mercantil Grancolombiano*, to obtain money to pay its debts.[29]

In Rwanda, the effects of this first coffee crisis of the 1990s were even more devastating.[30] Rwanda was primarily a rural society, with 90 percent of its labor force engaged in agriculture. About 70 percent of rural households cultivated some coffee. Coffee accounted for 80 percent of Rwanda's export earnings, and a large proportion of state revenues. The low coffee prices sparked famines in the countryside, at the same time that the decline in revenues crippled the state's ability to respond. As export earnings declined, the external debt soared, prompting a mission from the World Bank and a structural adjustment program that began in 1990. As if this were not enough, also in 1990, the Rwandan Patriotic Front invaded from their bases in Uganda to the north. The RPF were refugees and their descendants, who had left Rwanda in the 1960s after a Hutu-dominated government was established following independence. The Hutu-Tutsi conflict goes back to colonial rule by Belgium, when the minority Tutsi were used as agents of colonial administration and domination over the majority Hutu. The moderate Hutu president, Habyarimana, tried to juggle responding to the economic crisis and implementing World Bank adjustments with negotiating a settlement to the civil war and implementing democratic reforms, also demanded by international donors, but it was too much to handle. In April 1994 his plane exploded, probably shot down by militant Hutus, as he returned from peace negotiations, and the genocide began. About half a million Tutsi were slaughtered, and as many as two million people became refugees (out of a total population of about eight million).

Obviously, the prolonged period of low coffee prices was not the sole cause of the escalating guerilla war in Colombia or the genocide in Rwanda. But it was a contributing factor, and arguably, neither of these outcomes would have been nearly as severe in the absence of a coffee crisis. The low prices had devastating effects, if not quite so dramatic, in many other coffee producing countries as well. The producing states had liberalized their coffee sectors and exhausted their reserves, and were less able to cushion their growers from the low prices, or from any future fluctuations in the market. Few new investments were being made in coffee, and in some countries, growers were beginning to uproot their coffee trees to plant other crops. As the domestic economic impacts of low world prices began to spread and become more severe, the second phase of a new Polanyian double movement began—growers pressured their states to do something about the crisis. Producing states increasingly turned back to attempts to construct a new international regulatory regime.

New Efforts at Regulating the Market

The early efforts were sporadic and uncoordinated; all producers had been caught off guard by the severity of the price crash. Uganda, the most coffee-dependent country and one of the most severely affected, began discussions with other producers, particularly in Africa, about the possibility of forming a cartel, almost as soon as the quotas had ended. The five Central American producers, who had played a key role in the demise of the ICA and had expected to benefit from a free market, signed an agreement in December 1989 to withhold 15 percent of their exportable production. But without the participation of Brazil and Colombia, this initiative had little chance of affecting the level of world prices. And Brazil and Colombia were in no mood to cooperate to ease the suffering of the dissident producers who, in concert with the United States, had been responsible for the end of the quota system. None of the consuming states felt that there was much to be gained from a new round of negotiations so soon after the 1989 impasse. This situation continued through 1990 and 1991—the producers made feeble attempts to reduce their exports, and the consumers displayed little interest in new negotiations. The most that they could agree on was to continue to extend the 1983 ICA (without economic clauses) to keep the ICO alive as a forum for future discussions.[31]

By 1992, the consuming countries, even the United States, were beginning to be concerned about the economic impacts of continued low prices on the producing countries. The TNC coffee importers and roasters were beginning to report that the quality of coffees available worldwide was declining, as the reduced maintenance began to have an effect.[32] The United States was being pressured by Colombia, as it played an increasingly central role in the Bush Administration's "war on drugs" in the Andean region; the Colombians pointed out that they were losing more income through low coffee prices than they were gaining in aid from the U.S. anti-drug efforts.[33] They also pointed out that the EEC had exempted the Andean countries from import tariffs on coffee in 1990, to help support their anti-drug efforts.[34]

Through the spring and summer of 1992 and into early 1993, the momentum toward a new ICA seemed to be picking up. Producers grudgingly accepted the consumers' concept of a "universal quota," which would cover all exports regardless of their destination. Then the consumers, led by the United States, refused to play any role in the policing of the quotas or to restrict their imports from non-member exporters. Producers argued that this would remove incentives for coffee producing countries to join the ICO, and would create the conditions for a new two-tier market. A compromise was reached whereby the consumers would be free to accept all coffee imports, but would report sufficient information to the ICO so that it could determine whether producers were exceeding their quotas. Next, the producers accepted consumers' demands for a selectivity system, which would adjust the quotas for different types of coffees depending on world demand for them. But the negotiations ultimately broke down in March 1993 over the issue of "continuity," or the power of the ICO Coffee Council to review and revise the selectivity mechanism. Consumers wanted to minimize this power to make the agreement more "market-oriented"; producers feared that without this power, a new ICA would institutionalize the prevailing low level of world market prices for the duration of the agreement.[35]

The producing states felt betrayed by the consuming states. They felt that they had given in to most of the consumers' demands, but had gotten little in return. The United States, as the clear leader of the consumers in this round, came in for particularly harsh criticism. Myles Frechette, the head of the U.S. delegation, admitted that the producers had unilaterally conceded to more than

90 percent of consumers' demands. But he defended consumers' intransigence by stating that, "according to the exporters' scorecard, it was the importers' turn to make concessions, regardless of the magnitude of the concessions, and whether or not the proposals were consistent with a new market-oriented agreement."[36] In other words, the United States was only prepared to agree to an ICA that would further institutionalize a market free from political regulation. Colombia in particular felt that it had had a firm commitment from the United States to negotiate in good faith toward a new agreement, but that the United States had put the interests of its own coffee TNCs ahead of this commitment at crucial stages of the negotiations.[37]

This sense of betrayal unified the producers, and after March 1993 momentum toward unilateral action by the producers began to build rapidly. Brazil and Colombia agreed to freeze their current stocks, as well as continuing to retain 10 percent of their exports. The Central Americans, including even recalcitrant Guatemala, agreed to retain 15 percent of their exports. And the Inter-African Coffee Organization called a meeting for August in Kampala to discuss the formation of a coffee cartel. Agreement was reached August 17, 1993 in Kampala, by twenty-four exporting countries, soon joined by Indonesia, bringing their share of world green coffee exports to 85 percent. They formed the Association of Coffee Producing Countries (ACPC), and agreed on a retention plan that required all members to withhold 20 percent of their exportable production from the market. This agreement went into effect with the new coffee year on October 1, 1993.[38] The retention plan was based on the level of the ICO Indicator price, and set a price floor of 75 cents per pound. If the price stayed above 75 cents for twenty consecutive days, the retention percentage would be cut from 20 percent to 10 percent. If the price stayed above 80 cents, the retention would be cut to zero; and if the price stayed above 85 cents, countries would be allowed to sell from their retained stocks.[39] Given that prices were generally over $1.00 per pound through the 1980s under the quotas, this seemed like a very moderate goal.

Even though the ACPC controlled about 85 percent of coffee exports, some major producers remained outside the agreement, and this created problems for its potential success. Mexico, the fourth largest producer, was by far the largest one that did not join the ACPC, because it did not want to jeopardize the passage of the North American Free Trade Agreement (NAFTA). Ironically, the peasants of Chiapas, where about half of Mexico's coffee is grown, did not think that NAFTA was such a great deal, and timed the start of their rebellion to coincide with its entry into force, on January 1, 1994. The Zapatista rebellion severely cut into Mexico's production, minimizing the effects of Mexico's non-membership on the amount of coffee available outside the ACPC.[40] The Zapatista rebellion was in part a response to the structure of the coffee commodity chain in Chiapas. Peasant growers who produced most of the coffee there were unhappy with the low prices they had always received for their coffee from agents of the large coffee processors and exporters who came in from outside the region. This sense of exploitation was obviously heightened by the low world market prices that prevailed through the early 1990s. But the rebellion had much broader and deeper roots than just this: racial discrimination, widespread poverty and economic exploitation, and a fear that the opening of Mexico's markets under NAFTA would devastate peasant producers of food crops (Castells, Yazawa, and Kiselyova 1995–1996).

The other large bloc of producers that did not join the ACPC were the Asian countries, particularly Thailand and Vietnam.[41] These countries were "nontraditional" exporters of coffee—they had only begun to extensively plant coffee in the 1980s. Their coffee exports were growing rapidly in the early 1990s, and agreeing to the retention would have hampered their efforts to expand and diversify their exports. Further, as new exporters, they had no history or experience of cooperation with other "traditional" exporters in the ICAs, and less commitment to the principle of producers' collective action. The largest Asian producer, and the third largest producer overall, Indonesia, was reluctant to participate, because it felt that its ability to expand coffee exports had been stifled under the quotas. This was why it had joined with the "other milds" group in 1989 to oppose a new ICA. But Indonesia felt some solidarity with other producers, and finally did join the ACPC, and began to comply with the retention on April 1, 1994.

World market prices began to rise in the fall of 1993, even before the retention went into effect, and continued to rise through the spring of 1994. While the retention undoubtedly decreased the supply of coffee on the market, its effects were multiplied by declining production worldwide, the result of three years of reduced maintenance and uprooting of trees. But before the full effects of retention and declining production could be felt, the market was once again rocked by frost in Brazil.

The 1994 Frost

On the night of June 25, 1994, a severe frost struck the southern coffee regions of Brazil. It was immediately described as the worst since the 1975 frost. Then, about two weeks later, on July 10, another frost hit. It killed additional coffee trees that had only been weakened by the first frost, as well as striking new areas not hit by the first frost. As had been the case in 1975, the main effect was not on the 1994/95 harvest, which was well underway, but on the following year's crop. Brazil's production in the year preceding the frost had been about 28 million bags, similar to its level of production before the 1975 frost, but by this time, Brazil accounted for only about a quarter of total world production. The frost had struck at a particularly bad time, after the prolonged period of low prices had begun to affect production. The Brazilian crop was already suffering because of a prolonged dry spell preceding the frost, and this probably increased the frost damage. The 1994/95 crop was expected to be smaller than that of 1993/94, and exportable production was expected to be below total world demand for coffee for the third straight year, resulting in a further drawdown of

Figure 5.1: ICO Indicator Price for Green Coffee and Average Retail Price of Roasted and Ground Coffee, Monthly Average, January 1993–December 1996

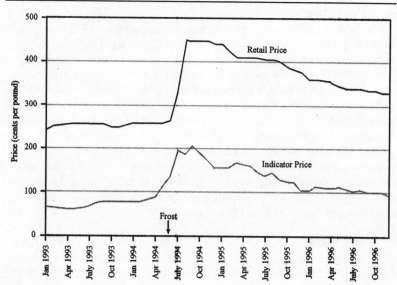

stocks. Prices had already begun to turn upward in 1994 because of the expected shortage and the ACPC retention plan.[42]

Speculation about the amount of damage to Brazil's crop abounded. Early estimates from sources in Brazil began to circulate almost immediately at the CSCE, and they put the damage from the first frost at 10 million bags. The earliest published estimate was by the private forecasting organization Accu-Weather, which estimated the loss from the first frost at 30–40 percent of the 1995/96 crop, with the second frost destroying an additional 10–15 percent. The Brazilian National Coffee Department (NCD), the successor to the IBC, released its estimate of a production decline of 40 percent on July 27. The USDA-FAS representatives were in the field assessing the damage caused by the first frost when the second one hit. The FAS did not release its estimate until August 12, and it was for a decline of 30–40 percent in the 1995/96 crop. The NCD forecast was for a harvest of about 16 million bags, while the FAS estimated 17–20 million. The Brazilian government officially disputed the FAS forecast, saying that it was underestimating the frost damage. Then the German commodity analysts F. O. Licht weighed in with their estimate of 18 million bags on August 26.[43]

Coffee prices responded to the frosts immediately. On Monday, June 27, the first day of trading after the frost, coffee futures rose 25 percent. The next day, the coffee roasters reacted. Folger's raised the price of its 13-ounce cans by 40 cents, and Maxwell House's went up by 35 cents. There was a second price increase in early July, even before the second frost hit, and a third one shortly after

Table 5.2 Brazilian and Total World Production and Exports of Green Coffee around the 1994 Frosts

Year	Production Brazil	Production World	Exports Brazil	Exports World
1993/94	28,500	93,223	17,022	72,044
1994/95	28,000	98,126	16,544	65,371
1995/96	16,800	89,743	12,728	75,033
1996/97	28,000	102,665	18,619	83,085

Sources: USDA, Foreign Agricultural Service, *Tropical Products: World Markets and Trade*, various issues, 1994–1999. The figures for both production and exports refer to coffee years, October 1–September 30. All figures are in thousands of bags of 60 kg.

the second frost. The upper line in figure 5.1 shows the trajectory of retail coffee prices in the United States. The July increase in the wholesale price of coffee was a record-breaking 42.8 percent, driving the U.S. Department of Labor's Producer Price Index up by 0.5 percent for the month, and raising fears of renewed inflation. Once again, these price increases generated consumer protests, and Richard Kessel, Executive Director of the New York State Consumer Protection Board wrote two letters to Attorney General Janet Reno urging an investigation of the manufacturers' price increases. They had come so rapidly that they couldn't possibly reflect actual cost increases, he argued.[44]

Coffee futures prices were extremely erratic. After climbing for more than a week after news of the first frost, they began to fall as traders second-guessed the initial reports from Brazil about the extent of the damage. Then they rose on a forecast of more cold weather in Brazil, and fell when the Brazilian government announced an auction of some of its coffee stocks. Then the second frost hit, prompting a new round of increases. After another week of increases, GNI, a London broker, in its "International Futures and Options Briefing" newsletter, said that the reports of frost damage had been exaggerated, and a CFTC report showed that large speculators were buying heavily, betting on further increases. These reports sent prices down again for several days. Then, when Brazil's NCD released its official estimate of the damage, prices soared again, because it was worse than anyone had expected. As the date approached for the release of the FAS official estimate a couple of weeks later, prices fell again, as traders expected it to be more optimistic than the official Brazilian estimate. When it wasn't much more optimistic, prices rose again. And so on.[45]

Table 5.2 shows Brazilian and total world production and exports for this period. The final production figure for 1995/96 turned out to be closer to the Brazilian NCD estimate than to that of the FAS. Brazil made up some of the difference from stocks, and its exports were only about 4 million bags lower than in 1994/95. Total world exports were actually higher in 1995/96 than in 1994/95, as other countries, particularly Colombia and the Central American countries, increased their exports. They had been building up stocks since the ACPC retention plan had gone into effect in late 1993, and they were able to take advantage of the higher prices and sell off these stocks. The lower line in figure 5.1 shows the ICO indicator price during this period. After a rapid run-up following the frosts, it slowly drifted downward over the next two years.

A comparison of the events following the 1994 frosts with those following the 1975 frost (discussed in chapter 4) shows clearly how the structure of the chain had changed, and how the TNCs were able to use their market power, financial power, and access to information to take advantage of the situation. There are several reasons why the reaction of prices to the 1975 frost was more drastic than to the 1994 frost. One was the severity of the frost. The 1975 frost caused more lasting damage to production in Brazil than did the 1994 frost; after the latter one, production recovered to previous levels within a year. Another reason was that Brazil accounted for a lower percentage of total world production in 1994 than in 1975, so the impact of the frost on world coffee supplies was smaller. In addition, there was panic buying at all levels following the 1975 frost: importers, roasters, retailers, and consumers were all hoarding coffee, and that prolonged the run-up of prices. This also caused a steeper decline after prices peaked, because everyone used up their extra supplies before buying more. The Congressional Research Service estimated that this panic buying was the primary factor that drove prices up about twice as high as they would have been if they had been based solely on availability of supplies.[46] A major reason for the panic buying was uncertainty—no one knew how much coffee would be available, and after many months of price increases, people started to expect the worst. Importers were willing to pay more to be sure of obtaining coffee, and passed the higher prices up along the rest of the commodity chain. As importers and roasters paid the higher prices, they drove futures prices up by hedging their purchases.

The dynamic following the 1994 frost was completely different. Futures prices jumped immediately and roasters followed with immediate wholesale price increases that would cover their increased costs of buying green coffee in the future. Traders and roasters had their sources in Brazil, who were closely monitoring the situation. They had a better idea of the extent of the frost damage and of the size and condition of Brazil's coffee stocks than they had had in 1975. In fact, there was almost too much information about conditions in Brazil available in 1994. In addition to the NCD and FAS, there were numerous estimates of the frost damage floating around in 1994. Commodity traders like ED&F Man and GNI published their estimates; analysts such as F. O. Licht published theirs; and even Accu-Weather released one. This plethora of information, and the fact that commodity funds and other speculators carried much more weight in the futures exchanges in 1994, caused a highly volatile situation in the futures prices. And this was translated into volatility of actual green coffee prices, because by that time the futures price determined the physical price. Despite this volatility, there was no prolonged run-up of prices to cause hoarding. The market was moving much more rapidly; after quickly climbing to a peak only a few months after the frost, futures and green coffee prices quickly began drifting downward. However, wholesale and retail prices remained high.

Another major difference was that there was no attempt by producers to manipulate the market once prices began to decline in 1994, as they had done in 1977–1979. The volume of trading on the CSCE was around 10–12,000 contracts per month in 1978; by 1995, it was around 160,000 per month. The amount of money needed to attempt to squeeze the market in 1995 would have been astronomical. And once again, information systems were much better in 1994. Brazil and El Salvador were able to pull off their operation in 1977 in relative secrecy. There were rumors floating around, but no one really knew what was happening at the time. The details only came out a few years later. Such a level of secrecy would have been impossible in 1994, particularly regarding the buying of large quantities of physical coffee and shipping them from one place to another. In fact, by 1994, the largest traders were in a better position to manipulate the market than states or firms in the producing countries. Their integrated strategies involved both buying physical coffee and buying coffee on paper (futures) and these could be combined in a variety of ways to their advantage. For example, they might sell futures contracts to lower the price slightly, and then quickly fix the price of some physical coffee that they had bought at the lower price. With the huge amounts of coffee they dealt with, even a movement of a fraction of a cent could generate a significant profit.

The most striking difference between 1975 and 1994 is revealed by comparing figure 4.1 from the previous chapter to figure 5.1. Figure 4.1 showed retail coffee prices generally following the trajectory of physical green coffee prices, with a lag. The gap between the two lines narrowed from the beginning of 1974 through the point where green coffee prices were roughly equal to retail prices in March 1977. This shows that, while retail prices were increasing, coffee producing countries were able to increase the share of these prices that they retained. Since it took several months for green coffee to get from the producing countries to the supermarket shelves, the coffee manufacturers were never losing money, but they were being squeezed. Figure 5.1 shows a different pattern. Roasters' responses to the increase in green coffee prices were much faster in 1994. In 1975, the first increase in wholesale price was announced by General Foods, eleven days after the frost. In 1994, Folger's increased its prices three days after the first frost struck, and the only reason it took that long was that the frost hit on a Saturday night. There were no futures traded for more than a day after news of the frost was first reported. Futures prices jumped on Monday, the next trading day, and the roasters raised their prices on Tuesday. The phenomenal 42.8 percent increase in wholesale prices for the month of July stands out in figure 5.1, so that the lower line briefly approaches, but comes nowhere near, the upper. Even as green coffee prices were increasing in 1994, producing countries were not able to significantly increase their share of total income. Part of the reason for this was that green coffee and futures prices reached their peak so quickly after the frost, and began to trend down. Further, the ability of TNC manufacturers to maintain their retail prices in the face of declining green coffee prices is clear from the gap between the upper and lower lines after the frost. The differences between these two figures are literally a graphic illustration of the way the balance of power had shifted away from states and firms in the coffee producing countries and toward the giant coffee TNCs.

Nevertheless, producing states and coffee growers were able to begin to recoup some of the losses they had suffered during the preceding four years. Coffee prices drifted slowly downward through 1995, and hovered around $1.00 per pound through 1996. Total world production remained below total world demand, the result of the low prices during the first coffee crisis. The ACPC acted to try to halt the price declines by reinstating the retention program, which had been cancelled immediately after the frosts struck, but it had little effect. Prices were still roughly double what they had been during the first crisis. Although they were on a downward trend, the producers weren't suffering as much as they had earlier, so they had less incentive to comply with the retention. Then, in 1997, prices quickly spiked again, briefly breaking the $3.00 barrier in May. The reasons for this sudden spike are unclear, and a number of explanations were offered by people in the coffee trade. Brazil's 1997/98 crop was forecast to be lower than the previous year's, and Colombia's crop had been damaged by heavy rains. Roasters had further reduced the amount of working stocks they kept on hand, in order to reduce costs. They relied even more heavily on the importers for just-in-time delivery of coffee; if a shortage arose, some importers might not have been able to deliver. In this situation, rumors of a shortage might have been enough to provoke a spurt of panic buying. Finally, there were reports of commodity funds taking large long positions (i.e., buying futures contracts), betting on a frost in Brazil in June or July.[47] In retrospect, it is likely that this price spike was more speculative than real, because once it was over, prices quickly went into a downward spiral, from which they had not yet recovered at the end of 2003. The ACPC continued to draw up new retention plans to try to stem the tide, but was unable to do so, and finally admitted failure and disbanded in October 2001.

The Second Coffee Crisis, 1998–?

World Bank structural adjustments had forced many producing countries to liberalize their coffee sectors, exposing their small coffee growers more directly to fluctuations in the world market. During the first crisis, this had helped small growers in some countries, who were able to receive a higher percentage of the low world market prices. In fact, even in the midst of the crisis, liberalization increased the prices some growers were receiving, and they responded by planting more coffee (Akiyama 2001). When the frosts drove prices rapidly upward in 1994, growers in many countries responded with a massive increase in coffee planting. Before liberalization, the state coffee agencies and marketing boards would have increased their taxes and revenues and saved some of this money as insurance against the next period of low prices. This would have reduced the price increase received by growers, and reduced their incentive to plant more coffee. But after liberalization, they were no longer able to do this.

The coffee produced by these newly planted trees began to hit the market in 1997–1998, sparking a second coffee crisis. By the end of 2000, prices had fallen below the levels reached at the depth of the first crisis, and they continued to fall.

By far the most phenomenal increase in production was registered by Vietnam, a country that had been a minor exporter just a decade earlier. In the late 1980s, Vietnam had received funding from East Germany and the Soviet Union to increase its coffee production.[48] This assistance had more than doubled its production by the time the frosts struck, and it was the third largest Asian coffee producer, behind Indonesia and India. In the early 1990s, the Vietnamese government began a resettlement program, encouraging ethnic Vietnamese to move to the Central Highlands. The Central Highlands were sparsely populated, mainly by indigenous peoples who had historically resisted rule by the Vietnamese. The area was on the border with Cambodia, and presented a security risk from the perspective of the government. The resettlement allowed the government to relieve population pressures in other regions of the country, and at the same time, bring the Highlands more firmly under government control. As it turned out, the Central Highlands also had an ideal climate for coffee cultivation. The government encouraged settlers to plant coffee, because it would also provide a valuable source of foreign exchange and revenues for the government. When prices shot up in 1994, little further encouragement by the government was needed. Migrants flocked to the Highlands, and forests were cleared and coffee planted so rapidly that environmental problems were created—deforestation, erosion, and water shortages. Between 1994/95 and 1999/2000, production tripled, and Vietnam had passed Colombia to become the world's second largest producing country.[49]

Media reports on the coffee crisis have repeatedly blamed the World Bank for funding the increase in coffee production in Vietnam, but there is no apparent evidence to support this claim. There is some evidence that large coffee traders have encouraged this development, and they have certainly taken advantage of it to drive world market prices down to record low levels. Most of Vietnam's coffee is low-quality robusta. It has very low production costs and can afford to sell its coffee cheaply. Japanese trading companies have been big customers, because robusta is ideal for producing the coffee extract used in Japan's canned coffee market (coffee extract is the stage of instant coffee prior to drying). Vietnam's coffee also has a reputation for poor quality, as a result of improper processing by growers and handling by traders (part of the reason its production costs are so low). A large proportion of Vietnam's exports go to Singapore, a major coffee transshipment point for Asian coffees. All of the major coffee traders have offices there, and it is widely suspected that Vietnamese coffee is cleaned up in Singapore and reexported as coffee from a different origin. The flood of Vietnamese coffee puts downward pressure on the price of robusta coffee on the world market. The major coffee manufacturers then blend a higher proportion of robustas into their coffee blends, lowering the demand for the different types of arabica coffee, and lowering their prices as well. Access to this large supply of cheap robusta coffee, combined with their dominant positions in the world market, enables the large traders to demand lower prices from all producing countries.[50]

While most attention has focused on Vietnam, it is not the sole cause of the crisis. Production in India and Uganda increased by more than 30 percent between the early 1990s and the late 1990s, while Guatemala's production increased by about 20 percent, and Ethiopia's by about 25 percent. Brazilian production recovered rapidly from the frosts, and it produced a bumper crop in 1998/99, further adding to the oversupply. Liberalization and increased prices were partly responsible for these production increases, but so were World Bank pressures on indebted countries to increase their exports in order to pay back their debts. The Bank had long had in place a policy restricting lending that would encourage increased planting of coffee, because of the "adding up" problem. While one relatively small coffee exporting country could increase its export earnings by increasing coffee production, if this path were followed by a number of small exporting countries at the same time, it could backfire. The increased production could be enough to cause world market prices to fall, meaning that each exporting country would earn less income from exporting more coffee. In 1994, the Bank abandoned this policy.[51] Bank lending to directly fund coffee production was apparently not a major cause of the crisis. But clearly, the Bank's economists should have been aware that simultaneously pressuring a number of indebted coffee producing countries to increase their exports of whatever they could find to export, in order to make debt payments, might well have the effect of driving down world market coffee prices.

It has been estimated that there are 10 million small farmers around the world who grow coffee, producing about 70 percent of the world's supply, and about 25 million people who depend directly on coffee for their livelihoods. For these people, the results of this second crisis of the decade have been devastating. Thousands of coffee farmers in Guatemala, Honduras, and Nicaragua have abandoned their farms and headed to the cities in search of food, or headed north with hopes of finding work in Mexico or the United States. In Kenya, farmers who have been losing money on coffee production have replaced their coffee trees with subsistence crops. At the end of July 2001, coffee farmers in Colombia blockaded major highways across the country, warning that unless their debts were cancelled, 80,000 of them would lose their farms because they would be forced to default on their loans. There have been reports that Colombian coffee growers have started to plant coca and opium poppies because they could not make ends meet with their incomes from coffee production.[52] And probably the most visible sign of the severity of the crisis in Colombia was that the FNC was forced to cut its advertising budget and retire Juan Valdez, who had been the symbol of Colombian coffee since 1959.[53]

The changes in the structure of the coffee commodity chain that occurred during the 1980s and 1990s had major implications for the governance structure. From the times that the various coffee producing countries had attained their independence from colonial powers, up through 1989, the coffee chain had been divided into two distinct segments, with producing states exercising governance over the segments located within their own borders, and core-based coffee trading and manufacturing companies controlling the rest of the chain. During the 1980s, the major coffee traders began to gain footholds in the producing countries, by taking over exporting companies or setting up new exporting subsidiaries. During the 1990s, the abilities of producing states to govern the segments of the chains within their borders were significantly weakened by liberalization and privatization. Producing states were pitted against one another by World Bank and IMF policies that used control over financing to discourage market intervention and push export expansion. As a result, the segmented governance structure was increasingly removed. The entire chain, from the coffee fields to the consumer's cup, came under the control of the TNCs. While the producing states still were able to exercise some control over the segments of the chains within their borders, they were no longer able to maintain international solidarity and influence world market prices. Therefore, they were no longer able to protect their coffee growers from the wild fluctuations in world market prices caused by financial speculation, or from the prolonged periods of historically low prices that prevailed during most of the 1990s. Increasingly, small peasant farmers producing coffee using family labor on one side of the market were directly confronting giant transnational conglomerates with state of the art information technologies, access to virtually unlimited financial resources, and a clear picture of the entire global coffee situation on the other side. It was no contest. By the end of the 1990s, as chapter 7 will demonstrate, the share of the coffee consumer's dollar that returned to the places where coffee was produced, and to the people who produced it, had shrunk to near insignificance. Meanwhile, a different kind of struggle was being waged over instant coffee.

Notes

1. Information on the consolidation of the coffee manufacturing TNCs in the following paragraphs has been drawn from the following sources: *Tea and Coffee Trade Journal* March 1982, p. 28; August 1982, p. 26; September 1985, pp. 30–31; July 1988, pp. 35–36; January 1989, pp. 16–22; April 1989, pp. 6–7; July 1989, pp. 6–7; September 1989, p 72; December 1989, p. 41; December 1991, p. 40; January 1992, p. 103; November 1992, pp. 39–46; December 1992, pp. 16–21; April 1993, p. 76; May 1999, p. 96; *World Coffee & Tea* March 1967, pp. 44–46; April 1989, p. 16; January 1990, pp. 28–30; January 1991, pp. 26–31; Landell Mills April, 1991; Stopford 1992; *Boletín Cafetera* May 15, 1993; Fitter and Kaplinsky 2001; Mattera 1992; *New York Times* June 23, 1990, p. 31; March 9, 1999, p. C2; June 9, 1999, p. C4; June 10, 2001, Section 3, p. 10; *Washington Post* September 28, 1985, p.1; *Los Angeles Times* October 22, 1999, p. C1; *Business Wire* June 8, 1999; December 5, 1999; December 14, 2000; *PR Newswire* November 7, 1989; December 1, 1995.

2. In 2001, Philip Morris attempted to remove the taint of tobacco from its food products by "spinning off" Kraft (which includes Maxwell House and all of its coffee operations) as a separate company. However, Philip Morris retained about 84 percent of

Kraft's common stock, and about 98 percent of the voting rights. In a further reorganization in 2003, the Altria group was formed. It consists of three divisions, Philip Morris (tobacco), Miller (beer), and Kraft (food processing). This seems to be a further attempt to isolate its tobacco operation from the rest of the company in such a way that it can be cut loose if it becomes a liability, without damaging the operations or the profits of the other divisions. I will continue to refer to the entire company as Philip Morris, since that name is widely known.

3. *Tea and Coffee Trade Journal* August 1990, pp. 52–55; January 1991, pp. 52–56; June 1991, pp. 16–18; February 1992, p. 47; July 1994, p. 5; March 1996, p. 6; May 1996, pp. 50–62; F. O. Licht December 23, 1993; Landell Mills April 1991; *Boletín Cafetera* May 15, 1993; *Financial Times* April 29, 1997, p. 10.

4. *Tea and Coffee Trade Journal* January 1986, pp. 96–99; August 1990, pp. 58–61, 96–99; January 1992, pp. 122–23; December 1992, p. 19; Carl Peel, "What Happened to the Greenies?," *Tea and Coffee Trade Journal* September 1996, pp. 124–29; *World Coffee and Tea* November 1980, pp. 14–16; January 1981, pp. 38–40, 80–81, 86–87; November 1981, pp. 12–14; November 1982, pp. 12–15; November 1983, pp. 20–22; November 1984, pp. 8–10; January 1985, pp. 30–34; November 1985, pp. 8–11; August 1990, pp. 28–30; Chalmin 1987, chapter 6.

5. Information on Neumann Kaffee Gruppe from *Tea and Coffee Trade Journal* January 1988, p. 111; April 1990, p. 60; June 1990, pp. 46–49; *Financial Times* December 2, 1987, p. 32; *Business Times* (Singapore) June 4, 1993, p. 2; company web site, www.trxfutures.com.

6. Information on Volcafe from *Tea and Coffee Trade Journal* April 1989, p. 44; June 1989, p. 40; *Financial Times* March 16, 1989, p. 45; May 9, 1989, p. 31; *New York Times* March 25, 1983, p. D2; company web site, www.volcafe.com.

7. Chalmin 1987, chapter 6; company web site, www.edfman.com.

8. Company annual report, 2000, accessed on the company web site, www.gs.com.

9. *Financial Times* June 7, 2000, p. 42; *Saint Paul Pioneer Press* June 6, 2000; company web site, www.ecomtrading.com.

10. The exception to this is Neumann, as stated above. Sources for the information in this paragraph not footnoted elsewhere are: *Tea and Coffee Trade Journal* December 1981, p. 46; June 1984, p. 41; September 1986, pp. 24–27; July 1990, pp. 18–20; December 1990, p. 15; January 1992, pp. 122–23; Carl Peel, "What Happened to the Greenies?," *Tea and Coffee Trade Journal* September 1996, pp. 124–29; *World Coffee & Tea* November 1984, pp. 8–10; January 1991, pp. 10–12; F. O. Licht December 15, 1987; June 11, 1993; Landell Mills April 1991; *Ward's* 1994.

11. Subsidiary locations from company web sites, op cit.

12. *Tea and Coffee Trade Journal* January 1986, pp. 96–99; August 1989, pp. 2–3; *World Coffee and Tea* November 1983, pp. 20–22; January 1985, pp. 30–34; November 1986, p. 13.

13. A coffee futures contract is an agreement to deliver a lot of coffee (37,500 pounds on the New York Exchange, five metric tons in London) at a specified future date at a set price. A coffee importer who had just purchased 37,500 pounds of coffee from a producing country, at a fixed price, for delivery in, say, three months, would hedge, or protect himself against the price of coffee going down during that three month period (and thus having to resell the coffee at a loss), by selling one futures contract. This contract would obligate someone else to take delivery of the coffee in three months, at a price high enough to cover the fixed price plus his costs for the transaction. If the price of coffee went down, he could still resell the coffee without losing any money. If the price of coffee went up, he could make a profit on selling the coffee, but would have to use

some of that profit to buy back the futures contract he had sold, at a higher price. The importer thus trades off the possibility of making a profit on a price increase for insurance against a loss caused by a price fall. The transaction works exactly the same way, but in reverse, for someone who contracts to sell coffee and wants to protect himself against a price rise. I have deliberately used the male pronoun in these discussions of coffee futures trading, because the vast majority of coffee traders are still male.

14. Kay Roggenkamp, "Coffee Futures Volume May be Damaged by Coffee Agreement," *World Coffee and Tea* September 1981, pp. 30–34; *World Coffee and Tea* November 1983, pp. 18–20.

15. An options contract is the right (but not the obligation) to buy or sell one futures contract at a set price. As a hedging instrument, it works in basically the same way as a futures contract. Thus an importer who has purchased physical coffee and wants to protect himself against a price decline, would purchase a "put" option, the right to sell a futures contract at a given price at some future date. If the price of coffee falls below that price, the importer could exercise the option and sell the futures contract at an above-market price to recoup his losses on the physical coffee. If the price rises, the importer would not exercise the option and it would expire; he would lose the cost of the option, or the premium, which is analogous to a premium paid to buy insurance. See ITC (1992) for more details. However, one futures contract is a contract for delivery of 37,500 pounds of coffee; at $1.20 to $1.45 per pound in the late 1980s, this was a very expensive contract (although the contracts are actually purchased on margins, for a small percentage of this total). In contrast, a coffee option was selling for around 10 cents per pound at the same time.

16. *Tea and Coffee Trade Journal* August 1981, pp. 12, 33; September 1986, pp. 17–19; January 1992, pp. 23–24; Carl Peel, "What Happened to the Greenies?," *Tea and Coffee Trade Journal* September 1996, pp. 124–29; *World Coffee and Tea* September 1984, p. 10; November 1986, pp. 20–22.

17. John Heuman, "Futures Markets: Commodity Funds, Speculators, and Influences," *Tea and Coffee Trade Journal*, November 1999, pp. 46–49.

18. Ibid.

19. Ibid.; ITC 1992, chapter 14. The older "coffee men," who have been involved in the trade for decades, often look down on the younger speculators, who, they say, don't even know what a coffee tree looks like, and couldn't find Colombia on a map.

20. *Tea and Coffee Trade Journal* June 1985, pp. 19–24; *World Coffee and Tea* November 1980, pp. 12–13; June 1984, pp. 8–9; personal interviews.

21. For example, the importer would buy coffee from the exporter at a differential of five cents under the "C" contract, and sell it to the roaster at three cents under.

22. ITC 1992; *World Coffee and Tea* January 1987, p. 62; personal interviews.

23. *World Coffee and Tea* January 1987, pp. 65–66; Marazzi 1984; Kuchiki 1990; John Heuman, "Futures Markets: Commodity Funds, Speculators, and Influences," *Tea and Coffee Trade Journal* November 1996, pp. 46–49.

24. These figures were calculated from ICO data.

25. ICO statistics; F. O. Licht April 4, 1990, p. 22; ED&F Man August 3, 1989; *World Coffee & Tea* September 1989, pp. 8–13.

26. *Tea and Coffee Trade Journal* June 1992, p. 62.

27. *Tea and Coffee Trade Journal* June 1992, p. 26.

28. This story is taken from an article in the major Colombian newspaper, *El Tiempo* April 17, 1994.

29. F. O. Licht March 15, 1993; *Latin American Economy and Business* May 1993, p. 27; Osorio 1994.

30. Information in this paragraph is drawn from Uvin 1996; Percival and Homer-Dixon 1996; Chossudovsky 1996; and Andersen 2000.

31. *World Coffee & Tea* December 1989, p. 27; January 1990, p. 18; F. O. Licht June 22, 1989, p. 308; October 20, 1989, p. 30; January 24, 1990, pp. 133–34.

32. *Tea and Coffee Trade Journal* January 1992, p. 54.

33. U.S. Senate (1990), hearings on "Drug Policy in the Andean Nations." This was the main topic at the second session, January 18, 1990, at which the Ambassadors of Colombia, Bolivia, and Peru testified. It is also mentioned in an exchange of letters between U.S. President Bush and Colombian President Barco in September 1989, reprinted as ICO document ICC 54-1, and in a letter from Bush to Colombian President Gaviria in August 1992, stating the U.S. commitment to negotiating an new ICA (F. O. Licht, October 7, 1992; *World Coffee & Tea* August 1992, p. 27.

34. *World Coffee & Tea* February 1991, p. 22.

35. F. O. Licht July 7, 1992; December 18, 1993; April 19, 1993.

36. F. O. Licht February 26, 1993, p. 186.

37. F. O. Licht, April 19, 1993. There was also a change of U.S. administration at a crucial stage just before the negotiations broke down. But U.S. negotiators insisted that they had full instructions from their government and that the change would not hamper their participation. This was probably accurate; Clinton's early focus was almost exclusively on domestic matters, and his trade policies, coordinated by the Office of the U.S. Trade Representative, were, if anything, more neoliberal than his predecessor's.

38. *Financial Times* August 18, 1993; *Wall Street Journal* August 18, 1993; F. O. Licht September 27, 1993; January 11, 1994.

39. *Journal of Commerce* August 18, 1993; F. O. Licht October 12, 1993.

40. *Journal of Commerce* July 8, 1993; January 20, 1994; May 2, 1994.

41. *Journal of Commerce* August 9, 1993, August 24, 1993.

42. *Tea and Coffee Trade Journal* August 1994, p. 5; *World Coffee and Tea* August 1994, p. 5; September 1994, p. 5; October 1994, p. 5; *New York Times* June 28, 1994, p. D1; June 29, 1994, p. D1; July 12, 1994, p. D13; *Financial Times* June 28, 1994, p. 30; July 12, 1994, p. 1; USDA, FAS *Tropical Products: World Markets and Trade*, June 1994.

43. *World Coffee and Tea* August 1994, p. 5; October 1994, p. 5; *Financial Times* July 12, 1994, p. 1; August 13, 1994, p. 2; August 16, 1994, p. 13; August 27, 1994, p. 12; *Journal of Commerce* July 28, 1994, p. B8.

44. The 13-ounce cans were a legacy of the 1975 frosts; as coffee prices climbed over an extended period following that frost, the TNCs tried to disguise the extent of the price increases by switching from a standard one-pound can to the 13-ounce size. So Folger's 40-cent increase actually amounted to an increase of almost 50 cents per pound. *New York Times* June 28, 1994, p. D1; *Financial Times* July 16, 1994, p. 9; *Buffalo News* June 29, 1994; *Arizona Republic* June 30, 1994, p. C1; *Journal of Commerce* July 25, 1994, p. B6; *Business Week* August 1, 1994, p. 20; *Chicago Sun-Times* July 14, 1994, p. 52; August 11, 1994, p. 4; *PR Newswire* July 2, 1994.

45. *New York Times* June 28, 1994, p. D1; June 29, 1994, p. D1; June 30, 1994, p. D17; July 8, 1994, p. D11; July 9, 1994, p. 43; July 11, 1994, p. D2; July 12, 1994, p. D13; July 26, 1994, p. D16; August 16, 1994, p. D13; *Washington Post* July 12, 1994, p. C1; *Financial Times* July 20, 1994, p. 30; July 28, 1994, p. 28; August 13, 1994, p. 12; August 16, 1994, p. 17.

46. *New York Times* November 14, 1977, p. 53.

47. *Tea and Coffee Trade Journal* September 1997, pp. 12–17.

48. ICO "Coffee in Vietnam," document EB 3259/91, Rev. 1, February, 1991.

49. Production figures for this paragraph from USDA, Foreign Agricultural Service, *Tropical Products: World Markets and Trade* June 1994; December 1995; December 1998; June 2001. Other information taken from Greenfield 2002; *Forbes* Vol. 163 Issue 10, May 17, 1999, p. 174; *Far Eastern Economic Review* Vol. 158 Issue 36, September 7, 1995, pp. 62–64; *Time* South Pacific Edition, Issue 13, April 2, 2002.

50. Greenfield 2002; *Tea and Coffee Trade Journal* November 1993, pp. 86–91; May, 1995, p. 24; November 1995, pp. 90–94; *Far Eastern Economic Review* September 7, 1995.

51. Schiff 1995; World Bank 1993; personal communication, Panos Varangis, August 27, 2001.

52. Oxfam 2001; *San Francisco Chronicle* May 20, 2001; *Washington Post* September 3, 2001; October 30, 2001; Agence France Press July 31, 2001; Associated Press July 28, 2001; July 29, 2001; August 1, 2001; *Houston Chronicle* November 22, 2001.

53. *New York Times* November 24, 2001.

Chapter 6

The Struggle for Control of the Instant Coffee Commodity Chain

The preceding three chapters have focused on struggles over the governance structure of the coffee commodity chain. As outlined in chapter 1, because of the way the chain was structured for most of the postwar period, struggles over governance, or what I have called the collective action strategy, predominated. However, the invention of technology to mass-produce instant coffee just before World War II opened up new possibilities. As discussed in chapter 2, green coffee was the form in which coffee was traditionally traded internationally, because it stored and traveled well, while roasted coffee rapidly went stale. Instant coffee was the first processed coffee product, ready for final consumption, which could be stored for long periods, and which could therefore be produced in coffee growing countries and exported to the major consuming markets. The invention of instant coffee created a new niche in core markets, and at the same time, opened the possibility of producers located in coffee growing countries competing for a share of this niche. By building their own factories, producing states and firms could upgrade along the chain, and extend their control into the higher value-added processing operations that had been the exclusive reserve of the major coffee manufacturers. However, at the same time, this development also opened the possibility of manufacturers locating their own factories in the producing countries, moving their control further backward along the chain, and gaining access to shares of the income that had been controlled by Third World processors and exporters, and producing states. The invention of new instant coffee technology therefore set off a different kind of struggle, which involved what I have called the forward integration strategy. This struggle proceeded alongside the struggle over governance, but it was also influenced and at times constrained by the fact that the instant coffee chain was a strand of the larger coffee commodity chain. In order to understand how this forward integration struggle developed, we first need to understand how the instant coffee strand of the chain evolved.

A Brief History of Instant Coffee

The early history of instant coffee is linked to wars; military commanders had long sought a way to give their troops in the field a caffeine boost without having to carry along cumbersome brewing equipment.[1] The earliest experiments with, and patents for, instant coffee date to the Civil War; further experiments were conducted during the Spanish-American War. As an outgrowth of these experiments, a European immigrant named George Washington produced the first commercially viable instant coffee in the United States beginning in 1906. The G. Washington Coffee Company continued to sell instant coffee in the U.S. market into the 1940s.[2] Instant coffee received a further boost during World War I, when the U.S. Army purchased it for some of its troops in Europe. By most accounts, this early instant coffee was of poor quality and had a somewhat foul taste. The first major advance in instant coffee production occurred in the 1930s, when Nestlé technicians, in consultation with Brazilian coffee officials trying to find ways to dispose of their huge coffee stockpiles, realized that the spray-drying technology they used to produce powdered milk could be adapted for the production of powdered instant coffee. Nestlé built an instant coffee factory in the United States in 1939.

Commercial development of instant coffee for the consumer market was interrupted by World War II, but at the same time, the U.S. government provided a huge stimulus to the development of the industry by making instant coffee a standard component of the rations given to U.S. troops, and purchasing massive quantities of it. Eighty percent of this coffee was distributed to U.S. troops, and 20 percent was distributed to U.S. POWs by the Red Cross. Nestlé, G. Washington, and the few other small producers that existed at the time could not begin to meet this demand, and about ten new manufacturers went into business during the war. U.S. military purchases not only created an instant demand, stimulating the creation of these firms, but they also exposed millions of young men to instant coffee as a convenient consumer product.

In the postwar period, U.S. consumption of instant coffee increased rapidly, reaching about 20 to 25 percent of total U.S. coffee consumption (which was itself increasing) by 1960. The companies that had manufactured it for the military competed for shares of this expanding market. Three major players rapidly emerged: Nestlé, Borden (another producer of spray-dried milk), and General Foods, whose Maxwell House division was already the leader in the U.S. market for roasted and ground (R&G) coffee. Also in the early 1950s, ten medium sized roasting firms that served regional markets, mostly in the east, pooled their resources to form Tenco, an instant coffee manufacturer, to produce instant coffee to be packaged under each of the investing companies' labels. Tenco rapidly became the third largest instant coffee manufacturing company, after Nestlé and General Foods, producing "private label" instant coffees for dozens of small roasters and grocery chains, in addition to the ten original investors.[3]

Instant coffee was on the cutting edge of the "durable foods" (Friedmann, 1991a) introduced to the U.S. market during the 1950s, along with other convenience foods such as frozen orange juice concentrate, Birds-eye frozen vegetables, and TV dinners. It had a long shelf life, was quick and easy to prepare (no special equipment needed), convenient (no spent grounds to dispose of), and cheaper per cup than brewed R&G coffee. These claims all figured prominently in the advertising campaigns of the major manufacturers. In 1954, world coffee prices rose sharply following a Brazilian frost in 1953. In a country just coming off wartime price controls (ceiling prices on green coffee imports had just been lifted in 1953), price became the major selling point for instant coffee.

Instant coffee manufacturers responded by switching from arabica to robusta beans as the basis of their instant coffee blends and pushing up their extraction rates. Robusta beans yielded higher percentages of soluble solids, and were available at lower prices on the world market. African production (mostly robusta) was increasing rapidly during the 1950s, making this switch feasible. In the 1940s and early 1950s, instant coffees had been "filled" with soluble carbohydrates because of the low yields of the early extraction technology. In the early 1950s, manufacturers began to introduce "100% pure" instant coffee. The higher extraction rates achieved in the 1950s allowed manufacturers to replace this filler by extracting the less soluble and less flavorful solids from coffee, literally squeezing more solids out of the same amount of beans. These solids were not extracted in normal brewing and did not add anything to the flavor of the instant coffee (in fact they may have detracted from it), but they did help to lower its price relative to R&G coffee.

The United States was the major consuming market for instant coffee in the 1950s, but world consumption rapidly expanded. Nestlé, based in Switzerland, was manufacturing it for the Swiss and French markets. It was also introduced into the U.K. in the 1940s, and became somewhat popular during the war when tea exports were sometimes scarce and tea was rationed. From there, it spread to Australia, New Zealand, and Canada. The U.S. military also played a role in introducing it to the Japanese market during the postwar occupation. The U.K., Canada, and Japan joined the United States as major consumers of instant coffee in the late 1950s and early 1960s. Both Nestlé and General Foods embarked on aggressive expansion programs as consumption spread. General Foods focused on building factories in the major consuming countries, but by this time, Nestlé was already involved in the production of instant coffee in the coffee growing countries.

The basic design of an instant coffee factory has not changed all that much since this initial rapid increase in production during the 1950s and early 1960s. Green coffee is first roasted and ground on site; it is more economical to perform this processing at the factory than to ship roasted coffee in from a roaster located elsewhere. This coffee is put into a battery of extractors (usually six or seven), and hot water is forced under pressure sequentially through these extractors. The water first enters an extractor in which the coffee has gone through five or six previous extractions, where the least soluble carbohydrates are extracted at high temperature. The water is then passed through the remaining extractors, in which each subsequent extractor contains coffee that has gone through one less extraction, finishing with one which is filled with freshly ground roasted coffee. The water temperature drops as it passes through each of the extractors. In this way, the water picks up the least volatile and least flavorful solids in the first extractor, and the most volatile and most flavorful solids in the last one. At this point the coffee extract is drawn off and the most extracted grounds are dumped and replaced with freshly ground coffee; and the process begins again. The coffee extract is now ready for drying. Advances in extraction technology during the 1960s and 1970s enabled producers to further increase the rate of extraction from about 33 percent (i.e., three pounds of coffee produced one pound of instant) which had been achieved by 1960, to almost 50 percent, but most of the other technological advances have come in the drying process.

The technique most widely used to dry the extract during the 1950s was spray drying. The extract was sprayed from the top of a huge cylindrical drying tower, where it was met by a blast of hot air, and the dried solids accumulated in a conical collector at the bottom. But this technique had some serious drawbacks. Much of the highly volatile and distinctive coffee aroma evaporated in the drying. Spray drying also produced a fine powder that did not dissolve easily in hot water. Therefore, in the 1960s, General Foods and Nestlé developed methods for freeze drying the coffee extract. This improved the recovery of the most distinctive and volatile coffee solids and oils during the drying process, and produced larger granules which looked more like R&G coffee, and also dissolved more easily. However, this method was also considerably more expensive than spray drying. At the same time, the major manufacturers were also working on ways to improve spray drying. They found that they could agglomerate the powder into larger granules to improve its looks and solubility, and aromatize it, or add back in some of the aroma-carrying oils after the drying process. This at least improved the aroma of spray-dried instant in the jar, if not its flavor in the cup.

The high capital intensiveness of instant coffee production led to a high concentration of market shares in the major core markets. Only the largest coffee processing firms had the capital to compete in the development of new technologies and the building of more modern production facilities. In addition, only the largest firms could afford the advertising and promotional expenditures necessary to compete on the national market. In the United States in 1951, the major manufacturers spent over $3 million on advertising; by 1962 their advertising expenditures on instant coffee had risen to over $43 million, for TV spots alone. But regional markets remained strong in the United States into the 1960s and smaller manufacturers were able to compete with the majors in these markets without trying for national distribution. While the majors increasingly focused their advertising on TV spots, the regional manufacturers were able to advertise much more cheaply in local newspapers. Private label processors like Coca-Cola's Tenco Division also continued to produce a number of small private-label brands, disguising somewhat the high degree of concentration in the market. But markets became increasingly national in the 1960s, smaller brands began to disappear or be acquired by the largest manufacturers, and by the 1970s, three or four national coffee companies accounted for over 80 percent of instant coffee sales in most major consuming markets (United States, Canada, Japan, Europe, Australia, and New Zealand) (UNCTAD 1984).

In the U.S. market, Borden proved unable to keep up with the rapid pace of technological innovation set by Nestlé and General Foods in the 1950s, and by 1960, was no longer a major producer of instant. Procter & Gamble, which had acquired Folger's in 1963, as the pace of innovation was beginning to slow, invested in instant coffee plants, and in the R&D needed to develop its own spray-drying capacity. Thus by the late 1970s, Nestlé, General Foods, and P&G controlled almost 90 percent of the U.S. instant coffee market; and Coca-Cola's Tenco Division accounted for most of the remainder.

By the 1970s, instant coffee consumption had also begun to decline in many of these countries, and instant coffee now has a relatively small share of most of the traditional consuming markets. But its consumption worldwide is still increasing. Because of its ease and method of preparation, it seems to be the coffee product most acceptable in traditional tea-drinking countries. The U.K., Canada, and Japan are the best early examples; in all three countries, instant was the form in which coffee was first introduced on the market. In the U.K., 90 percent of coffee consumption is still in instant form; in Canada it is about one third. Japanese tastes evolved rather rapidly toward higher-quality R&G arabicas, and now their consumption is divided between R&G, instant, and canned coffees, with the share of instant declining. However, the market share of canned coffee beverages is growing, and instant coffee or coffee extract is used in their production. More recently this pattern of instant coffee as the most readily adopted form of consumption has been seen in East Asian NICs such as South Korea and Taiwan. Instant coffee consumption has also increased in many Third World countries, including some coffee producers where coffee drinking has not been a part of the culture. In some cases, instant coffee, as a "modern" industrial product produced by firms in developed countries, with high brand name recognition, has become something of a status symbol, and is preferred over locally produced R&G by the middle and upper classes. In these cases, instant coffee plays a role in marking class differences similar to that played by specialty coffee in the U.S. market (see chapter 8).

Instant Coffee Production in the Coffee Growing Countries

Coffee growing countries, given their structural position in the traditional coffee commodity chain, faced major obstacles to selling large volumes of instant coffee in the core markets. First, a country would have to produce a sufficient volume of coffee. Any country which already earned significant income from green coffee exports would have to build an instant coffee export capacity alongside its traditional export trade. Thus, it would have to have the capacity to continue exporting green coffee while diverting a sufficient quantity into instant production to take advantage of economies of scale. The cases of Ecuador and India suggest that a minimum green coffee export capacity of about one million bags (60 kg. each) per year would be required to become a major instant coffee exporter.[4] Second, a country would have to have the basic industrial infrastructure necessary to operate a factory, such as good roads, reliable power generation facilities, and an adequate source of large amounts of water. Therefore, in the late 1950s, only about seven countries probably had the capacity to develop an instant coffee industry: Brazil, Colombia, El Salvador, Guatemala, Mexico, Côte d'Ivoire, Angola, and Uganda. By the late 1980s, about twenty major producing countries probably had the potential to become instant coffee exporters, based on these two criteria.[5]

Third, the state and/or local capitalists would have to have access to the capital and technology necessary to build a factory. In the 1950s and early 1960s, most of the key aspects of instant coffee production technology were controlled by core firms, and coffee growing countries would have had to get the technology from them. Thus the early factories were Nestlé subsidiaries or joint ventures with other core firms. The technology began to become more widely available in the 1960s, as the rate of technological change slowed. By the 1970s, most instant coffee technology was standardized, and most of the necessary components could be made in most of the major coffee growing countries. Key components of the technology that couldn't be produced locally could be purchased from core equipment supply or consulting firms.

Fourth, once an instant coffee factory had been established in a coffee growing country, it would have to sell the instant coffee in the core consuming markets. Here it would come into direct competition with the country's largest customers for green coffee, the national coffee companies. They controlled the core markets and defended them against all new entrants, with brand name advertising, discounts, coupons, and other tactics of oligopolistic competition. By the late 1950s, selling instant coffee produced in a coffee growing country directly to consumers in the core markets would have required a huge advertising budget to compete against the companies' established brands. In addition, coffee growing countries could not offer the blends of different types of coffee that were used by the major manufacturers; most countries produced only one type of coffee. Finally, the coffee companies potentially could threaten to boycott the green coffee exports from countries challenging their markets. Their global sourcing strategies (Friedmann, 1991a) allowed them to replace the coffee from any one origin with a suitable substitute from another origin, without significantly affecting the taste of the blend.[6] Thus, the coffee growing country faced a dilemma: the more aggressively it enacted policies to increase control forward along the chain into instant coffee processing, the more likely it was to face retaliation by the coffee companies against its green coffee exports.

If instant producers in the coffee growing countries couldn't sell their products directly to consumers in the core markets, the alternative was to sell instant coffee in bulk to core firms that would package and retail the coffee under their own brand names. When Brazil initially tried to use this strategy to gain a share of the U.S. market in the 1960s, it met strong opposition from most coffee companies and green coffee dealers. Once instant coffee production had been established in Brazil and several other coffee growing countries, most companies adopted a policy of using the instant or extract produced there as a component of their overall global sourcing strategies. But they used these purchases only as a supplement to their own production in their facilities in the core markets. This strategy by coffee growing countries involved settling for a marginal share of the market, and surrendering to a core firm some of the income that would have been gained from direct retailing.

Despite all of these barriers, five coffee growing countries have become significant exporters of instant coffee. Their stories illustrate the possibilities and the limits of the forward integration strategy. They have followed a variety of paths into instant coffee exporting.[7] In Brazil and Ecuador, the state has provided various incentives to local capitalists to encourage their entry into instant coffee processing. Côte d'Ivoire's export industry is a Nestlé subsidiary, which located there because of a different set of state incentives. Colombia and India have pursued more mixed strategies involving alliances of state and local capital, with some participation by Nestlé as well. These five countries display very different export patterns reflecting the different paths by which they moved into the instant coffee industry. In Brazil and Ecuador, local capitalists have exported instant coffee to the same core markets as their green coffee. Some Brazilian manufacturers have also sought new markets for their product. The destinations of Côte d'Ivoire's exports are determined by the global production and marketing strategies of Nestlé. Colombia, with more direct state involvement, has pursued a strategy of seeking out new markets for its instant coffee, while India has pursued a similar strategy with much less success, because the state chose to focus on exports to the former Soviet Union.

Table 6.1 shows the instant coffee exports of these five countries from 1976/77 to 1991/92.[8] Brazil is clearly the dominant exporter of instant coffee, to a much greater degree than it is in green coffee. Colombia, the second largest exporter of green coffee, was established as the second largest instant coffee exporter by the mid-1980s. Côte d'Ivoire was the third largest coffee producer, and the largest producer of robusta, when its instant coffee industry was established in the 1960s. It has generally maintained its third position in instant coffee exports, despite falling to fifth in green coffee (behind Indonesia and Mexico) in the mid-1990s. Ecuador is an interesting case of a relatively small coffee producer that has nonetheless become a significant exporter of instant. It exports a higher proportion of its coffee in instant form than any other country except Brazil. India was a relatively small exporter of both green and instant coffee until it rapidly expanded sales to the Soviet Union in the mid-1980s. Other minor instant coffee exporters not considered in detail here include Mexico, El

Table 6.1 Exports of Instant Coffee[a] by Coffee Producing Countries to All Destinations, 1976/77–1991/92

	1976/ 77[b]	1977/ 78	1978/ 79	1979/ 80	1980/ 81	1981/ 82
Brazil	2023	1599	2614	2087	2303	2322
Colombia	214	70	146	96	126	101
Côte d'Ivoire	97	101	265	99	76	179
Ecuador	24	16	56	85	176	215
India	18	20	35	53	52	95
All Others	58	104	153	166	155	85
Total	2434	1910	3269	2586	2888	2997
% Total Coffee Exports, All Forms	4.6	3.7	5.0	4.2	4.8	4.7

	1981[c]	1982	1983	1984	1985	1986
Brazil	2197	2247	2117	2199	1974	1949
Colombia	126	105	219	215	245	270
Côte d'Ivoire	77	196	219	176	224	202
Ecuador	182	244	207	169	150	147
India	65	94	77	56	59	29
All Others	158	109	119	89	94	98
Total	2805	2995	2958	2904	2746	2695
% Total Coffee Exports, All Forms	4.5	4.6	4.3	4.2	3.8	4.2

	1986/ 87[b]	1987/ 88	1988/ 89	1989/ 90	1990/ 91	1991/ 92
Brazil	1958	2139	2079	2706	1666	2053
Colombia	241	314	341	394	358	412
Côte d'Ivoire	183	245	299	279	194	349
Ecuador	160	134	142	180	183	241
India	32	48	174	301	97	136
All Others	98	83	83	106	133	154
Total	2672	2963	3118	3966	2631	3345
% Total Coffee Exports, All Forms	3.6	4.7	4.3	4.9	3.5	4.3

Sources: ICO documents. Instant coffee exports for 1976/77–1981/82 from EB 2380/84; 1981–1986 from EB 2857/87; 1986/87–1991/92 from EB 3398/93. Total coffee exports for 1976/77–1981/82 and 1981–1983 from WP Agreement No. 13/88 Rev. 2 (calendar year exports for 1981–1983 estimated from coffee year data); 1984–1986 from EB 3222/90 Add. 1; 1986/87–1991/92 from EB 3393/93.
[a]Figures in thousands of bags (60 kg each) of green bean equivalent. One thousand bags of green bean equivalent equals about 23 metric tons, or 50,875 pounds, of instant coffee, assuming the ICO conversion factor of 2.6 pounds of green coffee to one pound of instant.
[b]Coffee years, October 1–September 30.
[c]Calendar years.

Salvador, Guatemala, Nicaragua, and Indonesia.

Table 6.1 also shows the limited impacts that these efforts have had on the overall structure of the international coffee trade. Instant coffee has accounted for between 3.5 and 5 percent of total coffee exports by coffee growing countries over this entire period, and there is no discernible trend of increase in the proportion of coffee that is exported in processed form. The volume of instant coffee exports has increased somewhat, but so has the volume of green coffee exports. The exports of these five countries accounted for almost 60 percent of total world exports of instant coffee in 1989 (exports from the core consuming countries accounted for most of the remaining 40 percent); however, most of the instant coffee consumed in the core markets was being produced in those countries by the coffee TNCs. Instant coffee firms in these five countries were also competing with the TNCs for the new instant coffee markets which were opening in the 1980s and 1990s, with mixed results. The next section outlines how these five countries became instant coffee exporters, and how their exports shaped, and were shaped by, the evolving structure of the chain.

The Evolution of the Instant Coffee Chain

The development of mass production technology for instant coffee and the rapid increase and spread of its consumption during the 1950s and 1960s led to the creation of a new strand of the commodity chain. Because of the nature of instant coffee, there were a variety of possibilities for the structure of this new chain. Instant coffee factories did not have to be located near the point of consumption, as did R&G factories; they could also be located near the source of their raw material input, green coffee. Both the major coffee companies and the coffee producing states had interests in how the emerging chain would be structured, and pursued a variety of strategies to shape it. In this section, the evolution of the chain is traced through three distinct phases: an initial phase controlled by the coffee companies; a second phase dominated by producing state initiatives; and the current phase of globalization and competition over new markets.

Coffee Company Initiatives, 1950–1965

As the new chain emerged in the early 1950s, the technology for extracting and drying the soluble coffee solids that made up instant coffee was still rapidly evolving. It was controlled by the major manufacturers, as only they had the capital to invest in R&D and new plants. Three major U.S. companies undertook international initiatives during this period, each following a somewhat different strategy, shaped by their corporate identities.

General Foods had long been a major producer of R&G coffee, and it set up its instant coffee production on the model of its R&G production. Factories were located in the major core markets, near the point of consumption. The first factories were built in the United States and Canada, and later in the U.K. and in Germany, to serve the European market. General Foods was also the first company to build a plant in Japan. It did acquire a Mexican instant coffee producer in 1962, but did not actively seek to locate its factories in coffee growing regions.

Nestlé had long been transnational; it grew by locating production facilities in each new national market it entered. And it followed the same strategy with instant coffee. By the mid-1960s, Nestlé had plants in Australia, New Zealand, Canada, Austria, Denmark, France, Germany, Italy, Netherlands, Spain, Switzerland, and the U.K. But Nestlé was also active in Third World national markets, and built factories wherever there was a demand. By 1964, Nestlé had subsidiaries in Brazil, Colombia, Mexico, and Côte d'Ivoire, and a joint venture in India. All of these plants produced for local markets, except for the Côte d'Ivoire plant. The story of the Côte d'Ivoire plant illustrates the effects of the manufacturers' backward integration strategies on the producing countries.[9]

Côte d'Ivoire was an obvious location for an instant coffee factory, since it was at the time the world's largest producer of robusta coffee. In 1959, as the Ivoirien administration looked toward its imminent independence, it was eager to attract foreign capital, particularly in the processing of its primary commodities, and Nestlé obtained a number of generous concessions by agreeing to build a plant there. It received an exemption from export taxes for the export of some green coffee from the Ivoirien subsidiary to its French parent (a subsidiary of the Swiss company). This amount was linked to the output of the factory, and was gradually decreased over a twelve-year period, beginning in 1962 when the factory opened. Some of the instant coffee exported from the factory was also exempted from export taxes. In addition, by locating in Côte d'Ivoire, Nestlé gained access to lower quality coffees not suitable for export, such as beans broken during processing, or discolored beans. These were available at very low prices inside the country, and while not of export quality, they were still suitable for instant coffee production. Most of the original concessions granted to Nestlé have since been phased out, but it still enjoys access to low-price green coffee that is directly processed into instant. Nestlé's Côte d'Ivoire plant thus has considerably lower raw material costs than core-based factories.

Côte d'Ivoire's export pattern is radically different from those of the other major exporters, and reflects Nestlé's global strategy. The factory in Côte d'Ivoire was established mainly to serve a "regional" market: western and northern Africa, the Middle East, and Greece. Although all of these markets were small when the subsidiary was first established, they have all grown. Greece has always been the leading destination of Côte d'Ivoire's exports, but these exports grew rapidly during the 1980s. They account for about two-thirds of the instant coffee consumed in Greece, marketed through Nestlé's food products subsidiary in Greece. Small amounts have also been exported to Cyprus and to Europe. The other major markets for Ivoirien instant have been Senegal and the Middle East. But instant remains a relatively small proportion of total coffee exports, and it is controlled by Nestlé. In addition, the instant coffee factory has few linkages to the local economy; it has stimulated the development of industries producing packaging materials, but the instant coffee technology is all imported from Europe by Nestlé.

The third company, Tenco, was established by ten smaller regional coffee companies, which pooled their capital to be able to compete with the likes of General Foods in instant coffee production. Thus Tenco undertook the most innovative and ambitious strategy. It collaborated with International Basic Economy Corp. (IBEC), a Rockefeller company that invested in food processing industries in a number of Third World countries, and attempted to create an international network to produce and distribute instant coffee.[10] Other manufacturers imported green coffees from a number of different countries and blended them to produce instant. The Tenco-IBEC plan was to manufacture instant in a number of coffee growing countries and export it in bulk to the major consuming markets, where it would be blended and packaged for private label customers. These local brands could then be sold at lower prices than the majors' national brands. Tenco-IBEC built factories in El Salvador, Mexico, and Guatemala between 1955 and 1958, forming joint ventures with local capitalists—large coffee growers and/or local coffee roasting firms. Instant coffee from these factories became the first instant imported into the United States; until that time all instant consumed in the United States had been produced there (see table 6.2).[11] However, after Tenco was acquired by Coca-Cola in 1960, this strategy was not actively pursued; Coca-Cola reverted to a General Foods strategy of building in the core markets, establishing factories in Germany and the U.K.

During this initial phase of expansion, one reason for building instant coffee factories in the coffee growing countries was lower labor costs. But as instant coffee production became increasingly automated in the 1960s, labor costs were less of a factor, and skilled technical workers were needed to operate the factories; they were in greater supply in the core consuming markets. The high costs of green coffee in the mid-1950s sent Tenco in particular to the growing countries in search of lower raw materials costs. But as prices fell during the late 1950s, and TNCs in the core increased the robusta content of their blends, these cost advantages were also offset to some extent.

The production capacity that was established in the coffee growing countries during this period was relatively small and mostly locally oriented. The rapidly growing core consumer markets were being satisfied mainly by a rapid expansion of the core production facilities of the major manufacturers. Most of the Third World production capacity built during this period was intended to capture local markets. Further, it was under the control of the major companies and was integrated into their global strategies; it generally had few linkages to the local economies. In the case of Nestlé's Côte d'Ivoire plant and Tenco's Central American plants, the strategy was to gain a competitive edge by lowering the cost of raw material inputs. This comparative advantage of lower production costs formed the basis for producing state initiatives beginning in the mid-1960s.

Table 6.2 U.S. Consumption and Imports of Instant Coffee, 1956–1978

	1956	1957	1958	1959	1960	1961	1962	1963	1964	1965	1966	1967
Total Consumption	2511	2994	3139	3430	3598	3875	3982	3992	3993	3949	4010	4159
Imports	38	90	99	126	126	93	91	142	120	64	239	621
Imports as % of Consumption	1.5	3.0	3.2	3.7	3.5	2.4	2.3	3.6	3.0	1.6	6.0	14.9
Imports by Source												
Brazil	0	0	0	0	0	0	0	0	1	6	136	506
Colombia	0	0	0	0	0	0	0	0	0	0	0	0
Ecuador	0	0	0	0	0	0	0	0	0	0	0	0
El Salvador	37	64	54	57	56	41	1	2	3	7	17	23
Guatemala	0	0	8	33	56	14	3	7	15	8	32	20
Mexico	0	25	37	35	14	3	29	34	45	0	23	16
Nicaragua	0	0	0	0	0	36	52	55	36	42	20	5
Other Growers[a]	0	0	0	0	0	0	0	0	0	0	0	3
Argentina	0	0	0	0	0	0	0	0	20	0	0	4
Canada	0	0	0	0	0	0	5	42	0	0	0	0
France	0	0	0	0	0	0	0	0	0	0	7	39
Germany	0	0	0	0	0	0	0	0	0	0	0	2
Netherlands	0	0	0	0	0	0	0	0	0	0	0	0
Spain	0	0	0	0	0	0	0	0	0	0	0	0
Switzerland	0	0	0	0	0	0	0	0	0	0	3	0
U.K.	0	0	0	0	0	0	0	0	0	1	0	0
Other Consumers[b]	1	1	0	1	0	0	1	2	0	0	1	3

Continued on next page

Table 6.2 U.S. Consumption and Imports of Instant Coffee, 1956–1978 (continued)

	1968	1969	1970	1971	1972	1973	1974	1975	1976	1977	1978
Total Consumption	4252	4437	4648	4960	5202	5560	5203	4984	4415	3663	3633
Imports	511	911	809	827	1274	1558	1638	1107	1552	1281	1226
Imports as % of Consumption	12.0	20.5	17.4	16.7	24.5	28.0	31.5	22.2	35.2	35.0	33.7
Imports by Source											
Brazil	428	640	527	509	890	931	1154	829	1163	939	1007
Colombia	0	0	0	0	0	2	0	2	20	31	8
Ecuador	0	0	0	0	1	0	6	6	9	7	21
El Salvador	23	45	32	22	22	26	24	37	10	15	23
Guatemala	20	30	31	16	15	14	8	8	8	2	3
Mexico	7	13	6	10	17	14	1	0	18	2	34
Nicaragua	0	31	8	10	0	6	0	16	0	4	2
Other Growers[a]	0	0	0	0	0	66	20	0	9	18	7
Argentina	0	1	0	3	1	11	0	0	4	1	0
Canada	9	54	14	24	18	55	84	16	59	72	0
France	18	15	14	13	26	164	144	108	139	105	75
Germany	2	1	28	36	94	78	31	13	33	23	9
Netherlands	0	5	29	38	4	4	6	0	3	9	10
Spain	0	0	1	27	89	46	53	48	48	42	25
Switzerland	0	40	79	48	29	45	19	8	0	0	0
U.K.	0	35	36	71	58	82	87	10	3	5	0
Other Consumers[b]	4	1	4	0	10	14	1	6	26	6	2

Source: Pan American Coffee Bureau (1966), Tables IS-1, ISV-10, C-6, CP-15; Pan American Coffee Bureau (1967–1975), Tables S-1, C-2; Instituto Brasileiro do Café (1978), Tables IM-6, IM-7, PR-23, CO-3; (1979), Tables IM-11, IM-12, PR-23, CO-3. Imports in pounds have been converted into thousands of bags of green bean equivalent using the ICO conversion factor of 1:3.

[a]1967: Peru; 1973: Angola and Tanzania; 1974: Peru and Tanzania; 1976: Angola and Tanzania; 1977: Dominican Republic and Uganda; 1978: Honduras.

[b]Major sources are Portugal in 1972 and Belgium in 1976. These figures also include some rounding error from other entries.

Producing State Initiatives, 1965–1975

By the mid-1960s, instant coffee was far enough advanced in the product life cycle that production technology was not rapidly changing and did not require a huge R&D effort. The technology could be acquired from core engineering firms by any investors with the necessary capital. Under these conditions, Brazil took the lead in developing an instant coffee export industry, and was soon followed by Colombia, Ecuador, and India. But it was the explosive growth of Brazil's exports that led to conflict with the manufacturers that had controlled the chain up to that point.[12]

By the early 1960s, Brazil was into the "secondary ISI" phase of its development strategy, and the state was beginning to look for ways to diversify its exports (Haggard 1990). Brazil was by far the world's largest coffee producer and coffee still accounted for over 40 percent of its total export earnings. Developing the capacity to produce instant coffee for export thus seemed like a logical step in the evolution of its development strategy. Brazil was also the world's second largest coffee consumer, after the United States, and had always had a large internal market for coffee and a number of large local roasting companies. One of Nestlé's first Third World subsidiaries to produce instant coffee was built in Brazil in 1952. This subsidiary produced mainly for the local market, but instant coffee had only a small share of the total Brazilian market. Several other major manufacturers, including Tenco, developed plans to build factories in Brazil in the late 1950s, but abandoned them after having trouble getting licenses and permission to import equipment.

Beginning in 1960, the state coffee agency, the IBC, announced a series of measures to encourage local capitalists to build instant coffee factories, including sales of green coffee from the massive IBC stocks, and guarantees to purchase 80 percent of the output in the first year and decreasing percentages thereafter. But the most important measure was an exemption from the export tax that was applied to all green coffee exports. The first two Brazilian manufacturers, Dominium and Cacique, opened in 1965. After that, production expanded rapidly, with Vigor and Frusol opening in 1966 and five additional plants opened by 1969. A small amount of instant was exported to the United States in 1965, but exports grew rapidly as the new plants went into operation and by 1969, the Brazilian product had captured 14 percent of the total U.S. instant coffee market (see table 6.2).

The "Brazil powder," as it was called by the U.S. industry, had several significant advantages over instant coffee manufactured in the United States. The most important was cost. Brazilian manufacturers could buy non-export-quality coffee beans, or "grinders," from the IBC for significantly less than export-quality coffee. When combined with the export tax exemption, this meant that Brazilian manufacturers could deliver instant to the U.S. market at a cost of about 50–60 cents per pound less than U.S. producers. This was a huge difference at a time when the average retail price of instant coffee on the U.S. market was about $2.50 per pound. Further, the Brazil powder was of higher quality than most instant coffee being sold on the U.S. market, since it was made from Brazilian arabicas, while the coffee blends used in the manufacture of instant by the TNCs had high percentages of harsher-tasting robustas. The "grinders," being used by the Brazilian manufacturers were mainly broken beans; they did not meet export criteria, but had taste qualities similar to those of the average grades of Brazilian export-quality coffee. The Brazil powder was all spray dried at this time, and so the TNCs could offset the quality disadvantage somewhat through spray drying, but this only added to the production cost; the Brazil powder was still cheaper and better tasting.

The rapid growth of Brazilian exports created a division in the U.S. coffee industry. Most green coffee importers were strongly opposed, because the Brazil powder could be sold directly to instant coffee manufacturers, bypassing the green traders. But some importers soon decided that they could deal in instant coffee as well as green, and began buying from producers in Brazil for resale to U.S. manufacturers, or to smaller firms wanting to package their own private labels. General Foods was one of the leaders of the opposition to Brazilian imports, but Nestlé, with a plant in Brazil, did not take a strong position either way. Coca-Cola/Tenco, the pioneer in importing instant coffee produced in the coffee growing countries, strongly supported the Brazilian policy. And two other large U.S. producers, Hills Bros. and Chock Full o' Nuts, closed down their instant coffee factories and began to import the Brazil powder and package it under their own labels.

The height of this controversy coincided with the renegotiation of the International Coffee Agreement (ICA) in 1968 (see the discussion in chapter 3). The U.S. State Department took a hard line in these negotiations, insisting on including a mechanism in the Agreement to deal with the problem of "unfair competition," that is, the fact that Brazil exempted instant coffee from the green coffee export tax. This resulted in the inclusion of Article 44 in the new ICA, which prohibited "discriminatory treatment in favor of processed coffee as opposed to green coffee" by the exporting countries. Ironically, most of the importing countries which signed the ICA (though not the United States) imposed much higher import tariffs on processed coffee than they did on green coffee, but were apparently not troubled by this form of "discriminatory treatment." Once the ICA went into force, the United States used Article 44 to compel Brazil to impose a 13-cent per pound export tax on instant coffee destined for the U.S. market. The members of the U.S. coffee industry who had originally opposed the Brazilian policy were not satisfied; they argued that this tax did not begin to offset the cost advantage of the Brazilian manufacturers.

Meanwhile, the U.S. Congress, sympathetic to industry complaints, held up the legislation enabling U.S. enforcement of the export quotas under the 1968 ICA. This forced the State Department, which had agreed to the 13-cent tax, to seek further concessions from Brazil. In March 1971, an agreement was finally reached which satisfied most of the remaining opposition. The United States agreed to implement the 1968 ICA, and Brazil agreed to sell 560,000 bags of green coffee per year to U.S. instant coffee manufacturers, exempt from the

regular green coffee export taxes. The green coffee traders were satisfied because this coffee was to be sold through normal trade channels. General Foods
was placated, because under the allocation formula agreed on, it stood to receive
almost half of this coffee. Nestlé, not a major purchaser of Brazilian coffee,
nonetheless got almost a quarter of it. But not everyone was happy—Hills Bros.
and Chock Full o' Nuts, which were no longer manufacturing instant in the
United States, received none. This agreement marked the end of the Brazil powder controversy, but it was soon rendered moot when the 1968 ICA quota system was suspended in 1972.

By this time, the economics of instant coffee production in Brazil had
changed. The high demand for grinders on the Brazilian market in the late 1960s
had driven their price up nearly to the level of export-quality coffee. Two frosts
in Brazil in 1969 and 1972 had reduced the supply of Brazilian coffee and increased the price advantage of robustas. And the rapid expansion of production
capacity in Brazil had outstripped the growth of markets for Brazilian instant.
Then, just as the market was recovering from the 1972 frost, the devastating
frost of 1975 hit. Brazilian coffee was so scarce that the Brazilian manufacturers
had to begin importing African robustas for use in their factories. Soon after
this, Brazil began planting its own robusta coffee, and is now one of the world's
largest producers of robusta, most of which is used by the instant coffee manufacturers. Nonetheless, as a result of state initiatives and investments by local
capitalists, Brazil had eleven instant coffee producers with significant installed
capacity by the late 1970s. They produced mainly for export and had gained a
foothold in the U.S. and other core markets.

Brazil remains the major exporter of instant coffee among the coffee growing countries, and it exports a relatively high proportion of its coffee, between
10 and 20 percent, in instant form. The United States has always been the largest
importer of Brazilian instant coffee, as it has been for green coffee. The U.K. is
the second largest importer; instant coffee represents a much larger proportion
of the U.K.'s coffee imports than for any other major importer, because of its
high level of instant consumption. The U.K. imports go mainly to Brooke Bond
and Lyons-Tetley, the third and fourth ranked firms in the U.K. market; Nestlé,
which controls over half of the U.K. market, manufactures all of its instant locally, and General Foods, which controls another quarter, manufactures its instant locally or imports it from other consuming countries. In general, Brazilian
instant coffee exports go to the same major consuming markets to which its
green coffee exports go.

Colombia is the second largest coffee grower, after Brazil.[13] By the mid-
1960s, it still depended on coffee for over 60 percent of its export earnings, but
had begun a drive to diversify its exports. Colombia is the second largest coffee
consuming country among the coffee producers, but its internal market is nowhere near the size of Brazil's. Nestlé also built an instant coffee subsidiary in
Colombia in the early 1950s to produce for the domestic market. Its success induced a large domestic roaster, Colcafé, to open an instant factory in 1960. Colcafé produced primarily for the local market, but began to export small quanti-

ties. The Colombian quasi-state agency which controlled coffee policy, the FNC, was originally opposed to the export of instant coffee, because they felt that it generally lowered taste standards for coffee, and that high quality was the major selling point of Colombian coffee (exemplified by the Juan Valdez ad campaign). But by the late 1960s, it was clear that instant coffee was an important product in core markets, and that Brazil's move into instant coffee exporting had been successful, so the FNC decided to begin producing instant coffee for export. To maintain the image of Colombian coffee, they decided to produce high quality instant, and so built a freeze-dry plant which opened in 1973.

The destinations of Colombia's instant coffee exports reflect the effects of this more direct state involvement. While the two largest importers of Colombian green coffee are the United States and Germany, the largest importer of instant is Japan. FNC strategy has been to leave established markets, particularly the United States, to the private exporters, while focusing its efforts on finding and expanding new markets for its coffee. Thus, Colcafé sends most of its exports to the United States and Canada, as well as to the U.K. and Germany. The FNC had already become one of the largest exporters of green coffee to Japan, a relatively new and rapidly expanding market, and the move into instant was a natural step. More recently, the FNC has rapidly expanded its exports of coffee extract, and most of this has also gone to Japan, for the production of canned coffee.

Ecuador was much less dependent on coffee than Brazil or Colombia; it obtained almost half of its export earnings from bananas. As in Colombia, Ecuador's instant coffee industry also began with production for the local market. In 1957, the state enacted an Industrial Development Law to encourage import substitution. Ecuador was already importing some instant coffee for local consumption, while the raw material needed for its production was available locally. The Law thus established protective tariffs against instant coffee imports, and made credit available for the import of machinery needed to manufacture it. A group of local capitalists involved in food processing for the local market formed Solubles Instantaneous (SiCafé) in 1960, and began to produce instant coffee in 1962. Production was intended for local consumption, but in the late 1960s instant coffee export boom, SiCafé was able to find export markets for its product. This success induced other capitalists to invest. In the late 1970s, the Noboa Group, the largest financial-industrial group in Ecuador and the leading agro-exporters, built another factory to produce instant coffee for export.[14] In this case, SiCafé was a textbook "infant industry." It began by supplying the local market behind tariff walls, but soon began to find export markets and quickly became a major exporter. Its success later drew another producer into the industry.

The United States is the major importer of both green and instant coffee from Ecuador, but its instant coffee exports are more dispersed than its green exports; the United States imported 63 percent of Ecuador's total coffee exports in 1989, but only about a third of its instant. Germany and Japan import both green and instant from Ecuador, but proportionally more instant than the United

States. Ecuadorean exporters have also sought markets in Eastern Europe (the former Czechoslovakia, Poland, and Romania), and made some sales to Russia.

India is a major tea-producing and tea-exporting country, but has also grown some coffee in the southern part of the country since the early colonial period.[15] The first instant coffee factory was built in the south by local capitalists in 1957. Brooke Bond built India's second plant in 1961, and Nestlé opened a joint venture with local capitalists in 1963. These manufacturers were initially established to produce for the local market. But the USSR was a major trading partner of India in the 1960s, and when the USSR started buying instant coffee in the 1960s, India was a logical source. India's instant coffee exports were small at the time (the equivalent of 15,000–20,000 bags of green coffee), but almost all of them went to the USSR, with small amounts also sold to Yugoslavia. Since the Indian Coffee Board was the sole exporter of coffee, it must have purchased the instant from these producers for export. And much of this trade was on barter terms, with the USSR supplying oil and manufactured goods in return for Indian tea, coffee, and other agricultural commodities. A fourth locally owned firm, Asian Coffee Ltd., opened in 1989; it would be the last major instant coffee plant built by a producing country. The bulk of India's instant coffee exports have always gone to the USSR; even when it stopped buying from Brazilian firms in 1974, it continued to import instant from India. India has also exported some instant to the U.K., probably reflecting Brooke Bond sales to its British parent.

The state of the world coffee market in the mid-1960s facilitated these developments. Production was increasing and consumption stagnating. The first ICA imposed export quotas and forced many large growing countries to build up coffee stockpiles. Low quality coffee, unsuitable for export, but suitable for instant coffee manufacture, was readily available at low prices on the internal market. Although instant coffee exports were counted against the ICA quotas, they had higher unit value than green bean exports. Under these conditions, with state encouragement, Brazil's instant coffee industry mushroomed and captured large shares of the U.S. and Canadian markets by 1970. In addition, a few of these firms, led by Cacique, began to seek out new markets, particularly in the USSR. India also began to export to the USSR during this period. In Colombia, these conditions, and Brazil's early success, convinced the FNC to move aggressively into freeze-dried production for export. In Ecuador, these market conditions enabled SiCafé to find export markets when it sought them. Meanwhile, exports from the Tenco-IBEC Central American plants stagnated or declined under Coca-Cola ownership in the 1960s, as the original plans for a worldwide manufacturing network were abandoned in favor of the General Foods strategy of building in the consuming markets.

During this second phase, initiatives by coffee growing states shaped the expansion of their capacities to export to the core markets. State policies created a "comparative advantage" to induce local capital into production for export. In Brazil and Ecuador, instant coffee exports were exempted from taxes applied to green coffee exports to give local manufacturers a cost advantage. In Colombia, the quasi-state FNC invested capital earned from its control over green coffee exports in the development of an instant coffee export capacity. And in India, the state arranged barter deals with the USSR, which enabled it to export coffee in return for products that it needed to import.

These initiatives by producing states greatly expanded instant coffee production capacity in the coffee-growing countries. Through the late 1960s and early 1970s, exports of instant from these plants into the core markets grew rapidly. And unlike the exports from Central America and Côte d'Ivoire in the earlier phase, these exports were controlled by local capitalists and producing states, and they had more linkages to the local economy. While some major manufacturers and the U.S. state initially opposed Brazil's initiative, by the late 1970s an accommodation had occurred. Producing states and local capitalists could not afford the advertising expenditures needed to introduce their own brands into the core markets. So they sold their instant in bulk to the majors or to smaller firms, who packaged and sold it under their own brand names. The TNCs found that they could integrate this product into their global sourcing and marketing strategies, while maintaining their control over the major core markets. The struggle then moved into new markets opening in the 1980s.

Globalization in the 1980s

There was less incentive to expand instant coffee exports in the late 1970s. After the Brazilian frost of 1975, there was a shortage of green coffee, and importers were willing to pay high prices to get it. The coffee growing countries were earning high incomes from green coffee exports without any additional investment in processing it. Brazil and a few other countries had won shares of the major consuming markets, but were not seeking to expand them. New instant coffee factories were being built, but they were not yet significant contributors to the international trade. The major expansion of international trade during this period was among the consuming countries. Most of this trade was controlled by the major manufacturers, and represented attempts to enter new markets or to serve established markets through a global sourcing strategy. However, by 1980, coffee production had again exceeded worldwide demand and prices had fallen from their late-1970s peaks; quotas were again in effect, creating the potential for a new expansion of instant coffee exports from the coffee growing countries.

In the 1980s, the manufacturing and marketing of coffee were being globalized, as described in the preceding chapter. One aspect of this globalization in instant coffee involved the growth of linkages between the TNCs and the established producers in Brazil and Colombia. Iguacu, the second largest Brazilian producer, is now 40 percent owned by Marubeni, one of the largest Japanese *sogo shosha*, or general trading companies; the remaining 60 percent share belongs to a group of coffee growers. Another Brazilian producer, Vigor, was purchased by Marcellino Martins, one of the country's largest green coffee exporters, which was later acquired by ED&F Man, one of the world's top five green

Table 6.3 Imports of Major ICO-Member Instant Coffee Importing Countries, 1986/87–1991/92

	1986/ 87	1987/ 88	1988/ 89	1989/ 90	1990/ 91	1991/ 92
Total World Exports	4778	5426	5755	6429	5356	6379
From Coffee Growers	55.9%	54.6%	54.2%	61.7%	49.1%	52.4%
United States						
Total Imports	969	954	1220	1110	847	964
From Coffee Growers	69.2%	74.2%	79.7%	79.5%	69.1%	66.3%
From Big Three[a]	66.2%	73.0%	78.6%	77.5%	66.2%	65.4%
United Kingdom						
Total Imports	731	748	709	706	805	871
From Coffee Growers	51.5%	51.4%	45.9%	49.0%	44.4%	45.6%
From Big Three	50.1%	50.7%	45.6%	48.4%	42.8%	42.6%
France						
Total Imports	399	344	424	381	367	365
From Coffee Growers	6.7%	10.7%	11.1%	11.2%	13.7%	14.5%
Germany						
Total Imports	288	287	333	336	372	391
From Coffee Growers	36.6%	37.6%	51.1%	50.0%	44.4%	42.9%
From Big Three	34.0%	36.2%	50.4%	50.0%	44.4%	42.7%
Japan						
Total Imports	283	322	318	250	259	226
From Coffee Growers	75.2%	72.1%	75.7%	69.9%	75.7%	74.0%
From Big Three	64.7%	65.2%	69.8%	64.4%	68.0%	70.4%
Greece						
Total Imports	128	156	212	226	230	247
From Coffee Growers	62.8%	88.1%	93.6%	90.0%	88.9%	87.6%
From Côte d'Ivoire	55.2%	81.2%	89.8%	87.0%	85.4%	85.7%
Netherlands						
Total Imports	107	109	107	113	109	103
From Coffee Growers	52.1%	52.4%	41.6%	39.7%	34.7%	30.0%
From Big Three	51.4%	52.3%	41.1%	38.0%	33.9%	29.1%
Belgium/ Luxembourg						
Total Imports	101	107	87	95	95	78
From Coffee Growers	1.4%	0.8%	0.0%	0.4%	4.0%	2.6%
Ireland						
Total Imports	82	108	88	99	81	44
From Coffee Growers	0.4%	0.0%	0.3%	0.3%	0.0%	0.0%
Italy						
Total Imports	65	66	75	72	79	94
From Coffee Growers	2.8%	2.5%	2.1%	3.0%	2.6%	6.6%
Spain						
Total Imports	0	40	77	85	87	102
From Coffee Growers	–	20.0%	33.1%	3.1%	8.5%	11.9%

Continued on next page

Table 6.3 Imports of Major ICO-Member Instant Coffee Importing Countries, 1986/87–1991/92 (continued)

	1986/ 87	1987/ 88	1988/ 89	1989/ 90	1990/ 91	1991/ 92
Denmark						
Total Imports	20	22	24	27	32	40
From Coffee Growers	3.1%	2.5%	1.3%	2.5%	1.7%	3.8%
Switzerland						
Total Imports	27	30	25	20	22	16
From Coffee Growers	44.4%	45.7%	40.0%	45.0%	36.4%	37.5%
From Big Three	44.4%	45.7%	40.0%	45.0%	36.4%	37.5%

Source: Imports into ICO-Member countries from ICO EB 3399/93; exports from coffee growers from EB 3398/93. Total imports are expressed in thousand bags (60 kg) of green bean equivalent.
[a]Big Three = Brazil, Colombia, and Ecuador.

coffee importers. Dominium ran into financial difficulties soon after it was formed, and was taken over by the Central Bank of Brazil and later sold to Mitsubishi. Coca-Cola owns one small plant and is a partner in another with Iguacu. Thus, while Brazilian capital still controls the majority of the instant coffee industry, the coffee TNCs have increased their share of ownership since the industry was originally established. The Colombian FNC also formed a partnership with Marubeni in the early 1980s. It modernized its freeze-dry plant and greatly expanded its capacity; Marubeni provided capital and technology in return for a minority share of the firm. Production capacity was further expanded in the late 1980s.

The coffee growing countries that had built their export capacity in the 1960s and 1970s maintained a share of the "traditional" consuming markets in the 1980s despite globalization, but it was a limited share. This is shown in table 6.3. This table shows the total volume of international trade in instant coffee in the late 1980s and early 1990s, and the imports of the major ICO-member importers during these years. Unfortunately, there are no good data on the total consumption of instant coffee in these importing countries, but in almost all of them, imports represented a relatively small share of consumption. Almost all of them had local factories that satisfied most of the local demand.

Table 6.3 shows that the coffee growing countries accounted for over half of total international trade in these years. These figures somewhat overstate the importance of growing country manufacturers, because some of these exports came from Nestlé subsidiaries (e.g., in Côte d'Ivoire) or Coca-Cola or Marubeni joint ventures. Table 6.3 shows that many of the large ICO member importers got most of their instant coffee imports from other consuming countries; the large majority of this was intra-firm trade controlled by the TNCs. Several ICO member importers got significant shares of their imports from coffee growing countries: United States, U.K., Germany, Japan, Greece, Netherlands, and Switzerland. As we have already seen, Greece got the bulk of its instant imports from the Nestlé plant in Côte d'Ivoire. All other major importers from the growing

Table 6.4 Imports of Other Major Instant Coffee Importers (ICO Non-Members)

	1985	1986	1987	1988	1989	1990
Canada	277	307	306	283	274	208
Australia	178	160	114	138	168	161
USSR	0	252	251	282	672	NA
Hungary	66	65	120	88	0	100
Other Eastern Europe	81	72	123	58	10	74
Taiwan	29	25	41	67	96	105
Hong Kong	31	30	47	57	63	87
Malaysia	74	64	18	15	16	17
South Korea	0	1	0	2	23	35
Saudi Arabia	112	76	100	75	84	67
United Arab Emirates	29	25	26	13	20	34

Source: ICO EB 3399/93. Total imports are expressed in thousand bags (60 kg) of green bean equivalent.

countries, among ICO members, got virtually all of these imports from what I have called the "Big Three": Brazil, Colombia, and Ecuador.

Another aspect of globalization in the 1980s was the increase of instant coffee consumption in "non-traditional" markets, particularly the East Asian NICs and the Middle East. Established producers located in Brazil, Colombia, and Ecuador were better positioned to compete directly with the TNCs for these new markets than they had been to enter the "traditional" home markets of the TNCs. Table 6.4 shows the major non-member importers of instant; unfortunately the ICO has no data on the sources of their imports. The import patterns of Canada and Australia, both of which left the ICO in the late 1980s or early 1990s, are similar to those of the other ICO members shown in table 6.3—almost all of their imports come from other consuming countries or the "Big Three." The rest of the importers listed in Table 6.4 are new markets; the markets where the "Big Three" have competed with the TNCs for shares of growing markets for instant coffee. In the 1980s, consumption of instant coffee in these new consuming markets began to expand. The coffee growing countries had a further incentive to sell to these markets, because most were not ICO members, thus instant coffee exports to these markets would not count against the export quotas. Despite these factors, coffee growing instant coffee exporters have had only limited success in selling to these new markets. In part, this was due to the global presence of the TNCs, which had already established retail networks for their other consumer products in these new markets. For example, the Korean coffee market, with a high share of instant coffee consumption, is dominated by a joint venture between General Foods and Japan's Ajinomoto. Nestlé and Coca-Cola, the leaders in the Japanese canned coffee market, have formed a joint venture to distribute canned coffee throughout East Asia.

The opening of the Eastern European and Soviet markets in the late 1980s provided a further opportunity for these coffee growing exporters to capture new markets. These countries were also not ICO members. In the more stable Eastern

European countries (Poland, Hungary, Czechoslovakia), the European-based TNCs had the advantage of proximity and moved in quickly. The USSR and former Soviet republics have been the place where coffee growing countries have had the most success recently. In part, this was due to the instability of the market, which made the TNCs reluctant to invest. It was also due to the Soviet practice of barter arrangements with Third World states, which formed links between Third World producers and Soviet importers. This was a major factor in India's heavy sales to the USSR.[16]

Brazilian manufacturers have gained shares of the markets in some other Eastern European countries such as Romania. They have also had considerable success in the USSR, before its collapse, and more recently in Russia and the former Soviet republics. Brazilian manufacturers began selling to the USSR in the late 1960s, as Brazilian capacity was increasing rapidly and exports to the United States were threatened by the dispute over "discriminatory treatment." Cacique was the major supplier at this time. In 1974, an instant coffee factory was opened in the USSR and Brazilian sales stopped. But when the USSR again began to import large amounts of instant coffee in the mid-1980s, Brazil, and Cacique in particular, was a natural source. In the 1980s, Cacique and Iguacu were the major suppliers, and at times, Cacique shipped half its total exports there. These firms were hurt badly when these exports were disrupted by the collapse of the USSR in 1991, but Russian buyers again began importing large amounts of instant in 1993, much of it from Brazil. And unlike the bulk instant shipped to the core markets to be repackaged under other brand names, most of the instant sold by Cacique to Russia is packed for final consumption, under Cacique's own brand names.[17]

India was also hurt by the disruption of Soviet imports in 1991; its sales were increasing rapidly in the late 1980s, but crashed in 1991. Indian exports to the USSR were not as large as those from Brazil, which accounted for almost 75 percent of total Soviet imports in 1989, but India's Soviet exports were a much larger percentage of its total exports than Brazil's. Hence, the impact of the crash on India was more severe. But because of the way Indian exports were traded, this impact was also more indirect. The Coffee Board was able to begin finding some new markets for its exports after 1989, in some core markets and Eastern Europe, particularly in Poland. And once Russian buyers returned to the market in 1993, Indian exports there increased as well.

China is another huge potential market. Some coffee is grown in Yunnan, and there is a small local market for coffee, virtually all of it in instant form. Nestlé has established an instant coffee factory there, and there is also a state-owned plant. Colombia's FNC recently set up a joint venture with Japan's Mitsui to manufacture instant coffee and extract in China; some of this product will, at least initially, be exported to Japan.

It remains to be seen how big these new markets will ultimately become, and whether the early entry of Brazilian, Colombian, and Indian producers will help them to compete against the TNCs there. While the successes of instant manufacturers in the coffee growing countries have been limited thus far, they have gained market shares and early brand name recognition in some large markets with potential for rapid growth.

After the end of the ICA in 1989, the economics of instant coffee production shifted radically. With a glut of coffee on the market for most of the 1990s, the TNCs have had access to plentiful supplies of green coffee at very low prices. In addition, most producing countries have eliminated or drastically reduced their export taxes on green coffee, under pressure from the IMF and World Bank, and in an effort to maximize the incomes of their small coffee growers. This has destroyed the comparative advantage in raw materials costs on which the instant coffee industries of the producing countries were built. The established producers in Brazil and Colombia are operating with fully depreciated plants and are able to produce at costs low enough to compete with the TNCs. However, any new production capacity in producing countries is unlikely to be economically competitive because of the huge start-up costs. In addition, the markets in the major consuming countries are changing. As in the R&G segments of these markets, specialty and gourmet instant coffees are becoming more popular. These instants are often freeze-dried, decaffeinated, and/or contain added flavoring, all produced with technologies where the TNCs still hold a competitive edge. This further limits the ability of manufacturers located in the producing countries to find markets for their products[18] (Hone 1993).

The results of the struggle over the instant coffee strand of the commodity chain contrast with Gereffi's analysis, based on apparel chains, of the possibilities for upgrading in commodity chains, as outlined in chapter 1. Based on the experiences of East Asian firms in the apparel industry, Gereffi's analysis is relatively optimistic about the chances for successful forward integration. However, as Gibbon (2001) has pointed out, these successes have been based on the externalization of less profitable activities by the major TNCs that "drive" the chain. Thus, East Asian firms were able to move from simple assembly operations to "full-package" supply because the major apparel TNCs decided that operations such as procurement of fabric and cutting of pieces to be assembled were not profitable enough, and spun them off to the East Asian firms, in order to concentrate on their "core" competencies. These activities, such as designing and branding, were "core" in a double sense. They were "core" in a business sense, in that they were what the TNCs did best; but they were also "core" in a world-systems sense, in that they involved advanced technologies controlled by the TNCs, and were highly profitable. In the coffee chain, all of the operations carried out after the green coffee stage were core activities, in this double sense, and the major coffee companies had no interest in spinning them off to firms located in the producing countries. When a few producing countries were able to move into instant coffee processing, the TNCs accommodated them by integrating some of the output into their global sourcing strategies. But the case of the Brazil powder shows that the TNCs were not going to allow firms in the producing countries to move beyond being minor suppliers of bulk instant; they were prepared to defend their core markets by any means necessary.

There is one aspect of the instant coffee case which is consistent with all previous analyses of upgrading or forward integration: the importance of state action. State policies to enhance the chances for upgrading, and actions to make local firms more competitive, figure prominently in Gereffi's upgrading strategies. Gibbon points out that state action becomes even more important in cases where the lead firms in the chain are not externalizing less profitable functions. This is borne out by the case of instant coffee. State action played a central role in the few producing countries that were able to become significant producers of instant coffee. And it can be argued that the country where the most aggressive state action was taken is the one that is in the best position in the current market situation. Colombia, where the quasi-state coffee growers' federation practically created the instant coffee export industry, has ended up with a modern freeze-dry plant that can still compete with the upgraded production facilities of the TNCs. Brazil is still by far the largest producer of instant, but most of its production is of the older spray-dry variety, which is falling out of favor. The great irony of this situation is that the United States and the multilateral institutions, the IMF, World Bank, and WTO, are moving to prohibit exactly the kinds of state action that built the instant coffee industries of the producing countries: tariffs, subsidies, and "preferential" treatment. These international trade policies aimed at removing state "interference" in economic activity are foreclosing the possibilities of further upgrading in coffee and other tropical commodity chains. In so doing, they are once again moving to lock many peripheral countries more firmly into their old colonial roles in the world economy, as suppliers of raw materials to manufacturers located in the core.

As noted at the beginning of this chapter, the collective action strategy predominated in the coffee commodity chain, because of the way it was structured. In particular, the segmented governance structure focused struggles between producers and consumers on the world market and the price of green coffee. The major players in these struggles were the producing and consuming states, although firms on both sides of the world market also played key roles. The struggle over the instant coffee commodity chain was different. It was over which side of the world market the instant coffee industry would be located on, and who would control it. Firms in the producing and consuming countries were the key players in this struggle, with states playing more of a facilitating role for their firms (although there was direct state action to create an export firm in Colombia). Producing country firms and their states were ultimately overmatched in this struggle as well, but they were not as decisively defeated as in the collective action struggle. They were able to hold on to some of the gains they had made by moving into instant coffee processing, with at least the potential for further expansion into new markets. The gains in this struggle were more lasting because they revolved around control of a more advanced processing stage of the chain, rather than around the accommodation between governance structures where they met at a fixed point on the chain. At the same time, there are parallels in the ways that both struggles were impacted by globalization and financial expansion beginning in the 1980s. In the collective action struggle, once the governance of producing states was weakened, the coffee TNCs were able to extend control backwards into the producing countries by getting involved in coffee exporting. And in the forward integration struggle, the TNCs were able to take over a share of the instant coffee manufacturing capacity that had been constructed in the producing countries. Both of these moves further weakened the abilities of producing states to make coffee policies that would promote national development. Having analyzed the processes and outcomes of these struggles, it is time to turn to a key question raised in the introduction: Who benefits?

Notes

1. This section is based on the following articles in *Tea and Coffee Trade Journal*: by William Kappenberg, August 1952, pp. 22–24; by Michael Sivetz, February 1985, pp. 5–10, and June 1985, pp. 3–4; by Dan Bloch, February 1985, pp. 10–12; by Ralph Colton, July 1982, pp. 16, 38–39; by Samuel Lee, October 1988, pp. 3–4; I have also drawn on the following articles from *Tea and Coffee Trade Journal*: October 1952, p. 22; August 1954, p. 20; August 1956, p. 26; August 1957, p. 30; August 1958, p. 22; February 1986, pp. 6–10; February 1988, p. 18; also *World Coffee and Tea* September 1963, p. 40; Hone 1993; and U.S. Federal Trade Commission 1966.

2. In the 1940s, it was acquired by American Home Products Corp., which continued to sell G. Washington instant coffee in the northeast region in the 1950s. In 1961, Tenco purchased the original G. Washington plant in New Jersey, and the brand disappeared from the market (*Tea and Coffee Trade Journal* April 1954, p. 66; *World Coffee and Tea* March 1961, pp. 27–28).

3. Tenco was acquired by Minute Maid, the leader in the frozen orange juice industry, in 1959. Minute Maid was in turn acquired by Coca-Cola in 1960, which thereby became the world's third largest instant coffee manufacturer (*Tea and Coffee Trade Journal* September 1959, p. 85; *World Coffee and Tea* January 1961, p. 20). Coca-Cola subsequently sold Tenco to Tetley Tea, who in turn sold it to Chock Full o' Nuts, which was subsequently acquired by Sara Lee (*New York Times* November 18, 1981, p. D4; June 9, 1999. p. C4; *PR Newswire* November 7, 1989; *Business Wire* June 8, 1999).

4. According to an official of Brasilia, one of Brazil's largest instant coffee manufacturers, an annual output of 4000 metric tons of instant is the minimum size necessary for an "efficient and economical" factory (quoted in *World Coffee and Tea* March 1983, p. 16). Such a factory would use an input of 173,333 bags of green coffee to produce this output, assuming a 2.6:1 ratio of green to instant (the ICO conversion factor). Thus a country exporting one million bags would have to divert almost 20 percent of its total exports into instant coffee production (or increase production by almost 20 percent). Investing in instant coffee production would be very risky for a country with green coffee export capacity much smaller than this.

5. All of the top five green coffee exporters in the late 1980s, Brazil, Colombia, Indonesia, Mexico, and Côte d'Ivoire, had these requisites, and all produced some instant coffee. Other large exporters which had them were Costa Rica, Ecuador, El Salvador, Guatemala, Honduras, India, Papua New Guinea, Peru, Kenya, Ethiopia, Cameroun, Uganda, Zaire, and Vietnam.

6. Brazil and Colombia were the two exceptions; Brazil because it was such a large producer and its coffee was the basis of most blends sold in the U.S. market, and Colom-

bia because its Juan Valdez 100% Colombian marketing strategy, which began in 1959, created a distinctive image for its coffee.

7. Three of these five countries also grow both arabica and robusta coffees (Brazil, Ecuador, and India); thus they can offer a wider range of instant coffee blends to their customers.

8. The ICO collects data on both calendar year and coffee year (October 1–September 30) bases. Because reports are generated from this data primarily in response to requests from members, reports on a particular topic, such as instant coffee exports, do not necessarily use the same type of year as the basis for reports generated over a long period of time. For this reason, the 16-year period considered here is broken up into three overlapping sub-periods.

9. The story of the Côte d'Ivoire plant is based on Masini et al. 1979; see also Dinham and Hines 1984, pp. 66–67.

10. *Tea and Coffee Trade Journal* December 1956, p. 102.

11. Table 6.2 shows that the only significant imports of instant coffee into the United States during this initial period of expansion came from the Tenco-IBEC plants in Central America. The imports from Canada shown in Table 6.2 in the early 1960s were probably transfers between Nestle and General Foods production facilities; they were more than offset by U.S. exports to Canada. Altogether, these imports accounted for less than 5 percent of U.S. instant coffee consumption. And during this period, the United States was a net exporter of instant. Most U.S. exports in the late 1950s went to Canada, but exports to Japan increased rapidly after 1961, when Japan lifted import restrictions on instant.

12. The following account of the growth of the Brazilian instant coffee industry is drawn from Fisher 1972, chapter 9; Cordell 1969; Krasner 1973a; Lucier 1988, pp. 139–47; Sivetz in *Tea and Coffee Trade Journal* June 1985, pp. 3–4; *Tea and Coffee Trade Journal* August 1952, p. 22; October 1953, p. 26; December 1959, p. 52; *World Coffee and Tea* December 1960, pp. 15–17; April 1966, pp. 25–30; November 1966, pp. 25–30; November 1967, pp. 23–39; November 1968, pp. 24–26; November 1969, pp. 38–39; April 1970, pp. 25–29; August 1970, pp. 79–81; November 1970, pp. 47–49; May 1971, pp. 35–40; October 1984, p. 32.

13. Information on Colombia's instant coffee industry is drawn from *World Coffee and Tea* February 1961, p. 20; June 1962, pp. 66–67; April 1971, p. 26; *Tea and Coffee Trade Journal* February 1990, pp. 14–16; April 1991, pp. 36–37; June 1993, pp. 26–29.

14. Hidrobo 1992; Fierro Carrión 1991; *Tea and Coffee Trade Journal* April 1959, p. 62.

15. This account of India's development of instant coffee production is drawn from *World Coffee and Tea* May 1961, p. 22; June 1963, p. 66; June 1971, pp. 43–44; *Tea and Coffee Trade Journal* January 1991, p. 64, and Hone 1993.

16. *Tea and Coffee Trade Journal* May 1994, pp. 24–27; May 1995, pp. 64–67; May 1996, pp. 50–62; November 1996, pp. 88–94.

17. *World Coffee and Tea* March 1993, pp. 6–11; *Tea and Coffee Trade Journal* October 1991, pp. 86–87; July 1995, p. 7.

18. Exports of coffee extract from Colombia to Japan are the only prominent exception.

Chapter 7

Outcomes of the Struggles:
Where Does Your Coffee Dollar Go?

Follow the money.

—"Deep Throat," in Woodward and Bernstein's
All the President's Men

The analysis in the preceding chapters has focused on struggles over the structure of the coffee commodity chain and the politics of its governance. As noted in chapter 1, the most important object of these struggles has been control over shares of the income and profits that are available along the chain. Thus, a good way to assess the outcomes of these struggles is to look at how they have changed the distribution of income and profits over time. In other words, these struggles determined how much you paid for your coffee, and where your dollars went. This chapter obeys Deep Throat's admonition to follow the money. It looks at the dollars spent by consumers in the major markets for coffee and analyzes where those dollars went. It identifies the winners and losers that resulted from the various changes to the structure and governance of the coffee chain that have been detailed in the preceding chapters.

First, the analysis focuses on the marketing channel through which the bulk of the coffee flows: the roasted and ground coffee blends and instant coffee produced by the major manufacturers and sold through supermarkets and other retail stores. Next, it looks at how producing countries benefited from their attempts to integrate forward along the instant coffee strand of the chain. These analyses show that various actors within the coffee producing countries did reap some benefits as a result of these struggles. However, by the 1990s, most of these benefits had been lost.

The Distribution of Income from R&G and Instant Coffee

Fortunately, the coffee chain has a relatively simple structure (see Figure 2.1). This makes it easier to follow the money. And, because the ICAs established the International Coffee Organization (ICO) to monitor and collect statistics on the coffee trade, among other things, there are good statistics available over a relatively long period of time on prices at various stages of the chain. For the major consuming markets, the price data collected by the ICO include the average retail prices of roasted and ground coffee blends produced mainly by the major coffee companies and sold primarily through supermarkets. These sales account for the majority of coffee consumed in the United States and in most other major consuming markets, so this is a logical place to begin the analysis.

For estimation purposes, the coffee chain can be divided into three major stages: 1) the growing and initial processing of coffee on the farm; 2) processing up to the green coffee stage and exporting, by processors and exporters within the producing country, who are either local capitalists or state agencies; and 3) the importing of green coffee and the production and sale of roasted coffee to consumers in the core markets. The first two stages of the chain are under the control of individuals, firms, and agencies in the producing countries, and the third stage is under the control of TNCs based in the core. This division of the chain into three stages thus allows us to estimate what percentage of the consumer's coffee dollar returns to the people who grow the coffee, what percentage is returned to other participants, including states, within the producing countries, and what percentage remains within the consuming countries. The bulk of this latter share goes to the coffee companies.

The analysis begins with the total amount of money spent by consumers in the core markets to purchase coffee products for final consumption. This is equivalent to the total amount of income available to be divided up among participants all along the coffee chain. In order to make the results more intuitively comprehensible, this total income can be represented by the average retail price of a typical pound of R&G coffee in the core markets. The share of this total income that remains within the consuming country is estimated by the average retail price of coffee minus the average price of imported green coffee.[1] The share of income that remains within the producing countries is represented by the average export price of green coffee,[2] and is divided into the average price paid to coffee growers[3] and the additional share of value added within the country—the export price minus the growers' price. This method of estimation necessitates adding a fourth, residual category, which includes shipping costs, and weight losses that occur during the roasting of the coffee.[4]

Once the shares of income going to each of the three major stages in the chain are calculated, we can attempt to estimate the profits at each stage. This is a bit more difficult, as data on costs of production are much harder to obtain, particularly for the major coffee manufacturers. After the profits are estimated, we can add them up along the chain and estimate the shares of the total profit that are controlled by participants at each of the three major stages. Finally, we can attempt to identify the types of rents that predominate at each stage of the chain.

Tables 7.1 and 7.2 present the results of this initial step in the analysis—the average retail price for a pound of R&G coffee is broken down into the shares remaining in the consuming countries; returning to the coffee growers; received by intermediaries, including the state, in producing countries; and the residual category. A further complication is introduced by the time periods for which the data are available. The limiting factor here is the data on prices (both retail and growers'), which are available as calendar year averages for 1971–1980, as monthly averages for the last month of each quarter for 1975–1985, and as coffee year averages after 1985. To use the full range of data available, I constructed two overlapping sets of estimates, a calendar year series 1971–1980 (table 7.1) and a coffee year series 1975/76–2000/01 (table 7.2).[5]

There were two types of changes in the world market during the period considered here which might have altered the division of income between producing and consuming countries. One was fluctuation in the world production of coffee, caused primarily by bumper crops or natural disasters in Brazil.[6] As described in chapter 2, there tends to be a two-year cycle in which a large crop one year is followed by a smaller one the next, as the trees "rest." In addition, there is the longer tree crop price cycle, due to the fact that new trees take three to five years to mature and begin bearing fruit. Generally, we would expect shortages, leading to high or rising prices, to shift income to producers; while oversupply, leading to low or falling prices, would tend to shift income to consumers. The second type of change was in the regulatory regime governing the world market. As discussed in chapters 3–5, export quotas were in effect between 1962 and 1972, and again between 1980 and 1989. During 1972–1980, quotas were suspended, first due to lack of agreement between producing and consuming states, and then because of the 1975 Brazilian frost. And in 1989, the quota regime came to an end. Most econometric analyses of the world coffee market have concluded that the quotas increased world market prices above equilibrium levels (Edwards and Parikh 1976; Vogelvang 1988; Herrmann 1986; Akiyama and Varangis 1990; Bohman and Jarvis 1990). Thus, we would expect producers to get higher shares of the total income when quotas are in effect than when they are suspended.

The data in Table 7.1 begin just before the end of the first quota period in 1972. These data show that about a third of the total income returned to the producing countries, with growers receiving about two-thirds of that, or roughly 20 cents of each coffee dollar. Through the early 1970s, a little over half of the total coffee income remained in the consuming countries. Since prices were stabilized through most of the 1960s by the quota system, we can project that the distribution of income observed here probably had prevailed at least since 1965. However, with only two years' worth of data on the situation during this early quota period, we should not place too much weight on this extrapolation. The data show no significant shift in income due to the end of the first quota regime. However, because of frosts in Brazil in 1969 and 1972, world market prices were rising during this period, possibly offsetting any income losses producers

Table 7.1 Where Did Your Coffee Dollar Go in 1971–1980?

	Distribution of Coffee Income for Calendar Years									
	1971	1972	1973	1974	1975	1976	1977	1978	1979	1980
Retail price[a]	123.2 (100%)	129.1 (100%)	151.0 (100%)	169.7 (100%)	183.7 (100%)	328.0 (100%)	425.1 (100%)	401.8 (100%)	387.1 (100%)	417.2 (100%)
Value added in cons. countries[b]	71.5 (58.0)	74.4 (57.6)	82.4 (54.6)	93.2 (54.9)	108.3 (58.9)	112.4 (47.2)	178.8 (42.1)	206.5 (51.4)	199.8 (51.6)	215.9 (51.7)
Transport costs and weight loss[c]	13.9 (11.3)	12.8 (9.9)	17.0 (11.2)	18.8 (11.1)	20.8 (11.3)	20.3 (8.5)	50.4 (11.8)	47.3 (11.8)	41.8 (10.8)	53.6 (12.8)
Value added in prod. countries[d]	15.3 (12.4)	17.0 (13.2)	19.4 (12.8)	22.7 (13.4)	15.1 (8.1)	34.7 (14.6)	91.7 (21.6)	67.9 (16.9)	66.8 (17.2)	70.4 (16.8)
Paid to growers[e]	22.5 (18.2)	24.9 (19.3)	32.3 (21.4)	35.0 (20.6)	39.5 (21.5)	70.5 (29.6)	104.2 (24.5)	80.1 (19.9)	78.8 (20.4)	77.3 (18.5)

Source: Calculated from International Coffee Organization, *Quarterly Statistical Bulletin*, various issues. Amounts shown are in U.S. cents per pound of ground roasted coffee, with percentage distribution in parentheses.

[a]Weighted average of retail prices in ICO member importing countries, weighted by disappearance of all forms of coffee in each country, expressed in green bean equivalents.

[b]Retail price minus 1.19 X unit value of imports. Unit value of imports (c.i.f.) is a weighted average for all ICO member importing countries, weighted by total volume of coffee imports in green bean equivalents. ICO estimates that it takes 1.19 pounds of green beans to produce one pound of roasted coffee, due to weight loss in the roasting process.

[c]Cost of green coffee in a pound of roasted coffee as calculated in note b above minus the unit value of exports.

[d]Weighted average of unit values of exports (f.o.b.) from all ICO member exporting countries, weighted by the total volume of coffee exports in green bean equivalents, minus the average price paid to growers as calculated in note e below.

[e]Weighted average of prices paid to growers in each ICO member exporting country, in national currency units converted to U.S. cents per pound using prevailing exchange rates, weighted by total volume of coffee exports in green bean equivalents.

Table 7.2 Where Did Your Coffee Dollar Go in 1975/76–2000/01?

	Distribution of Coffee Income for Coffee Years (October 1–September 30)								
	1975/76	1976/77	1977/78	1978/79	1979/80	1980/81	1981/82	1982/83	1983/84
Retail price[a]	200.6 (100%)	362.4 (100%)	371.4 (100%)	337.1 (100%)	385.4 (100%)	310.7 (100%)	292.7 (100%)	288.9 (100%)	304.5 (100%)
Value added in cons. countries[b]	93.9 (46.8)	135.2 (37.3)	163.0 (43.9)	161.1 (47.8)	170.8 (44.3)	155.4 (50.0)	146.7 (50.1)	142.7 (49.4)	144.9 (47.6)
Transport costs and weight loss[c]	19.2 (9.6)	43.5 (12.0)	51.8 (13.9)	38.9 (11.5)	53.3 (13.8)	48.9 (15.7)	42.2 (14.4)	42.3 (14.6)	42.7 (14.0)
Value added in prod. countries[d]	26.5 (13.2)	85.4 (23.6)	71.3 (19.2)	58.1 (17.2)	79.2 (20.5)	41.8 (13.5)	39.1 (13.4)	44.3 (15.3)	56.0 (18.4)
Paid to growers[e]	61.0 (30.4)	98.3 (27.1)	85.4 (23.0)	79.0 (23.4)	82.3 (21.3)	64.5 (20.8)	64.6 (22.1)	59.7 (20.7)	60.8 (20.0)

Continued on next page

Table 7.2 Where Did Your Coffee Dollar Go in 1975/76–2000/01? (continued)

	Distribution of Coffee Income for Coffee Years (October 1–September 30)								
	1984/85	1985/86	1986/87	1987/88	1988/89	1989/90	1990/91	1991/92	1992/93
Retail price[a]	299.7 (100%)	429.6 (100%)	448.3 (100%)	427.4 (100%)	417.1 (100%)	415.5 (100%)	439.2 (100%)	443.3 (100%)	438.6 (100%)
Value added in cons. countries[b]	141.5 (47.2)	228.9 (53.3)	288.8 (64.4)	286.4 (67.0)	276.6 (66.3)	322.2 (77.5)	344.8 (78.5)	362.0 (81.7)	357.6 (81.5)
Transport costs and weight loss[c]	45.0 (15.0)	43.1 (10.0)	49.0 (10.9)	33.4 (7.8)	42.7 (10.2)	31.2 (7.5)	27.2 (6.2)	25.8 (6.8)	28.2 (6.4)
Value added in prod. countries[d]	48.0 (16.0)	60.0 (14.0)	37.7 (8.4)	44.3 (10.4)	34.6 (8.3)	11.2 (2.7)	17.7 (4.0)	11.2 (2.5)	11.4 (2.6)
Paid to growers[e]	65.2 (21.8)	97.6 (22.7)	72.8 (16.2)	63.3 (14.8)	62.8 (15.1)	50.9 (12.2)	49.5 (11.3)	43.9 (9.9)	41.3 (9.4)

Continued on next page

Table 7.2 Where Did Your Coffee Dollar Go in 1975/76–2000/01? (continued)

	Distribution of Coffee Income for Coffee Years (October 1–September 30)							
	1993/94	1994/95	1995/96	1996/97	1997/98	1998/99	1999/00	2000/01
Retail price[a]	471.9 (100%)	632.7 (100%)	569.6 (100%)	542.2 (100%)	548.6 (100%)	521.1 (100%)	476.5 (100%)	399.1 (100%)
Value added in cons. countries[b]	357.4 (75.7)	430.8 (68.1)	416.7 (73.1)	380.8 (70.2)	380.0 (69.3)	393.7 (75.5)	365.9 (76.8)	316.7 (79.4)
Transport costs and weight loss[c]	26.5 (5.6)	60.4 (9.5)	51.4 (9.0)	47.4 (8.7)	53.2 (9.7)	40.0 (7.7)	36.5 (7.7)	33.3 (8.3)
Value added in prod. countries[d]	25.6 (5.4)	26.8 (4.2)	11.2 (2.0)	19.2 (3.5)	11.8 (2.1)	11.6 (2.2)	13.9 (2.9)	7.5 (1.9)
Paid to growers[e]	62.4 (13.2)	114.7 (18.1)	90.3 (15.8)	94.8 (17.5)	103.6 (18.9)	75.8 (14.6)	60.2 (12.6)	41.5 (10.4)

Source: Calculated from International Coffee Organization Documents EB3338/92, EB2793/87, WP Agreement No. 14/88 Rev. 2, WP Agreement No. 15/88 Rev. 2, "Coffee Statistics October–September 1985/86 to 1990/91" and ICO, *Quarterly Statistical Bulletin*, various issues, and additional data provided by the ICO. Amounts shown are in U.S. cents per pound of ground roasted coffee, with percentage distribution in parentheses.

[a]Weighted average of retail prices in ICO member importing countries, weighted by disappearance of all forms of coffee in each country, expressed in green bean equivalents, for 1975/76 to 1993/94. For 1994/95 to 2000/01, the weights are total imports of all forms of coffee, in green bean equivalents.

[b]Retail price minus 1.19 X unit value of imports. Unit value of imports (c.i.f.) is a weighted average for all ICO member importing countries, weighted by total volume of coffee imports in green bean equivalents. ICO estimates that it takes 1.19 pounds of green beans to produce one pound of roasted coffee, due to weight loss in the roasting process.

[c]Cost of green coffee in a pound of roasted coffee as calculated in note b above minus the unit value of exports.

[d]Weighted average of unit values of exports (f.o.b.) from all ICO member exporting countries, weighted by the total volume of coffee exports in green bean equivalents, minus the average price paid to growers as calculated in note e below.

[e]Weighted average of prices paid to growers in each ICO member exporting country, in national currency units converted to U.S. cents per pound using prevailing exchange rates, weighted by total volume of coffee exports in green bean equivalents.

may have experienced from the end of the quotas.

The devastating Brazilian frost of June 1975 had a dramatic effect on world market coffee prices. As described in chapter 4, retail prices of coffee rose sharply through 1976 and into 1977, dramatically increasing the total amount of income available to be distributed along the chain. As expected, rising prices shifted income toward producers; consuming countries' share of total income fell below half, and producers' share exceeded 40 percent. Growers' shares increased to about 25–30 cents of the coffee dollar. Producing states also increased their shares, particularly in 1977, as they raised taxes to try to lessen the inflationary effects of the export boom. Thus in coffee year 1976/77 and calendar year 1977, the share of income retained by producers exceeded that retained in consuming countries, but as prices began to fall after 1977, producer and consumer shares reverted to roughly their previous levels (tables 7.1 and 7.2).[7]

When quotas were reinstated in 1980, producers' and consumers' shares stabilized at about these same levels. This seems contrary to expectations that the quotas would benefit producers. However, world market prices were falling in 1980, as the new trees planted during the 1976–1977 coffee boom began to produce, and the reimposition of quotas may have forestalled an even deeper cut in producers' share of income. Further, shipping costs appear to have increased after 1980, which may have resulted from the second oil price shock in 1979 and the global recession of the early 1980s. These developments may also have caused further reductions in income for producers if the quotas had not been in effect.[8]

Quotas were suspended once again in early 1986, following a severe drought in Brazil that lowered output and raised world market prices. Prices peaked in the spring of 1986 and declined gradually thereafter, leading to a reimposition of quotas in late 1987, near the beginning of the 1987/88 coffee year. The suspension of quotas in a rising market in 1986 coincides with a shift of more than 10 percent of total income from the producers to the consumers. But when the quotas were reinstated in a falling market in late 1987, this division of total income was maintained. Table 7.2 shows that TNCs were able to increase retail prices during 1985/86 in response to the increases in world market prices for green coffee; but when green coffee prices declined in 1987, retail prices dipped only slightly. After this shift, almost two-thirds of total income remained in the consuming countries; producing countries' share declined to about one-quarter, and growers received about 15 cents of the coffee dollar. Once again, this shift of income to consumers is contrary to expectations that producers should benefit from a rising market. As noted in chapter 4, the 1986–1987 price increase was about 24 percent less than it would have been if the quotas had not been in effect prior to the increase (Akiyama and Varangis 1990), and this probably reduced the producers' benefits from the temporary shortage. In addition, the global consolidation of the coffee TNCs was underway at this time, and their rising market power is seen in their ability to maintain retail prices in the face of declining green coffee prices, increasing their share of income in 1986/87.

After the negotiations to renew the ICA broke down in 1989 and quotas were again suspended, world market prices crashed, falling by 50 percent within six months. Retail prices declined slightly, and then actually increased in 1990/91 and 1991/92 as green coffee prices continued to decline, reaching historic lows in the summer of 1992. Table 7.2 shows that the 1989 price crash coincided with an additional 10 percent shift in total income from producers to consumers. The share remaining in consuming countries exceeded three-quarters, while the growers' share decreased to about 10 cents of the coffee dollar. The growers' share was prevented from falling further by the drastic cuts in export taxes taken by producing states, as well as the beginnings of liberalization and privatization of the coffee agencies and marketing boards. This is shown by the decline in value added within the producing countries from about 8–10 cents to only about 2–3 cents of each coffee dollar.

These two shifts, of roughly 20 percent of total coffee income over a period of less than five years (1985–1990), contrast sharply with the relative stability of the distribution of coffee income observed over at least the previous fifteen years. The shift of income accompanying the 1976–1977 coffee boom was roughly 10 percent, but it was temporary, and the prefrost distribution was quickly reestablished and stabilized when it was over. While both of the later 10 percent shifts coincided with suspensions of the quota system, one was in a rising market and one in a falling market. Thus, the suspension of the quotas and the loss of benefits they provided to producers is not a sufficient explanation of these shifts. In 1986–1987, the quotas were quickly reinstated, but the shift was not reversed. The most plausible interpretation is that the quota suspensions destabilized what had been a relatively orderly market, enabling the TNCs to use their market power to increase their shares of income. In both cases, the TNCs were able to maintain or even increase the levels of retail prices during periods when world market prices for green coffee were falling.

The 1994 Brazilian frosts again shifted income back toward producers. The share remaining in consuming countries fell to about 70 percent, while growers received about 15–20 cents of the coffee dollar. The shares of income going to other participants in the coffee producing countries increased slightly, to 3–5 cents on the dollar, but as liberalization and privatization continued, these shares remained very low. Some of the remaining coffee agencies and marketing boards increased taxes to recover assets lost while trying to support growers during the 1989–1993 crisis, and some local processors and exporters also increased their margins. The distribution of income stayed fairly stable as shortages persisted through 1995–1996, and as prices spiked again in 1997. However, as the second coffee crisis developed after 1997, the distribution of income returned to its pre-1994 level: about 80 percent of the total income was retained in the consuming countries, the growers' share fell back to about 10 cents of every coffee dollar, and the share of value added in producing countries was about 2 cents of every dollar.

One way to make the current level of returns to growers more concretely understandable is to recall that the average mature coffee tree produces enough coffee cherries in one year to yield about one pound of roasted coffee beans. For all of his or her efforts in tending, maintaining, and harvesting one coffee tree over a period of one year, the average coffee grower in 2000/01 received a total of 41.5 cents. For the amount of time and effort alone involved in this activity, this is paltry compensation indeed. And this doesn't even begin to take into account the added costs that many growers incur, for fertilizers, pesticides, and seasonal labor to help with the harvest. Put in this perspective, it is no wonder that millions of coffee growers around the world are facing hunger, loss of their land, and for many of them, loss of the only livelihood they have ever known.

The analysis to this point has focused on the distribution of total coffee income between producing and consuming countries. The next questions are: what are the costs of production at each stage of the coffee commodity chain, and consequently, how much surplus is generated at each stage? In order to answer these questions, we must consider the specific systems of production and distribution in individual producing and consuming countries, and the structures of costs and surpluses they generate. This task is tackled in the next two sections.

The Distribution of the Surplus in the Producing Countries

In this section, estimates from previous studies of the costs of coffee production and processing in different producing countries are used to estimate the total surplus remaining in the producing countries and its division between the growers, the state, and others. A compilation of these results is presented in table 7.3. These studies used different sets of countries, different methods to decompose the export price into costs and surplus, and different methods of allocating the surplus among participants within each country. The task of making this data comparable across producing countries is made more difficult by the fact that their production systems vary widely. For instance, some growers sell fresh cherries directly to the processors, others wet-process the cherries into parchment coffee, and still others dry-process them. Intermediate processing of parchment or dried cherries into green coffee is sometimes performed by state agencies, sometimes by a few large exporters, and in other cases, by a myriad of small agents and traders. Nonetheless, table 7.3 presents the best estimates available of the amounts of surplus retained within producing countries, and of the distribution of this surplus. The variations between countries in the amount of surplus and its distribution, which are evident within each column of table 7.3, are due largely to the differing production systems. But comparing data for each country across time, within the rows of the table, gives us some indication of how changes in the amount and distribution of the surplus are related to the shifts in the distribution of income analyzed above.

Orlandi's (1978) estimates of the surplus in 1973, shown in the first column of table 7.3, are valuable because they are from the beginning of the period considered here, in the early 1970s, as the quotas which had been in effect under the first two ICAs were lifted. These estimates suggest that roughly half of the export price of green coffee was economic surplus which remained in the producing countries, and that the bulk of this surplus was appropriated by the states. The export prices shown here reflect differences in quality and world market prices of the three grades of arabicas produced by these countries. For Brazil, no data on costs of production were available. The state share, 39 percent of the export price, which can be considered as pure surplus, was collected through various forms of export taxation. Growers and exporters probably earned additional surplus, bringing the total surplus to about half of the export price. In Colombia, where the highest quality arabicas are produced, over 60 percent of the export price was surplus, and the quasi-state coffee agency, the FNC, took over 60 percent of that. Still, coffee growers received a share of the total surplus equal to about a quarter of the export price. No data were available on the costs of private processors and exporters, who handled about 60 percent of Colombia's coffee in the early 1970s. Their gross income amounted to only about six cents per pound, shown here as the processing cost, so they received a negligible share of the surplus per pound. In El Salvador, the state's and growers' shares of the surplus amounted to only 30 percent of the export price, and the state took two-thirds of it. However, the gross income of processors accounted for 18 percent of the export price, much higher than in Brazil or Colombia, and a large part of this is almost certainly surplus also. In El Salvador's plantation system, the processors are usually the largest plantation owners, who are sometimes exporters as well. Thus the total surplus was probably on the order of 45 percent of the export price, with the largest plantation owners taking a little over half of it, and the state taking most of the remainder. Based on the estimates from these three countries, we can say that in the early 1970s, probably about half of the export prices of coffee from producing countries represented surplus. However, it is difficult to generalize from these rough estimates for three countries to the situation in all other producing countries.

The rapid increase in retail prices of coffee following the devastating 1975 Brazilian frost created a flurry of interest in where consumers' coffee dollars were going, and spawned a number of studies attempting to explain why prices increased as much and as rapidly as they did. One of these studies was conducted by the U.S. Government Accounting Office (U.S. GAO 1977) for the House Agriculture Committee's Subcommittee on Domestic Marketing, Consumer Relations and Nutrition in 1977; this study attempted to estimate costs of production and profits in Orlandi's three countries as well as in Mexico and Côte d'Ivoire. These results are shown in the second column of table 7.3. As it turned out, the period on which this report focused was the acme of the coffee price boom that followed the frost, around April 1977 (the ICO indicator price peaked at its all-time high of 314.96 cents per pound in this month). This means that these figures probably overestimate the amount of surplus that went to the producing countries during the boom. In addition, the GAO based their estimates on the New York (cif) prices of the coffees from most countries; this method apparently assigns most of the transport costs to the exporters' surplus, resulting in a further overestimate of the surplus. Nonetheless, the data give us

Table 7.3 Estimates of the Total Surplus Retained in Coffee Producing Countries, and Its Division between Growers, the State, and Others

Country	1973		1977		ca. 1982		1987/88	
Brazil (A)								
Export price	51.3		369.0		115.7		97.5	
Production		NA	40.0		54.4		54.8	
Processing	3.3		1.5		6.8			NA
Total Surplus		NA	327.5	(89%)	54.5	(47%)	42.7	(44%)
Grower		NA	186.8	(57%)	0		-12.7	
State	20.0		101.3	(31%)	54.4	(100%)		NA
Others		NA	39.4	(11%)	0.1	(0%)		NA
Colombia (A)								
Export price	69.3		314.3		131.5		126.5	
Production	20.2			NA	77.7		73.2	
Processing	5.9		2.6		8.2			NA
Total Surplus	43.2	(62%)		NA	46.2	(35%)	53.3	
Grower	16.4	(38%)		NA	-10.0		2.2	
State	26.8	(62%)	207.4		55.2			NA
Others	0		16.2		1.0	(2%)		NA
El Salvador (A)								
Export price	58.0		300.0				129.6	
Production	26.6		35.5				58.5	
Processing	13.8		9.0					NA
Total Surplus	17.6	(30%)	255.5	(85%)			71.1	
Grower	5.4	(31%)	146.5	(57%)			6.2	
State	12.2	(69%)	83.0	(32%)				NA
Others		NA	26.0	(10%)				NA
Mexico (A)								
Export price			315.0				119.8	
Production			31.0				75.6	
Processing			18.0					NA
Total Surplus			266.0	(84%)			44.2	(37%)
Grower			107.0	(40%)			11.3	(26%)
State			136.0	(51%)				NA
Others			23.0	(9%)				NA
Costa Rica (A)								
Export price					119.7		119.7	
Production					49.9		64.5	
Processing					18.1			NA
Total Surplus					51.7	(43%)	55.2	(46%)
Grower					24.2	(47%)	5.1	(9%)
State					27.5	(53%)		NA
Others					0			NA

Continued on next page

Table 7.3 Estimates of the Total Surplus Retained in Coffee Producing Countries, and Its Division between Growers, the State, and Others (continued)

	1973	1977	ca. 1982	1987/88
Kenya (A)				
Export price			132.4	140.8
Production			70.8	96.1
Processing			24.9	NA
Total Surplus			36.7 (28%)	45.7 (32%)
Grower			24.8 (68%)	6.0 (13%)
State			10.6 (29%)	NA
Others			1.3 (3%)	NA
Rwanda (A)				
Export price			123.4	
Production			54.4	
Processing			16.3	
Total Surplus			52.7 (44%)	
Grower			23.3 (44%)	
State			28.4 (54%)	
Others			1.0 (2%)	
Cameroun (R)				
Export price			97.5	94.0
Production			40.8	88.5
Processing			17.7	NA
Total Surplus			39.0 (40%)	5.5 (6%)
Grower			5.0 (13%)	-20.5
State			34.0 (87%)	
Others			0	NA
Côte d'Ivoire (R)				
Export price		291.1	86.2	101.8
Production		NA	40.8	112.3
Processing		1.0	13.2	NA
Total Surplus		NA	32.2 (37%)	-10.5
Grower		NA	0.6 (2%)	-50.5
State		240.9	31.6 (98%)	NA
Others		0.4	0	NA
Indonesia (R)				
Export price			79.4	86.7
Production			36.3	69.0
Processing			36.3	NA
Total Surplus			6.8 (8%)	17.7 (20%)
Grower			2.6 (38%)	-9.0
State			4.0 (59%)	NA
Others			0.2 (3%)	NA

Sources: 1973 data from Orlandi (1978); 1977 data from USGAO (1977); 1982 data from de Graaf (1986); 1987/88 data on export price and price paid to growers provided by ICO; data on production cost from Landell Mills, as reported in *Carta Cafetera* (1990). (A) indicates a producer of arabica coffee; (R) indicates a producer of robusta coffee.

an approximation of the distribution of surplus within some major producing countries at the height of the boom.

The overall picture from these GAO data, as compared to Orlandi's, is that the large price increases of 1976–1977 greatly increased the total amount of surplus retained in the producing countries. Production costs increased somewhat between 1973 and 1977, but not nearly as fast as world market prices. The bulk of this surplus was divided between the coffee growers and the state, but their relative shares varied greatly across producing countries. In Brazil, the state's share of the surplus declined, which suggests that coffee growers reaped windfall profits during the boom. In Colombia, the total surplus increased, and the state's share alone amounted to two-thirds of the export price. The growers' share of the total surplus probably declined, but the absolute amount of surplus they received almost certainly increased. In El Salvador, there was a large increase in surplus, and most of it was apparently passed on to the growers. The total surplus in Mexico was similarly large, and the state took a little more than half of it. In Côte d'Ivoire, the state share alone, collected through its *Caisse de Stabilisation*, amounted to almost 83 percent of the export price. All coffee transactions were under the control of the *Caisse*, which set the prices that could be charged by traders and processors within the country. These figures indicate that the coffee price boom increased surplus in producing countries from about half of the export price to about three-quarters of a much higher price. In some countries the state took most of this increase by holding down internal prices or increasing taxes; in other countries most of the increase was passed on to coffee growers. It should be noted here that when states took most of the increased surplus, this was not simply a case of greedy state bureaucrats ripping off the peasants. There are sound economic reasons for states to heavily tax the increased incomes resulting from export booms, to prevent economic distortions known as the "Dutch disease" (Davis 1983; Bevan, Collier, and Gunning 1990).

The most comprehensive published comparative analysis of production and processing costs in the producing countries was conducted in the early 1980s by J. de Graaf of the Royal Tropical Institute in Amsterdam. De Graaf (1986) analyzed production, processing, transport, and export costs for eight major producers: Brazil, Colombia, Costa Rica, Kenya, Rwanda, Cameroun, Côte d'Ivoire, and Indonesia. In coffee year 1981/82 these eight producers accounted for 62 percent of total ICO member exports. These data are summarized in column 3 of table 7.3.

De Graaf's data show zero profits on average for Brazilian growers. He states that this is partly due to losses suffered by growers in Paraná, the state worst hit by the 1975 frost. It is reasonable to assume that profits per pound were relatively low, and de Graaf may have underestimated prices paid to growers. Using data from the ICO on prices paid to growers along with de Graaf's estimated production costs yields a plausible estimate of 3.5 cents profit per pound. Since most Brazilian production comes from large diversified farms, low profit rates may be sufficient; the farms produce large volumes of coffee, and coffee income represents only one component of their total income. Almost half of Brazil's export price was surplus, and virtually all of it went to the state. Since the growers probably made a small profit, the share of the state is overstated in these numbers, but it seems reasonable to conclude that the state (primarily the state coffee agency, the IBC) did capture most of the surplus in the early 1980s. These figures refer only to coffee that is exported; they do not include income and profit generated by Brazil's sizable internal coffee market.

The data show a negative profit for Colombian growers; again, de Graaf seems to have underestimated prices paid to growers. Using the ICO data on growers' price there is a very small positive profit. Either way, it seems safe to conclude that most of the surplus (only 35 percent of the export price in Colombia vs. about half in Brazil) went to the quasi-state FNC in the early 1980s. This is consistent with the estimate for the late 1980s shown in column 4, but it must be considered in light of the services provided by the FNC to growers (discussed in chapter 5).

The data for Costa Rica show a total surplus of about 45 percent of the export price, divided roughly equally between the growers and the state. A lower amount of surplus was retained in Kenya than in other arabica producing countries studied by de Graaf; only about a quarter of the export price was surplus. The data show growers receiving about two-thirds of this surplus. Rwanda is by far the smallest producer considered here; despite the fact that it is dependent on coffee for most of its export earnings, its production is an insignificant share of total world production. Table 7.3 shows an amount and distribution of surplus for Rwanda that is very similar to that of Costa Rica, another mild arabica producer. Surplus was divided primarily between the state and the growers, with the state getting a somewhat larger share.

Cameroun is a producer of both robusta and arabica coffee; arabica production accounts for about 25 percent of total production. The figures shown here are for robusta production; the data show that 40 percent of the export price was surplus, and almost all of the surplus was retained by the state, through its marketing board. Côte d'Ivoire was the world's largest robusta producer in 1981/82; the amount and distribution of the surplus here look very similar to those for Cameroun robustas; this makes sense since they have similar production systems.

Indonesia was the world's second largest exporter of robustas, behind Côte d'Ivoire, in 1981/82; about 5 percent of its total production was arabica. Indonesia stands out as a low-profit producer—surplus represented only about 8 percent of the export price, well below all other cases analyzed here. Indonesia's state did not intervene in the coffee sector to the same degree as other producing countries considered here. Growers got a larger share of the surplus than in the other robusta producing countries, but not as large a share as arabica growers. The state still took a large share, collected through export taxes on private exporters, but the surplus to be shared here was much less.

What is probably the most comprehensive comparative study of production costs ever conducted is not available to the public. It was conducted by Landell Mills Commodity Studies (LM) of the U.K. in 1987/88, and is available only by special subscription; it is information which has itself become a commodity. A summary of the results has been published in *Carta Cafetera* (15–30 Abril, 1990), the newsletter of the Colombian coffee exporters' association. The study covered 21 producing countries, 11 arabica producers, 2 robusta producers, and eight countries that produced both (although most are major producers of only one). The last column of table 7.3 presents data from this study only for countries included in one of the three previous studies reported here. Because the LM study focused only on production costs, these data were combined with ICO data on export prices and prices paid to growers to obtain estimates of the total surplus. The de Graaf and LM data provide a reasonably good basis for concluding that, during the 1980s, about one-third to one-half of the export price of coffee represented surplus which was retained in the producing countries.[9] Differences within this range depended mainly on the production systems, types and qualities of coffee grown, and the levels of world market prices for the different types and qualities. The LM data which have been published have no estimates of the state's share of the surplus, but even de Graaf's small set of countries suggests that this share varies considerably across producing countries, depending on the structure of the production system, and the state's role in it. What is interesting about these results is that despite the large shift in income shares between producing and consuming countries in 1986–1987 discussed in the previous section, there was apparently no decline in the amount of surplus retained in the producing countries.

This brief sketch of the situation in the 1980s sets the stage for what happened after 1989; although there are no data available for this period, it is possible to project what happened based on the above discussion. If the costs of production were more than half of the export price of coffee in the 1980s, and export prices fell by 50 percent during the 1989 price crash, then this crash wiped out the entire surplus. Growers could, and did, cut their production costs by cutting back on fertilizer, maintenance, and harvesting (picking less selectively or resorting to stripping, which lowered the quality of coffee they produced), but they couldn't match the fall in price. This is why growers worldwide were complaining by 1991–1992 that the prices they were receiving were below their costs. And this despite the fact that the states had also cut back their coffee income and their roles in coffee processing and export, and in some cases were providing subsidies to growers out of income they received from other sources (as noted above, the share of value added in the producing countries fell to about 2 percent in these years). Coffee acreage declined in many countries in the early 1990s, and the coffee trees which remained were less well maintained than they had been through the 1980s, creating the conditions for shortages in the mid-1990s. The 1993/94 increase in world market prices probably brought the income of producing countries back above their costs of production, but there are no systematic studies of costs of production in this period to indicate the amount of surplus which returned to producing countries. The data in table 7.2 suggest that most of the higher export prices during 1994–1997 were passed on to growers, but states may have marginally increased their shares. By 2000/01, the prices being received by most growers were probably once again below their costs of production.

The data on surplus analyzed in this section suggest that over most of the period considered here, the total surplus amounted to about 40–50 percent of the export price. There appear to have been two significant shifts. One was the coffee boom of 1976–1977, during which about 75 percent of the export price may have been surplus. However, this was only a temporary shift, and surplus probably returned quickly to its prefrost levels, as did income shares. The second shift occurred as a result of the price crash of 1989, which drastically reduced this surplus; indeed, it became negative for some countries by 1990, and probably for many more by 1992. The 1994–1997 period probably provided a brief respite when some surplus was available to participants in the producing countries, but by about 2000, the surplus was once again probably close to zero if not negative.

These data show that coffee growing was a profitable activity in the producing countries, probably at least from the mid-1960s to the late 1980s. This is the period during which the ICAs were working to regulate the market. Most of the profit during this period appears to have flowed to either coffee growers or producing states. Because coffee growing tends to be a smallholder activity, profits that go to coffee growers are spread widely over large rural areas, and probably have strong multiplier effects on local economies. Indeed, the coffee growing regions of countries like Colombia have usually been more prosperous than other rural areas. However, this has changed significantly since 1989. States have also extracted significant shares of this surplus, which have been put to a variety of uses. As discussed in previous chapters, many state coffee agencies put their share of the surplus to good use, providing credit, agricultural extension services, and coffee research which helped growers to upgrade their production. A few, most notably Colombia's FNC, used some of these profits to develop the coffee growing regions. However, in other cases, for instance in some African countries, this surplus was squandered as state marketing boards were turned into cash cows for corrupt public officials.

This section of the analysis has focused on the amount of surplus that remained in the producing countries. But we know little about the distribution of the surplus along the entire coffee commodity chain until we also estimate the amount of surplus retained within the consuming countries. This is the subject of the next section.

Surplus in the Consuming Countries

On the consuming side of the market, the production system and the structure of the coffee commodity chain are more similar across countries than is the case for producing countries. TNC coffee importers bring in the green coffee and sell it to coffee manufacturers. They process and package the coffee and sell it to retailers who in turn sell to the final consumers. The difficulties encountered in the previous section, where estimates of the surplus might differ widely across countries with different production systems producing different types and qualities of coffee, are less of a problem in the consuming countries. The globalization of coffee manufacturing has spread a similar system, and probably a similar distribution of profits, across all consuming countries. The main components in all countries should be the profits of importers, roasters, and retailers. However, obtaining the data to estimate these components turns out to be even more difficult than it was in the producing countries.

First, the largest players in these markets are now huge diversified TNCs, and it is almost impossible to sort out how much profits they make on their coffee operations as opposed to their other product lines. Second, information on costs of production can legally be considered a "trade secret" which does not have to be disclosed. The difficulty presented by this aspect of coffee manufacturing in the core is highlighted by the 1991 report of the U.K. Monopolies and Mergers Commission (MMC) on the prices of instant coffee. The MMC was asked to investigate Nestlé's pricing practices following the 1989 price crash, after which the retail prices of instant coffee generally remained at their pre-crash levels. In the U.K., over 90 percent of the coffee consumed is in instant form, and in 1990, Nestlé brands accounted for 56 percent of the retail market. The MMC was asked to investigate whether Nestlé's position in the market allowed it to make monopoly profits following the price crash. But almost all of the data on Nestlé's profits are suppressed in the public version of the report, because it "would not be in the public interest to disclose [them]." (MMC 1991, iv)

The only profit data left in this report are shown in table 7.4. The table shows profits as a percent of the total retail value increasing from a level of about 20 percent in 1985–1986 to about 30 percent in 1988–1989. It shows Nestlé's green coffee costs decreasing from about 40 percent of the retail price in 1985–1986 to 23 percent in 1989. Since Nestlé generally bought through importers, these costs already include the importers' profits. Thus we can tentatively conclude that, in the late 1980s, surplus retained in the consuming countries was in the range of 30–40 percent of the retail price.

The MMC report acknowledges that Nestlé's "profitability is considerably higher than that of industry in general or of other firms in its own industry" (1, also see 75). But it finds no evidence that Nestlé's market position enabled it to gain an unfair advantage over its competition. What is considered to be its competition in this analysis is instructive: the second largest share in the market (25 percent) is held by General Foods Ltd., the Philip Morris/Kraft/General Foods U.K. subsidiary; the other two companies considered in detail are Lyons-Tetley and Brooke Bond, both major players in the world tea market, based in the U.K. They produce or import instant coffee for sale in the U.K. market, and hold 8 percent and 6 percent shares of the market respectively. Thus all companies considered are large diversified TNCs who collectively benefit from their oligopoly position; together they account for 95 percent of the market. Although there are no "anti-competitive" discussions of pricing policy among these firms, none are

Where Does Your Coffee Dollar Go? 181

Table 7.4 Estimates of Nestlé's Profits as a Percentage of Retail Sales

	1985	1986	1987	1988	1989
Operating profit[a]	48.3	59.9	77.8	91.9	99.6
Total sales (wholesale)	231.7	261.4	256.2	268.3	276.7
11% Retail margin[b]	28.6	32.3	31.7	33.2	34.2
Retail sales (est.)	260.3	293.7	287.9	301.5	310.9
Profit % of wholesale	20.9	22.9	30.4	34.3	36.0
Profit % of retail sales	18.6	20.4	27.0	30.5	32.0
Green coffee costs as % of retail sales	40.4	39.9	29.9	24.7	22.9
Advertising and promotion as % of retail sales	3.4	3.1	4.2	4.5	4.3

Source: U.K. Monopolies and Mergers Commission (1991), table 4.4, p. 52.
[a]Calculated as return on capital X capital employed.
[b]I assume a gross retail margin of 11 percent of the retail price. MMC states on p. 23 that the gross margin on Nestlé's most popular brand was under 10 percent, and on GFL's, less than 11 percent. But minor brands had margins close to double those of the major brands.

needed; they all know what the other firms are doing and respond accordingly. In this situation, Nestlé doesn't need to resort to "anti-competitive practices" and none of its TNC competitors are likely to complain about Nestlé's higher profits, as long as theirs are sufficient.

The data thus suggest a significant increase in Nestlé's profits beginning in about 1986. This coincides with the increase in value added in the consuming countries that happened between coffee years 1985/86 and 1986/87, as shown in table 7.2. Although data for one TNC in one consuming market is not a good basis for generalization, it is tempting to conclude from this data that the TNCs, after a short lag, were able to increase retail prices to match the 1985–1986 rise in green coffee prices, and that they were able to maintain these retail price levels through the late 1980s despite the fact that green coffee prices had fallen back to their early 1980s levels by mid-1987. Thus, most of the 10 percent shift in total income to the consuming countries that occurred around 1986 consisted of increased profits flowing to the TNCs because of their increasing market power. When green coffee prices crashed in 1989, the TNCs were positioned to continue to maintain their wholesale/retail prices, leading to the additional 10 percent shift in value added toward the consuming countries that is shown in table 7.2. This shift probably led to a further increase in TNC profits, which is only hinted at in the MMC report.

An UNCTAD study (1984) also contains some data on the distribution of coffee income during the period 1974–1978 in one consuming country, the United States. UNCTAD concludes that "gross margins from the activities of trading, processing, and distributing companies could be as high as one quarter of the retail price of coffee" (38). This would amount to roughly half of the retained value in the United States. Since this period contains the 1976–1977 coffee price boom, it is reasonable to estimate that the surplus was about half of the retail price during the non-boom years, but substantially lower during the boom.

UNCTAD derived some of this data from the U.S. Census Bureau's Censuses and Annual Surveys of Manufactures, and it is possible to use these sources to put together a picture of how this distribution has changed over time. These data are shown in table 7.5. Since these data provide no estimates of retail value, it is difficult to compare them with the previous estimates. Nevertheless, the data show an increasing trend in manufacturing value added over time. The table shows a spike in raw material costs corresponding to the 1976–1977 coffee boom, as value added fell below 20 percent in 1977. But value added quickly returned to its prefrost level of around 35 percent. There are further increases corresponding to the 1986–1987 period of higher prices, and to the 1989 price crash—the same times that shifts of income shares from producers to consumers were noted above. The cost of raw materials rose again during the 1994–1997 period of higher prices, and value added fell to 40 percent in 1995, but then increased to 45 percent during the second crisis.

These figures include some other inputs besides green coffee—in 1987, green coffee accounted for 80 percent of material input costs; most of the rest were for packaging materials. But they show a definite trend toward higher value added in the consuming countries from around 35 percent of wholesale in the early 1970s to around 45 percent in the early 1990s. Labor costs were a minor component of total costs. The data show them falling during the 1970s and then rising slightly, as a percentage of wholesale sales. By 2000, labor costs accounted for about the same percentage of the wholesale price that they had in 1972. Other costs such as energy inputs also increased during this period, but they are also a minor cost—energy costs were about 1 percent of material inputs in 1987, increasing to 1.2 percent in 1997. Therefore, increasing costs cannot account for the increased value added by manufacturing over this period, and there must have been a substantial increase in the surplus. The data in tables 7.4 and 7.5 thus are broadly consistent; both suggest significant increases in the amount of surplus retained in the consuming countries, and both trace shifts in the surplus to the 1986–1987 and 1989–1990 periods during which income shares also shifted toward the consuming countries.

The Distribution of Benefits along the Commodity Chain

Pulling together the results presented in the three previous sections, we can summarize the changes in the distributions of income and surplus that have oc-

Table 7.5 Wholesale Sales, Cost of Raw Materials, Manufacturing Value Added, and Payroll Costs for Coffee Manufacturing Establishments in the United States, 1972–2000

	Wholesale Sales ($ 000)	Cost of Raw Materials[a] Value	Percent	Manufacturing Value Added Value	Percent	Payroll Costs Value	Percent
1972	2328.7	1503.1	64.5	825.8	35.5	131.5	5.6
1973	2570.3	1761.1	68.5	822.6	32.0	135.8	5.3
1974	2724.8	1845.5	67.7	905.9	33.2	139.4	5.1
1975	3161.6	2047.2	64.8	1108.0	35.0	149.3	4.7
1976	1623.6	3394.5	73.4	1257.6	27.2	153.4	3.3
1977	5616.4	4643.4	82.7	988.0	17.6	164.8	2.9
1978	6011.0	4342.0	72.2	1652.1	27.5	178.0	3.0
1979	5944.8	4222.5	71.0	1748.3	29.4	198.9	3.3
1980	6341.5	4459.9	70.3	1902.1	30.0	224.3	3.5
1981	5717.1	3791.4	66.3	1915.5	33.5	265.7	4.6
1982	5826.9	3749.0	64.3	2070.3	35.5	265.7	4.6
1983	5808.5	3710.8	63.9	2115.0	36.4	265.1	4.6
1984	6378.4	4178.3	65.5	2220.2	34.8	279.2	4.4
1985	6677.1	4211.2	63.1	2445.8	36.6	294.5	4.4
1986	7544.0	5140.2	68.1	2444.7	32.4	307.1	4.1
1987	6400.8	3775.2	59.0	2589.8	40.5	303.0	4.7
1988	6332.4	3526.8	55.7	2795.8	44.1	315.6	5.0
1989	6167.2	3491.6	56.6	2658.1	43.1	303.1	4.9
1990	6622.7	3004.9	45.4	3581.8	54.1	326.7	4.9
1991	5919.9	3035.2	51.3	2868.4	48.4	324.4	5.5
1992	5292.8	2530.0	47.8	2752.5	52.0	340.0	6.4
1993	5535.7	2587.8	46.7	2969.6	53.6	339.4	6.1
1994	6127.1	3277.5	53.5	2925.1	47.8	333.3	5.4
1995	6418.1	3855.2	60.1	2602.7	40.6	338.2	5.3
1996	6552.0	3689.9	56.3	2892.6	44.1	337.5	5.2
1997	7166.6	4100.2	57.2	3140.5	43.8	347.8	4.8
1997[b]	7974.9	4401.2	55.2	3644.7	45.7	445.4	5.6
1998	7716.7	4174.0	54.1	3514.6	45.5	422.3	5.5
1999	7466.3	4101.5	54.9	3388.0	45.4	449.8	6.0
2000	7229.2	3997.2	55.3	3219.2	44.5	433.0	6.0

Source: 1987 Census of Manufactures, Industry Series—Miscellaneous Food and Kindred Products (US Census Bureau 1990), Table 1a-1, p. 2CI-8; 1992 Census of Manufactures, Industry Series— Miscellaneous Food and Kindred Products; 1997 Economic Census, Manufacturing, Industry Series—Coffee and Tea Manufacturing; Annual Surveys of Manufactures, Industry Statistics, 1993, 1994, 1995, 1996, 2000. All sources except the 1987 Census obtained from the Census Bureau website, www.census.gov.
[a]There is some overlap between value of shipments and cost of raw materials, because the outputs of one establishment may be used as inputs in another establishment. For the coffee industry this overlap is minimal, but for some years, it causes the cost of raw materials plus manufacturing value added to be slightly greater than the total value of shipments.
[b]Beginning in 1997, tea blending and instant tea manufacturing establishments are combined with establishments producing roasted and instant coffee. Data from the 1997 Census allow comparison of figures calculated using the old and new definitions, shown on the first and second lines for 1997, respectively. Figures for 1998–2000 are based on the new definition.

curred over the past twenty years. In the early 1970s, a little more than half of the total income went to consuming countries, and about a third of it was surplus. About a third of total income went to producing countries, and about half of it was surplus. The result was that the total amount of surplus was roughly equally divided between the producing and consuming countries. The 1975 Brazilian frost and the subsequent coffee boom significantly shifted this distribution. Producing countries' share of the retained value briefly increased to more than half, and as much as three-quarters of this may have been surplus. Consuming countries' income dropped to near 40 percent of the total, and as little as 20 percent of this may have been surplus. What was a relatively small shift in income thus apparently masked what was a massive, but very brief, redistribution of the surplus. For a period in 1976–1977, the producing countries may have received as much as 80 percent of the total surplus available along the chain.

The situation seems to have quickly reverted to what it had been before the boom, and remained the same until 1986. Income in consuming countries was about half the total, with about a third, or maybe slightly more, being surplus; income in the producing countries was again about a third of the total, with a bit less than half of it being surplus. Thus the division of the surplus was again roughly equal, with the consuming countries probably having a slightly larger share than they had before the boom. The Brazilian drought of 1985, leading to price increases and the temporary suspension of quotas in 1986–1987, appears to have triggered another significant shift. The income of consuming countries rose to about two-thirds of the total, while the income of producing countries fell to about a quarter. Surplus in the consuming countries rose to probably around 40 percent of income, while surplus in the producing countries seems to have held steady at about 40 percent of income. However, because the total amount of surplus increased, the net result was a shift in the distribution of the surplus: about 60 percent of the total surplus available along the chain now went to consumers and about 40 percent to producers.

The next major shift recorded in these data was caused by the end of quotas and the price crash of 1989. Income in the consuming countries rose to about three-quarters of the total, while the income of producers fell to about 15 percent. Surplus in the consuming countries may have risen to about half of total income, while surplus in the producing countries fell to near, and sometimes below, zero. The Brazilian frosts of 1994 shifted a large amount of income, and probably surplus as well, back to the producing countries. But, as was the case in 1976–1977, this shift was temporary, and the distribution of surplus in the late 1990s as the second crisis developed looked about the same as it had been during the first crisis of 1989–1993. Almost all of the surplus was retained in the consuming countries. Many coffee growers were receiving less than it cost them to produce the coffee, many states had withdrawn from market intervention and had relinquished their shares of the surplus, and private exporters and processors were probably receiving very small profits.

From this summary of the results, it might seem that natural disasters in

Brazil have as much influence on the distributions of income and surplus as any of the economic or political factors that have been the focus of analysis in this book. This impression is correct to the extent that these disasters introduced exogenous shocks into the chain, to which all market participants had to respond. These shocks provided the opportunities for much larger shifts than would have been likely under "normal" conditions. The impression is incorrect to the extent that it is impossible to know what would have happened in the absence of other political and economic changes. In particular, the shifts in income and surplus from producers to consumers in the late 1980s and early 1990s occurred in a context of increasing market power of the TNCS on one side of the market, and the defeat of producers' attempts to regulate the market on the other. Without these political and economic changes, the exogenous shocks of natural disasters in Brazil might have caused only temporary shifts, as happened during the late-1970s coffee boom.

As for the division of the income and surplus within the producing countries, it is clear that the largest shares go to the coffee growers and the state. The relative sizes of these shares vary greatly across producing countries and over time; in some cases such as Brazil and Colombia, the state may take about half of the total income and an even larger share of the surplus. In other countries such as Indonesia, the state may only take about 10 percent of the income and less than a third of the surplus, leaving the bulk of both for growers. Intermediate traders and processors, and exporters, get relatively small shares of the income and surplus. However, to put this into perspective, we also need to consider volumes. The estimates in this chapter are all based on the production and export of a pound of green coffee. But a peasant grower producing one or two hundred pounds of coffee a year and earning a large share of the surplus per pound is still worse off than a large exporter who ships one or two hundred thousand bags (13–26 million pounds) per year, but earns only a very small profit per pound.

In the consuming countries, the main beneficiaries are the TNC roasters, who get the majority of the income and surplus *and* handle huge volumes of coffee. Some of this surplus is probably passed on to workers through higher wages, but this is undoubtedly a small share. The TNC coffee importers also earn a small share of the income, less than 10 percent of the total retail value, and a small share of the surplus. I have not been able to find any estimates of the importers' costs, in order to make an estimate of the importers' share of the surplus. But, as for the exporters, the TNC importers handle such large volumes of coffee that they can do quite well on a very small profit per pound. Finally, some consuming states also take a share of the surplus through taxes, which, in the case of some European countries, can be quite substantial.

Now that we have a rough idea of how the surplus is distributed along the chain, we can consider the different types and sources of rents received by different participants. The different types of rents were discussed in chapter 1, based on Kaplinsky (1998). For most of the period before 1986 (excluding the 1976–1977 coffee boom), when the total amount of surplus was roughly evenly

divided between producing and consuming countries, it is clear that the bulk of
the surplus retained in the producing countries was due to what I have called
regulation rents (see chapter 1). The gap between costs of production and world
market prices for green coffee was maintained by the ICA quota system and the
collective action of producers. The individual states, through the coffee agencies
and marketing boards, decided how these rents were divided between the state
and the coffee growers, the major recipients in most countries. The actual prices
received by growers in different countries, and consequently the amounts of
surplus, varied considerably, due to the operation of different types of rents discussed in chapter 1. For instance, growers in Kenya or Guatemala received some
resource rents because their soils and climates were conducive to producing the
highest quality arabicas. Growers in countries like Uganda with poor infrastructure and transportation links received lower profits because of negative infrastructural rents. And growers in Colombia and Central America received
technology rents from the technification of coffee production. But these were all
minor rents that determined the relative profitability of coffee production in different countries; the major source of rents for all producing countries was market regulation.

During the 1976–1977 coffee boom, prices soared because of shortages and
panic buying, and the shares of surplus going to the producing countries increased sharply. These increases can be classified as resource rents, resulting
from scarcity, or the perception of scarcity. As Kaplinsky (1998, 16) states, resource rents like these are generally unstable because the high rents stimulate
increased production. As we have seen, the coffee boom stimulated new planting in many producing countries, leading by 1980 to a reimposition of quotas
and a return to the situation where the main source of rents was market regulation.

The primary type of rents accruing to consuming countries are product and
marketing rents, which are based on product differentiation through brand
names and advertising. Kaplinsky's (1998) discussion suggests that the original
source of product and marketing rents for the national coffee companies of the
1950s and 1960s was economies of scale, which allowed them to undersell their
smaller competitors. But by the 1980s, Fordism was giving way to flexible production, and branding and advertising, along with product innovation to target
niche markets, was the major source of these product and marketing rents. By
1986, the major coffee companies had begun to go global, greatly increasing
their market power across the major consuming markets. The data presented in
this chapter suggest that it was this increased market power that enabled the coffee TNCs to increase their wholesale prices in response to the increase in green
coffee prices during 1985–1986, and then maintain those wholesale prices as
green coffee prices returned to their previous levels. Thus the shift of shares of
both income and surplus toward consuming countries observed around 1986
seems to be due to the ability of the coffee TNCs to use their market power to
increase the total amount of surplus available, and to capture all of this increase.

By contrast, the further shift of income and surplus to producers after 1989 appears to be due to the defeat of producers' collective action and a shift of the surplus formerly controlled by producing countries into the coffers of the TNCs. After 1989, the market power of the TNCs once again allowed them to maintain their wholesale prices, and capture what had been the regulation rents going to the producing countries, transforming them into increased product and marketing rents. The minor rents discussed above, resource, infrastructural, and technology, remained potential sources of rents for the producers. But in a situation where the TNCs were dominant, these minor rents no longer determined the relative profitability of coffee growing in different countries, but whether it was profitable at all—whether the prices paid to growers barely covered or fell below their costs of production. During the period 1994–1997, shortages again produced some resource rents for the producers, but these were short lived.

One additional type of policy rent in consuming countries deserves brief mention: taxation. All consuming states levy taxes on coffee, through sales taxes as in the United States or VAT taxes as in Europe, and in countries like the U.K. and Germany, this adds significantly to the cost of coffee to the consumer. The fact that core states receive a share of the surplus is usually overlooked in discussions of the role of the state in international commodity trade. These discussions tend to focus on the taxes taken by producing states as distorting factors in the world market, overlooking the fact that consuming states also raise revenues from taxes on coffee. And unlike the situation in the producing countries, where some of these tax revenues are used by state coffee agencies to provide services to coffee growers, tax revenues in the consuming countries go directly into the general budget. No one questions whether core states use their shares of the surplus productively, or squander them, for instance, on bloated militaries.

Benefits from Instant Coffee Exports

The preceding analysis gives us some sense of the benefits coffee growers and coffee producing countries were able to obtain through their involvement in the coffee chain. These benefits were mainly a result of the collective action strategy. Coffee producers were able to act collectively to maintain the ICA quota regime until 1989, and this market regulation returned significant shares of income and profits to the growers and producing countries. As we have seen, the flow of benefits to producers was also influenced by natural disasters in Brazil that produced temporary windfalls. However, by the 1990s, changes in the structure of the chain associated with globalization and the period of financial expansion, particularly the consolidation of control by the coffee TNCs and the weakening of producing states, had decisively shifted benefits toward consuming countries and the TNCs. As noted in the preceding chapter, some producing states engaged in another strategy to increase their benefits from the coffee chain: the forward integration strategy. Since the goal of this struggle over the instant coffee chain was the desire by both TNCs and producing states to capture larger shares of the income and surplus, the question now is: how successful were producing states in the struggle, as judged by their monetary gains? Using the preceding analysis as a benchmark, we can compare the gains from instant coffee production to those from green coffee exporting.

Unfortunately, very little data exist which would allow us to compare a country's earnings from instant coffee exports to those from green coffee exports, in order to estimate the payoff from the development of an instant coffee export capacity. The ICO converts data on exports of all different forms of coffee into green bean equivalents, and reports unit values of exports only for all forms of coffee combined. It also reports the retail price of instant coffee in importing country markets only when instant is the primary form consumed, that is, in the U.K., Australia, New Zealand, and Fiji. Further, there are no comparative studies of the costs of producing instant as there are for the production of green coffee. The data which are available suggest that the coffee growing countries did earn somewhat more from instant coffee exports than they did from green coffee, but that, at the same time, the TNCs were able to use these exports to maintain or increase their already sizable profit margins.

The best data available to address this question are shown in table 7.6. These data are from the period in which instant coffee was a relatively new phenomenon, and detailed statistics were being collected on it by the Pan American Coffee Bureau and Brazil's IBC. This table shows the unit values of instant coffee imports into the United States, the import prices of an equivalent amount of green coffee,[10] and the retail prices of instant coffee in the U.S. market. From the late 1950s through the mid-1960s, the average import price of instant coffee was declining. In part, this was a reflection of the worldwide coffee surplus; the world market price of green coffee was also declining during this period. Green and instant coffee prices got a temporary boost in 1964, as the export quotas of the first ICA began to have an effect, but the decline continued after that.

Prices got a further boost from the frosts in Brazil in 1969 and 1972, and then the 1975 frost rocked the market. Comparing the average import prices of instant and green coffee, we see that during the late 1950s and early 1960s, the average import price of instant was above the average import price of an equivalent amount of green coffee, at times by as much as $1.00 per pound. Most instant coffee imports came from the Tenco-IBEC plants in Central America at this time. After 1965, when the Brazil powder began to enter the U.S. market, the average import price of instant fell below the average import price of the equivalent in green coffee. This situation illustrates the cost advantage of the Brazilian manufacturers; as noted in chapter 6, Brazilian production costs were probably more than 50 cents per pound of instant lower than those of U.S. manufacturers. As discussed in that chapter, this cost advantage was created by Brazilian state export tax policies.

While the import price of instant coffee was declining through the 1960s, however, the retail price of instant in the U.S. market remained relatively stable, at about $2.50 per pound. This retail price was probably maintained by General Foods and Nestlé, who were already the price leaders in the market, and who

Table 7.6 Retail Price of Instant Coffee in the U.S. Market, Compared to Unit Value of Imports of Instant Coffee and the Equivalent Amount of Green Coffee, 1956–1978

Year	Retail Price of Instant Coffee[a]	Unit Value of Imports of Instant Coffee	Unit Value of Green Coffee Equivalent[b]
1956	396	292	210
1957	362	279	183
1958	325	259	150
1959	277	193	129
1960	262	176	123
1961	245	157	114
1962	242	119	108
1963	246	118	105
1964	284	136	141
1965	254	120	135
1966	242	104	120
1967	237	110	114
1968	238	97	111
1969	249	105	123
1970	279	132	168
1971	291	144	135
1972	291	138	156
1973	309	149	207
1974	369	165	219
1975	427	177	246
1976	546	260	447
1977	832	505	924
1978	874	436	495

Source: Pan American Coffee Bureau (1966), Tables IS-1, ISV-10, C-6, CP-15; Pan American Coffee Bureau (1967–1975), Tables S-1, C-2; Instituto Brazileiro do Café (1978), Tables IM-6, IM-7, PR-23, CO-3.
[a]U.S. cents per pound.
[b]Unit value of imports for three pounds of green coffee, which, with the technology of the 1950s and 1960s, would produce about one pound of instant coffee. Extraction rates had improved by the 1970s, so this may overstate the price of the amount of green coffee necessary to produce one pound of instant. For 1956–1965, the average price of "Other Mild" arabicas on the New York market is used—this is an average of prices for El Salvador, Guatemala, and Mexico. For 1966–1978, the average price of Brazil Santos 4 on the New York market is used. These choices for the reference price of green coffee reflect the major sources of instant coffee imports during these time periods.

manufactured almost all of their instant domestically. This growing gap between the retail price of instant in the United States and the price at which the Brazil powder was available was what convinced Hills Bros. and Chock Full o' Nuts to switch to the Brazilian import. At this import price, they could afford to sell their brands at a price below that established by General Foods and Nestlé, and make a handsome profit. The potential for this strategy on the part of their competition was what motivated General Foods to lead the industry campaign to limit Brazilian imports.

The prices of imported instant coffee remained below the prices of the equivalent amounts of green coffee through the 1970s. However, the data in Table 7.6 mask an interesting pattern.[11] During the 1970s, imports of instant from other consuming countries, particularly France and Canada, expanded. The import prices of the instant coffee from these sources were significantly higher than the prices of instant from Brazil and the other coffee growing countries. In some cases, they were even above the average retail price of instant on the U.S. market. Part of this difference may be accounted for by the fact that imports from the coffee growing countries were in bulk, while some of the product from the consuming countries was packed for final consumption. It may also be due to the fact that the latter imports consisted of more freeze-dried product than the former; in particular, Nestlé was importing freeze-dried from its French factory in the mid-1960s while it got its U.S. facilities into full production. But more generally, the imports from other consuming countries represented primarily an intra-TNC trade. By the early 1970s, Nestlé and General Foods had dominant positions in the Canadian and French markets, as well as the U.S. market. In this intra-TNC trade, the TNCs covered temporary shortages in one market by importing product from a subsidiary in another market. In these cases, the prices paid by the U.S. TNCs (at least on the books) probably approximated the prices to be charged in the U.S. market (the United States had no import taxes on instant coffee).

For the entire period after 1965, when producing state initiatives to promote forward integration became significant, the average import prices of instant from the producing countries was well below the import price of an equivalent amount of green coffee. Thus, Brazil and other producing countries obtained no additional income from exporting instant coffee instead of green coffee. In Brazil and other producing countries, the cost advantage of instant manufacturers was based on access to nonexport quality beans and exemptions from export taxes. Therefore, the income shares and profits earned by the instant manufacturers represented primarily a shift of income and surplus from the state to the manufacturers, rather than an overall increase in the amount of income earned by producing countries from their coffee exports.

One additional set of data provides a glimpse at the situation during the 1980s. These data concern the prices of instant coffee imported into Japan in 1984–1990, and are shown in table 7.7. They give the unit values of import for Brazilian and Colombian instant coffee imports into Japan. Since most Brazilian instant was spray-dried and most Colombian instant was freeze-dried, the Colombian product commanded a higher price. But the spread between these prices varied considerably, ranging from zero to almost $1.00 per pound over this period. In 1984–1985, prices were relatively stable; Brazilian instant cost about $3.00 per pound and Colombian instant was about $3.50. In 1986, as the effects of the Brazilian drought drove up all coffee prices, the prices of Brazilian and Colombian instant rose to a peak of $4.75 and $5.00, respectively, in July. In

Table 7.7 Unit Values of Instant Coffee Imports into Japan, 1984–1990

Year and Month of Sale	Brazilian	Coffee Year Average	Colombian	Coffee Year Average	Unit Values All Forms of Coffee
1984					
Jan.	290		370		
April	300		370		
July	295		365		
Oct.	305	295	360	368	357
1985					
Jan.	290		350		
April	280		345		
July	290		360		
Oct.	295	291	360	354	348
1986					
Jan.	275		355		
April	325		400		
July	475		500		
Oct.	460	342	460	404	460
1987					
Jan.	390		440		
April	385		425		
July	305		370		
Oct.	280	385	320	424	354
1988					
Jan.	275		350		
April	250		300		
July	270		340		
Oct.	275	269	370	328	334
1989					
Jan.	275		330		
April	270		380		
July	320		405		
Oct.	300	285	345	371	340
1990					
Jan.	265		310		
April	245		275		
July	245		295		
Oct.	275	264	275	306	221

Source: Landell Mills, *Commodity Bulletin—Coffee*, various issues. Unit values are cif, in U.S. cents per pound.

1987 and 1988, prices fell to slightly below their pre-drought levels, around $2.50–2.75 and $3.00–3.75 respectively. After the end of ICA quotas in 1989, instant coffee prices fell again, but not as rapidly as those of green coffee. The data for mid-1990 show a price of $2.45 for Brazilian, and $2.95 for Colombian.

Table 7.7 also shows the unit values of coffee imports into Japan, with all forms of coffee included. Since all forms of coffee are converted into green bean equivalents in these figures, they reflect the prices paid by Japanese importers for green coffee (the other forms of coffee included are primarily instant coffee and coffee extract, but about 88 percent of Japanese imports were in green bean form during this period). The table suggests that Colombians receive a price for their instant coffee which is roughly the same as they receive for an equivalent amount of green coffee, while Brazilians receive a bit less than what they receive for the equivalent amount of green coffee. These prices are certainly less than the Japanese manufacturers' production costs, since they use the imported green coffee as their input (despite the fact that these manufacturers use more of the lower-priced robustas). The profits of the Brazilian and Colombian manufacturers depend on the fact that they can buy non-export quality green coffee on the local market at lower prices. In addition, Brazilian manufacturers received subsidies or exemptions from export taxes from the state during most of this period.

These data indicate the benefits of instant coffee production in the growing countries for export to core consuming markets, both for the growing countries and for the TNCs. Manufacturers in the growing countries have been able to earn a profit from instant coffee exports, although there is no good data to indicate how large this profit is. It is clear that most of this profit has depended on state tax policies, and thus represents a transfer of surplus from the state. These manufacturers have also been able to expand their sales in some consuming markets and open new markets for their product. Manufacturing into instant coffee also produces multiplier effects in the economies of the growing countries, in the form of demand for instant coffee production machinery (most of which can now be produced in the growing countries), demand for packaging materials, and (some) increase in skilled jobs. But the TNCs have also benefited from this development, and the extent of their benefits is clearer in this data. Imports from the growing countries are generally available at prices below the cost of production in the core countries. And the market power of the TNCs has enabled them to maintain retail prices at a level comfortably above production costs while blending the growing country imports into their product to lower costs and increase profits.

In summary, from the 1960s through the 1980s, it appears that coffee production was a reasonably profitable undertaking. Small coffee growers, while they were not getting rich, were able to live, support their families, and enjoy a standard of living better than many other Third World agriculturalists. Coffee producing states were receiving revenues from coffee exports that allowed them to provide important services to the growers, and have some money left over to devote to other projects. Some growers, and some states, undoubtedly put the money they received from coffee to better uses than did others, but misuses and corruption were by no means a necessary product of the ICA quota system that supported this arrangement. By the 1990s, the situation had changed drastically. Producing states were receiving very little revenue, if any, from coffee; indeed, some states were subsidizing their growers to keep them on their land. Coffee growers were, at best, barely surviving; many were being driven out of business and off their land.

As has been emphasized in this chapter and preceding chapters, the actions taken, both individually and collectively by producing states were essential in maintaining a system where the benefits from coffee production were shared between producers and consumers. The breakdown of this system in the 1990s can be traced, on the one hand, to the strengthening of the coffee TNCs and the consolidation and extension of their market power; and on the other, to the weakening of producing states and the removal of their abilities to intervene in and regulate the market. The breakdown of the system has led to chronic over-supply and prolonged crises, as described in previous chapters and quantified in this one. The TNCs have been the major winners, reaping windfall profits, while small coffee growers struggle to stay alive.

As the coffee crises dragged on through the 1990s, and attempts by producing states to reinstate market regulation were thwarted, attention began to turn toward other means of increasing the income and surplus flowing to the producing countries. During the 1980s, a parallel market for specialty coffees developed; these coffees fetched significantly higher prices on the world market. This development in turn set the stage for the growth of organic and fair-trade coffees. The next chapter considers whether these new trading channels for coffee offer possible solutions to the coffee crisis.

Notes

1. The ICO data refer to roasted coffee, both ground and whole bean, sold through retail outlets. For countries where the bulk of coffee consumption is in instant form, primarily the U.K., the data refer to the retail price of instant coffee. To make these data comparable across countries, the ICO converts the retail price of instant coffee to its price equivalents for R&G coffee (one pound of instant is equivalent to about 2.2 pounds of R&G). Beginning in the late 1980s, roasted whole bean specialty coffees sold at higher prices became a significant new market segment in the United States; these prices are not included in the ICO data (which, for the United States, come from the U.S. Department of Labor's Bureau of Labor Statistics and are used for calculating the Consumer Price Index). The ICO data thus reflect the average prices of supermarket brands. The data also refer to coffee sold for home consumption; the additional income and profits generated by the sale of brewed coffee in restaurants or cafés is not included.

2. This export price includes the costs of other inputs, primarily fertilizers and pesticides. If these inputs are imported from core countries, including their costs in the export price would cause an overestimate of the share of total income retained by producing countries. Fortunately, coffee is produced with few imported inputs. Estimates by de Graaf (1986) suggest that imported inputs account for less than 10 percent of total robusta producing country income and less than 20 percent of total arabica producing country income. Therefore, the export prices used here somewhat overstate the share of income remaining in the coffee producing countries, but not by much.

3. Growers in different countries sell their coffee to processors at the next stage of the chain in various forms, including fresh cherries, dried cherries, and dried parchment

coffee (see the description of the coffee chain in chapter 2). To make the data on prices paid to growers comparable across countries, the ICO converts prices paid to growers for all forms of coffee to their price equivalents per pound of processed green coffee. For example, two pounds of dried cherries is equivalent to one pound of green coffee, so for growers who sell dried cherries to processors, the ICO price is one-half of the reported price per pound of dried cherries.

4. One main component of this residual category is the difference between the fob export and cif import prices. The fob (free on board) export price is the price an importer will pay for a load of coffee sitting in a ship at the port in the exporting country. The cif (cost, insurance, and freight) import price is the fob export price plus the costs of shipping the coffee from the exporting country to a warehouse in the port of the importing country, plus the cost of insuring the coffee in transit. These additional costs could be considered as costs of doing business for coffee importers and manufacturers in consuming countries. They are separated out because they are relatively small components of the total price easily calculable from the basic ICO data on average prices of imports and exports. In addition, these transport costs are not easily allocated between producing and consuming countries. The shipping lines, insurance companies, and banks involved are generally TNCs based in the core countries, but some of the larger exporters like Brazil and Colombia ship coffee on nationally owned lines and obtain their insurance and financing locally. The other main component of this residual is the weight lost in roasting; it takes 1.19 pounds of green coffee to produce one pound of roasted coffee. This weight loss does not really add to retained value in the consuming countries; by separating it out, I estimate the retained value in consuming countries as the retail price of a pound of coffee minus the cost of enough green coffee to produce that pound.

5. A final caveat to bear in mind is that it takes months, at best, to move coffee from the tree to the cup. Grower prices are usually set by crop years, which also vary across countries, with most Southern Hemisphere producers (including Brazil and Indonesia) beginning April 1, while Northern Hemisphere producers (Colombia, Central America, and most African robusta producers) begin October 1. It usually takes a few months to process this coffee into green beans ready for export, at which point, depending on whether quotas are in effect and on the size of the crop, it may be stored for as long as several years. Further, coffee which is sold and shipped to consumer markets may also be held in warehouses, as a part of working stocks or as a basis for speculation on the futures exchanges, for as long as a year, and occasionally even longer. In brief, although most of the coffee sold by growers in a given coffee year is processed and purchased for final consumption in that same year, a significant portion is not. This stored coffee, depending on world market price trends, may be a source of additional windfall profits, or losses, for exporters, importers, TNCs, or producing states who hold these stocks. There are no data available which would allow us to factor this complication into the calculations.

6. Brazil accounted for about one-third of total world production during the period considered here. Fluctuations in Brazilian production accounted for almost 70 percent of the variability in total world production over this period.

7. Table 7.2 shows a consumers' share about 5 percent lower than in table 7.1. This appears to be due to a change in the retail price series in the ICO data for the United States. Retail prices used in the calculations for table 7.1 are from the Market Research Corporation of America; those used for table 7.2 are from the Bureau of Labor Statistics of the U.S. Department of Labor. Differences in U.S. retail prices have a large influence on the weighted average because the United States accounted for about one-third of total world imports of coffee at this time.

8. These data do not tell the full story of the division of income in the early 1980s,

because of the two-tier market which opened after the quotas were reintroduced. The export and import unit values reported by the ICA for this period refer to the quota market, and so they overstate the income share of producers. See chapter 4 for details.

9. The LM data overestimate production costs for robusta producers, leading to negative estimates of total surplus and growers' shares. This overestimate seems based on unreasonably high estimated processing costs, but the source of this error can't be determined, since their methodology is not public. The editors of *Carta Cafetera* stated that the overestimates derived from errors in exchange rate conversion, but this doesn't explain why only the processing costs were affected.

10. Here I have assumed a conversion factor of 3 pounds of green coffee to one pound of instant, because the extraction rates were low in the early years of instant coffee. By 1978, extraction rates had improved, and this method probably overstates the import price of an equivalent amount of green coffee. For the green coffee price, I have used the New York price for "other milds" coffees (average of El Salvador, Guatemala, and Mexico) for 1956–1965, because most instant coffee imports were coming from Central America during this period. After 1965, most instant was imported from Brazil, so I have used the New York price for Brazils for 1966–1978.

11. See Talbot (1997) for more detailed data.

Chapter 8

Solutions? Specialty, Organic, and Fair-Trade Coffees

The previous chapters have analyzed struggles over the control of the coffee chain in the period since World War II. By the 1990s, these struggles had left the coffee TNCs in dominant positions and in control of most of the benefits available through participation in the chain. There seemed to be no way to reintroduce balance into the system, either through limiting the power of the TNCs, or through reintroducing some form of state regulation to counterbalance their power. As crises dragged on through the 1990s, activists concerned with the plight of small coffee farmers in poor countries turned their efforts to finding more market-based ways of redistributing benefits along the coffee chain.[1] This chapter considers the alternative marketing channels that developed as globalization spread, and that are increasingly looked to as a way out of the crisis: specialty, organic, and fair-trade coffees.

The Rise of Specialty Coffee

During the time of the national coffee companies, from the 1950s through the 1970s, price was the most important point of competition. The major companies strove to create brand loyalty, but they sought to entice consumers to try their brand initially because it was cheaper than their competitors'. This can be seen most clearly in the coffee price wars that Procter & Gamble touched off when they took their Folger's brand into the Eastern strongholds of General Foods' Maxwell House. But it is also apparent in the way the national companies competed against the smaller regional brands, eventually driving most of them out of business. Special promotional offers, cents-off coupons, and blanket advertising were the weapons in these price wars.

The focus on price led the coffee companies to look for the cheapest way possible to produce their coffee. This led first to the development of global sourcing strategies. Coffee companies looked for ways to produce a consistent blend of different types of coffee while getting each different type of coffee as cheaply as possible (see the discussion of the four different types of coffee in chapter 2). So, for instance, if a company's blend used a certain percentage of "other milds" coffee, and Salvadoran coffee was cheaper than Guatemalan or Costa Rican, that could be used. If cheaper "other mild" coffee became available from India, that could be substituted for the Salvadoran, and so on. The next step involved small changes in the blend itself. So, for instance, if a blend were based primarily on Brazils, the cost of the blend could be lowered by substituting a small proportion of African robustas for some of the Brazils. Other milds could be substituted for Colombian milds, and so on.

These measures allowed the major coffee companies to get small cost advantages on their competitors in the short run. And it enabled them to maintain a relatively consistent taste to their blend, in the short run. But over time, it led to a general cheapening of the blends, a general decline in the quality of coffee offered by all of the major companies (Pendergrast 1999). This trend was exacerbated by the coffee boom of 1976–1977, as consumers began to revolt at the huge increases in coffee prices. The coffee companies responded with some classical marketing gimmicks that amounted to telling consumers to brew weaker coffee. They switched from one-pound (16 ounce) cans to 13-ounce cans, in order to hold constant or minimize the increase in the price per can. Then they tried to convince consumers that they could brew just as many cups of coffee from the new 13-ounce cans as they could from the old one-pound cans. Folger's introduced a new, "flaked" coffee that they claimed had a higher yield than their old ground coffee (Pendergrast 1999). When prices began to go down after 1977, the companies generally stuck to their 13-ounce cans, and didn't go out of their way to encourage consumers to brew stronger coffee. This cheapening of the blends and weakening of the brews caused a general decline in the quality of supermarket brands of coffee, and, beginning in the 1960s, touched off a long-term decline in coffee consumption in the United States.[2] It also created conditions for the development of a new niche market that focused on taste rather than price.

Another key development was the transformation of the national coffee companies into global TNCs, handling massive volumes of coffee. As they began to produce their standard blends in larger and larger volumes, they began to demand, from coffee traders and producing countries, larger and larger quantities of coffee with consistent taste characteristics. Green coffee was increasingly treated as an industrial input. Consistency of taste in the blend became a more desired attribute than the taste itself; quantity trumped quality. The drive for technification by the Latin American producers helped to fill this need. In fact, one reason for the push for technification and its support by USAID probably was that it responded to the needs of the major coffee companies. Producing countries also were eager to adopt it in order to increase their yields, their production, and, they hoped, their profits, so it was not solely a response to the demands of the coffee companies. But the fact that the drive to increase yields by producers nicely dovetailed with the demands of the coffee companies probably helped to speed its adoption. There was, however, one problem: the taste of the high-yielding varieties was generally inferior to that of the traditional varieties that they replaced (Rice 1996). The older varieties had been developed for their taste; the newer varieties were bred primarily for productivity and resistance to disease. Taste was a secondary consideration, as long as the beans were acceptable to the TNCs. These new varieties produced larger volumes of coffee with consistent taste, but the taste was consistently mediocre.

The technification of coffee production has also had a number of negative environmental consequences. To understand these, it is necessary to understand how technification has changed the production of coffee. "Traditional" coffee production, in the areas of Latin America that have been affected by technification, involved mixed agriculture, in which coffee was planted under the shade of trees, such as plantain, banana or fruit trees, or other leguminous trees that fixed nitrogen in the soil. Coffee was also often interplanted with other food crops such as beans or tomatoes. This system had a variety of ecological benefits. The shade trees shed leaves, providing ground cover that kept weeds down as well as decaying to add organic matter back to the soil, acting as a natural fertilizer. This effect was enhanced by the leguminous trees that fixed nitrogen, thereby reducing or eliminating the need for fertilizer. The tree cover also provided a habitat for birds that fed on insects that attacked the coffee trees. The trees also produced some firewood, and the trees and other interplanted crops produced food for subsistence of the grower's family, or other crops that could be marketed between coffee harvests and in times of low coffee prices. "Modern" technified coffee production involves clearing the land and planting a monoculture of high-yielding coffee trees under direct sun. This allows the grower to plant coffee trees at a much higher density, and, with the higher yielding varieties, to obtain as much as six times more coffee per unit of land. But, with the natural fertilizers and pest control removed, the modern method, like all other green revolution technologies, requires much heavier inputs of chemical fertilizers and pesticides. The dense planting of coffee exhausts the soil more rapidly, increasing the need for fertilizer application. In addition, with the trees packed so closely together, it is much easier for diseases to spread once they get into a coffee field than was the case with the traditional method. Finally, the modern method doesn't produce any other crops that are useful to the grower (Rice and Ward 1996).

The environmental consequences of this change in production techniques have been serious. First, increased use of fertilizers means increased nitrate runoff into ground water and streams and other bodies of water. Second, increased use of pesticides has resulted in exposures of coffee workers and others to highly toxic chemicals, including some banned for use in the United States, because recommended protective gear is rarely provided. Coffee roasting usually burns off any pesticide residues on the green coffee beans, so, unlike many other fruit and vegetable crops produced with toxic chemicals in the Third World, the risk to coffee drinkers is slight. Third, the large-scale growing of coffee means large-scale processing. The wet method of processing, preferred in the areas that have been technified, uses large amounts of water, which are often discharged into local streams carrying organic pollutants. It also generates large volumes of coffee pulp, which produce additional organic pollutants. These problems are more easily handled when coffee is grown on a smaller scale. For instance, coffee pulp is often used as a natural fertilizer on small "traditional" farms. But when processing is done on a large scale, it generates too much pulp to be easily used, and the pulp is less effective than modern petrochemical-based fertilizers. Finally, traditional shade coffee provided a vital habitat for biodiversity, in an area where much of the natural forest cover had already been removed for intensive agriculture of other types. Studies have shown that traditional coffee production is very similar to natural forest cover, in terms of the variety of species it supports. In particular, it provides a habitat for many migratory songbirds common in North America. A series of studies by researchers at the Smithsonian Migratory Bird Center and others have linked the decline in North American songbirds to loss of habitat in the regions of Central America and northern South America, where these birds spend the winter (e.g., Perfecto et al. 1996; Greenberg, Bichier, and Sterling 1997; Rice and Ward 1996; Rice 1996; Wille 1994; Tangley 1996).

The technification of coffee production has also caused a polarization of the coffee sectors in some of the Latin American countries where this process has gone the farthest. Replanting with the new varieties required a large investment that took at least three years before it began to produce any returns. The size of the required investment was increased further by the necessity of applying fertilizers and pesticides. For these reasons, the switch to the new high-yielding varieties was only a possibility for medium-to-large growers, who had sufficient land planted in coffee to make the investment worthwhile, and access to credit to finance it. Smaller growers who couldn't afford to technify were further marginalized. They kept on producing coffee because the trees were there and kept bearing, and they could exploit family labor to pick it, but it became harder and harder to get a fair price for it.

All of these developments had cumulated by the 1980s to produce mediocre tasting supermarket blends of coffee and declining consumption. The stage was set for the development of a countertrend that would privilege quality over quantity, and in many ways return coffee to its roots, in the days before the rise of the big national roasters.

The pioneer in this development was a coffee roaster named Alfred Peet, who opened a small coffee shop, Peet's Coffee, in Berkeley, California in 1966. Peet bought the highest quality green coffee he could find, in small lots, roasted it individually in small batches, and then brewed it and sold it in his store. Through the late 1960s and the 1970s, a number of similar small, specialty coffee roasters went into business, mostly along the West Coast of the United States between San Francisco and Seattle. These specialty roasters were in many ways the negation of what the TNCs were becoming. They sought out the highest quality coffees from the different producing regions, regardless of price, and bought in small quantities to insure the highest quality. They roasted the coffee in small batches and saw coffee roasting as an art, the antithesis of the computer-controlled industrial process that roasting was becoming at the TNCs. And they sold the roasted coffee fresh, often roasting in small batches right in the store for immediate sale, as opposed to the vacuum-sealed cans of the TNCs, sitting on the supermarket shelves.

The specialty revolution took off slowly, but by the late 1980s it had become a booming business.[3] In 1979, there were 40 "micro-roasters" in the United States; by 1989, this number had risen to 385. In 1999, there were an estimated 1200 "roaster-retailers." Specialty coffee sales rose from $750 million in 1979, to $1.5 billion in 1989, and to $5.4 billion in 1999. By 1998, specialty coffee accounted for about 18 percent of total U.S. imports of green coffee (Andrews 1992; SCAA 1999). The specialty revolution was part of a larger revolution in consumption that was occurring at the same time, in which affluent and upwardly mobile groups sought to consume a variety of "special" products to display their urbane sophistication and good taste. In the face of a creeping standardization of class diets (Friedmann 1991a), coffee became a means for the elites in certain core countries to reassert class differences (Smith 1996; Reese 1996; Roseberry 1996). Coffee was a perfect product for this type of consumption, because it came from a number of "exotic" tropical countries, and allowed consumers to engage in a sort of vicarious tourism through the act of drinking coffee. This aspect of consumption was played up in the marketing of many of the specialty roasters, such as Starbucks (Smith 1996).

The specialty roasters were willing to pay higher prices to obtain the highest quality green coffees available, and were also able to charge their relatively affluent customers much higher prices for their hand-crafted, single-origin coffees than the TNCs charged for their standard industrial blends. The growing demand for high-quality coffee stimulated increasing supplies, and opened a new marketing channel. Specialty coffees are carefully tended, traditional (nontechnified) varieties produced in regions which are particularly well suited to coffee growing, such as the Antigua region of Guatemala or the Sulawesi highlands of Indonesia. Combinations of climate and soil characteristics in these regions produce fine coffees with distinctive flavor characteristics, analogous to the distinctive flavors of wines produced in famous European wine regions. Specialty roasters, as well as some growers, have sought to play on the cachet of wine estates by advertising coffees from particular "estates" in these regions; probably the most famous of these is La Minita in Costa Rica's Terrazú region. Since the high quality green coffee was generally only available in small lots, it was not very profitable for the large coffee traders to handle it. So the growth of specialty coffee opened a market niche for smaller coffee trading firms specializing in coffee, in contrast to the multi-commodity TNC traders that supplied the TNC manufacturers. As small traders and small roasters were driven out of the mass market by the national companies through the 1970s and by the TNCs in the 1980s, the specialty trade opened up an alternative marketing channel where smaller businesses could survive and even prosper.[4]

The specialty coffee revolution opened a direct connection between coffee growers and coffee roasters, where the connection had previously been more indirect. Coffee growers sold to processors and exporters, who sold to importers, who sold to the roasters. In this situation, many coffee growers often had only the vaguest idea of how the coffee was ultimately used by consumers (Weiss 1996).[5] They certainly had little idea of what aspects of taste in the cup the roasters and consumers were interested in, or what variations in the techniques of growing and processing the coffee would produce them. The big coffee companies had never cared about these things; they were interested in large quantities of consistent (not necessarily high) quality at a low price, and this is what most growers were producing. So the specialty roasters began to travel to the producing regions, to talk to growers and see how the coffee was being produced, in order to increase the supplies of the high quality coffee they wanted to buy. This transfer of information about demand in the consuming markets, plus the knowledge that the specialty roasters were willing to pay extra for quality, allowed the coffee growers to respond. Growers and roasters began to work together to improve coffee quality. While many specialty roasters now deal directly with coffee growers, the coffee is still shipped by exporters and importers, who have the necessary expertise in handling, financing, and insurance for international trade.

The rise of specialty coffee as a reaction against the industrial standardization of the TNCs has thus produced two parallel segments of the coffee commodity chain. Industrial coffees are grown at lower cost with lower quality standards, although producing states do need to make some effort to standardize them to TNC specifications. They are shipped in bulk by the TNC importers, blended and roasted by the manufacturing TNCs, and sold on the mass market, mainly through supermarkets. Specialty coffees are carefully tended, produced in smaller quantities at higher cost, and with more direct involvement of the specialty roasters in quality control within the producing countries. They are imported by smaller traders, roasted in small batches by the specialty roasters, and sold for the most part in small specialty shops.[6]

As the specialty marketing channel has grown and become more profitable, it has also been taken over to some degree by coffee TNCs. This has happened in two ways: the industrial coffee TNCs have added specialty lines to their established brands, and a few specialty companies have grown into TNCs. Procter & Gamble has acquired Millstone Coffee, and Sara Lee acquired Café au Lait, a food service specialty company. Nestlé ventured into the specialty market by purchasing Sark's Gourmet Coffees, but later discontinued the brand. The TNCs have also developed lines of specialty instant coffees, such as General Foods International Coffees. The TNCs' specialty lines are sold mainly through supermarkets, alongside the industrial blends. Supermarket chains such as Safeway, and discount chains such as Price Club and Costco, have also developed their own house brands of specialty coffees. As these developments create a demand for larger volumes of specialty green coffees, quality may become compromised in the same way it has been in the supermarket brands. In addition, the development of flavored coffees allows lower quality coffee to be sold as specialty, because the flavoring covers up the taste of the coffee itself.

The most obvious example of a specialty company grown into a TNC is Starbucks. Starbucks began as a specialty roaster in Seattle's Pike Place Market in 1971. In 1987, Howard Schultz took it over and transformed it from a regional specialty company with 17 stores into a transnational with over 5000 stores and sales of $3.3 billion worldwide in 2002. Starbucks grew through an aggressive strategy of opening stores in new locations, but this strategy also included aggressive competition against other specialty companies. When Starbucks moved into a new city, it often located its store in the same block as, or across the street from, an established, smaller specialty roaster. In addition to trying to drive the competition out of business, it has also taken over some competitors, acquiring Coffee Connection in 1994, Pasqua Coffee and Seattle Coffee Company (U.K.) in 1998, and the Tazo tea company in 1999. It has formed partnerships and joint ventures with other TNCs. In 1996, it formed a joint venture with Pepsico to sell its Frappuccino drink, and a partnership with Dreyer's Grand Ice Cream to sell Starbucks coffee ice cream (both sold mainly through supermarkets). In 1998, it made a deal with Philip Morris, to get Starbucks coffee into supermarkets. There are other specialty TNCs, such as Diedrich (Coffee People, Coffee Plantation, and Gloria Jean's) and AFC (Seattle's Best Coffee), but they are dwarfed by Starbucks.[7] Although the volume of green coffee that Starbucks handles comes nowhere near that of the industrial coffee TNCs, it is still difficult to maintain high quality standards when dealing with the volumes of coffee that Starbucks does.

Organic and Fair-Trade Coffees

With these trends in place, the stage was set for the rise of organic and fair-trade coffees in the 1990s. Two additional developments in the core consuming countries also played an important role: the growth of the environmental movement and in particular, the organic farming movement; and the growth of the fair-trade movement, centered initially on handicrafts produced in the Third World.

Fair-trade coffee developed earlier than organic, mainly through the efforts of European activists concerned with development in Europe's former colonies.[8] They began to set up alternative trading organizations (ATOs) in European countries in the 1950s, to sell products produced in the Third World at prices that guaranteed the producers a fair return on their labor. The first fair-trade initiative in coffee was launched in the Netherlands by the Max Havelaar Institute. This initiative was designed to go beyond the alternative trade model of selling products in small fair-trade shops. The Max Havelaar fair-trade seal was offered to large national roasters if they would agree to buy some of their coffee on fair-trade terms. They could purchase the right to apply the seal to an amount of their roasted coffee equivalent to the amount of green coffee they purchased through fair trade. They could then charge more for this coffee, to recover their higher green coffee costs. The consumer, who paid more for the coffee, was assured that the difference in price was being returned to the coffee growers. The initial success of Max Havelaar led to the establishment of a similar certification in Germany, called TransFair.

This idea was slower to catch on in the United States. The first fair-trade coffee company in the United States was Equal Exchange, founded in 1986. It was an outgrowth of the Central American solidarity movement, and its initial goal was to circumvent President Reagan's embargo on trade with the Sandinista regime in Nicaragua. Equal Exchange exploited a loophole in the law that allowed Nicaraguan coffee roasted in Canada to be considered a Canadian product, not subject to embargo. Equal Exchange expanded from these beginnings to importing fairly traded coffees from other producing countries, although it did not seek fair-trade certification on the European model. There were ATOs established in the United States as well, most notably Global Exchange, but they focused on handicrafts and did not move into coffee as quickly as the European ATOs. However, in the mid-1990s, Global Exchange did play a key role in the founding of a national fair-trade organization on the European model. TransFair USA was founded in 1996, and TransFair certified coffee has become available in the United States in the last three to four years. Equal Exchange now has TransFair certification.

The idea that caught on more quickly in the United States was organic coffee. The organic movement was much larger than the fair-trade movement, but it also took longer to catch on in coffee. The organic movement grew out of a reaction against the mechanization of agriculture begun in the 1930s and 1940s in the United States. Along with that mechanization went increased application of fertilizers and other chemicals, and the organic movement arose out of the criticisms of the negative health and environmental consequences of this new production system. By 1972, the organic movement was an international institution, with the founding of IFOAM, the International Federation of Organic Agriculture Movements. IFOAM began issuing standards for production to be certified as organic in 1980, but it wasn't until 1995 that specific standards for organic coffee production were issued. However, coffee labeled as organic was being imported into the United States well before this.

While the specialty coffee revolution was initiated by people who were involved in the coffee industry, organic and fair-trade coffees were originally developed by people with no experience in coffee, for other political motives; environmental for the former, and economic development for the latter. Thus, while organic and fair-trade coffees have eventually found a home within the specialty sector, it has been a difficult marriage. The specialty roasters were motivated primarily by quality and taste. For the organic and fair-trade movements, now often lumped together under the umbrella label of sustainable coffee, quality and taste were secondary to the environmental and economic characteristics of the coffee. So, much of the early sustainable coffee didn't taste very good, and specialty roasters refused to carry it for that reason.[9] This led to a refrain repeated by several key figures in the specialty trade: "no coffee is 'sustainably' produced if it is not, first and foremost, a great-tasting coffee" (Castle 2001). Further, the specialty roasters worried that if they carried fair-trade or organic coffees, it would implicitly cast aspersions on their other coffees. Consumers might begin to question whether their other specialty coffees were environmentally harmful, or produced by exploited peasants (Castle 2001).

As a result of these initial conflicts, the sustainable coffee people came to understand the importance of quality and taste. And as the organic and fair-trade movements grew in the 1990s, some of the more socially conscious consumers of specialty coffee began to ask for sustainable coffees. Most specialty roaster-retailers now do carry some kind of sustainable coffee (Giovannucci 2001). However, there are still some bad feelings on both sides.[10]

There is no good data on the total volumes of coffee flowing through these alternative marketing channels; however, one recent survey (Giovannucci 2001) has estimated that, in the year 2000, about 9 million pounds of certified organic coffee were sold in the North American market, and about 15–18 million pounds were sold globally. It estimated 4.7 million pounds of fair-trade coffee were sold in North America and 29.1 million pounds globally. These figures, combined, represent considerably less than 1 percent of the North American and global coffee markets. These estimates confirm the predominance of the United States in the organic coffee market—U.S. sales account for at least 50 percent of total worldwide sales. Meanwhile, U.S. sales of fair trade coffee account for only about 15 percent of total worldwide sales, because fair-trade sales are much higher in Europe.

This geographic difference in the way that organic and fair-trade coffees have developed has led to a difference in the geographic locations of organic and fair-trade production. Organic coffee has been much more a North American initiative, and almost all organic production is located in Latin America. In 1999, it was estimated that 85 percent of the world's certified organic production was in Latin America, and 45 percent of it was in Mexico. Most of the rest was in Indonesia and Papua New Guinea; there was no certified organic production in Africa. For example, ISMAM (Indigenas de la Sierra Madre de Motozintla), a cooperative of over 1000 small-scale Mayan coffee growers in Chiapas, is the world's leading exporter of organic coffee (Nigh 1997). On the other hand, since the fair-trade movement started in Europe, there are many fair-trade coffee producers in Africa, although the majority of fair-trade coffee still comes from Latin America (which still accounts for the majority of world coffee production). The separate development of organic and fair-trade coffees has also led to a dual certification system, with different criteria and different certifying organizations for the two, despite the fact that there is substantial overlap: 40–50 percent of the world's organic coffee is produced by small growers' cooperatives on the International Fair-Trade Register.

Benefits of Organic and Fair-Trade Coffees

The most fundamental criterion for organic production of coffee, and other crops, is that no chemical fertilizers or pesticides can be applied, and initial certification requires repeated testing over a period of time to insure that there are no chemical residues in the soil. But the organic standards go far beyond this. Specifically, for coffee, IFOAM has developed a general set of guidelines that can be adapted to the specific conditions of coffee growing in different parts of the world. They include clearing and planting of land in ways that have minimal environmental impacts and prevent erosion; planting under shade whenever possible, building the soil by adding organic matter, promotion of ecological diversity, and recycling of processing wastes such as coffee pulp. They also require adherence to local laws regarding wages and working conditions (Rice and McLean 1999).

One of the major benefits of organic coffee is clearly environmental. However, it is really more a matter of maintaining the environment as it is, rather than significantly improving it. Most growers who go for organic certification are already producing in near-organic ways. While their conversion to organic does benefit the environment, the improvements are relatively marginal. The producers who have already technified their production are not rushing to convert to organic production. However, organic production does help to slow or stop the spread of technification. The growers earn more for producing organic coffee, but how much more depends on their marketing arrangements. Rice and McLean (1999) estimated the growers' premium at between 5 and 20 cents per pound. For fair-trade coffee that is also organic, the premium is set at 15 cents per pound. At a time when growers are receiving an average of only about 41 cents per pound for regular coffee (table 7.2), this is a significant premium.

The most important principle of fair-trade coffee is the minimum price, which is currently $1.26 per pound. However, this is the fob price (see chapter 7), and taking into consideration the costs of getting the coffee to port, about $1.00 gets back to the grower.[11] In the current market, this is still more than double the growers' price for non-fair-trade coffee. Only coffee produced by small growers organized into democratically run coops can be certified as fair trade. In addition, the buyers of fair-trade coffee commit to establishing long-term relationships with their suppliers, so that growers can count on a steady source of income. Finally, the buyers must provide credit, up to 60 percent of the value of the contract, at low interest, to the growers at the beginning of the season. This is an important requirement, because the grower incurs most of his or her expenses in the maintenance and harvesting of the coffee, before it is sold. Many small growers are forced to borrow from local buyers at usurious rates, or to sell their crop in advance at a very low price, because of the timing of these expenses. This requirement insures that growers are not put in a position of having to sell at a loss. In practice, however, once a growers' coop has established a relationship with a fair-trade buyer, the credit is usually not needed (Rice and McLean 1999; Waridel 2002).

Contradictions of Organic and Fair-Trade Coffees

These developments seem positive, and seem to offer some hope that globalization will allow consumers to connect more directly to coffee producers, in ways that counteract some of the worst negative consequences of globalization. However, fair-trade and organic coffees are also caught in a number of contradictions because they are still products of a globalized marketplace. Five of these contradictions, the yuppie syndrome, the oversupply problem, the tyranny of the "C" contract, the exclusiveness of certification, and bluewash, are discussed below.

The yuppie syndrome refers to the fact that these are niche products pitched at upscale markets. They are designed for more affluent consumers who define and display their value and their values through consumption. They will always have to be priced higher than the standard supermarket blends of coffee; this is inherent in the nature of the products. Fair-trade coffee, by definition, guarantees a fair return to the producer. To the extent that globalization has shifted the balance of power to TNCs and enabled them to drive down the prices of their raw materials, world market prices will never be fair prices. Arguably, organic coffee could be cheaper to produce in the long run, and therefore could be priced less than standard coffees. However, this will only occur when the full costs of industrialized production methods, including environmental damage and loss of biodiversity, are internalized in the price of coffee, an unlikely development as long as TNCs hold the balance of power. As long as these products are higher priced, they will not be a realistic option for a large percentage of the population who are living from paycheck to paycheck (and increasingly, not quite making it to the next paycheck). They will continue to be luxury items that exist alongside, without directly threatening the profitability of, the standard products of the TNCs.

At the production end of the chain, the yuppie syndrome generates an *oversupply problem*. Because the prices of organic, and especially of fair-trade, coffees are higher than world market prices, coffee growers would prefer to sell to these markets. This is less of a problem for organic coffee, because the price differential is smaller and the certification more costly. But there is currently more fair-trade coffee being produced than can be sold through the existing fair-trade channels, and the surplus is being sold at regular prices (Oxfam 2001). Fair-trade activists have turned their attention to increasing the demand for fair-trade coffee in the core markets. In 2000, under pressure from Global Exchange and other activists, Starbucks began selling fair-trade coffee beans in its stores. In 2001, it announced a commitment to buy one million pounds of fair-trade coffee over the following 18 months. On the one hand, this represents a very small fraction of Starbucks total coffee purchases. TransFair USA generally requires companies to commit to buying a minimum of 5 percent of their coffee through fair trade in order to use the TransFair label; Starbucks' commitment fell far below this level. On the other hand, TransFair was willing to make an exception for Starbucks because their commitment meant a significant increase in the total demand for fair trade. The largest fair-trade purchaser in the United

States, Equal Exchange, bought 1.2 million pounds in 2001.[12] More generally, simply raising the prices paid to growers without doing anything to control the amount of coffee being produced is an ultimately self-defeating strategy, as the history of the ICAs during the 1980s demonstrates.

The tyranny of the "C" contract (Rice and McLean 1999, 21) refers to the fact that world market coffee prices are still set with reference to the New York "C" coffee futures contract, and this influences the prices of all coffees traded internationally. Organic producers are typically paid a premium of 5 to 20 cents per pound above the price paid for regular coffee of the same type, but the regular price for that type is still set at a differential to the "C" contract price. Fair-trade producers are guaranteed a price floor, so that they receive a certain minimum price for their coffee even when world market prices are very low. This would seem to insulate them from the tyranny of the "C," and it does, but only to a limited extent. The prices of both organic and fair-trade coffees to the consumer are constrained somewhat by the prices of the TNC blends. While the types of consumers who purchase these coffees are willing to pay more, many of them are not willing to pay a lot more. The higher the price differential between organic and fair-trade coffees and the supermarket brands, the smaller the market will be, and the less will be the chances of attracting new consumers. Products being produced with an element of nonmarket logic (because protecting the environment or the livelihoods of coffee growers are seen as having intrinsic value) are still being priced in the market; in effect, the market determines the "price" of treating coffee producers and the environment fairly, and this "price" sets limits on how fairly they can be treated (Renard 1999).

The exclusiveness of certification refers to the fact that both organic and fair-trade certification tend to exclude certain groups from their benefits. Certification costs money. Consumers who are paying extra to buy coffee that is organically produced or fairly traded justifiably want to be sure they're getting what they paid for. With no standards and no certification, it would be easy for roasters to label products as organic or fair trade and charge more, even when they weren't. This certification needs to be done by a third party, independent of growers and importers, and that third party has to be paid for its services. Organic certification involves repeated visits to the farms where the coffee is grown, expensive lab tests to test for chemical residues, etc. It is much more costly, and the cost must be borne, at least initially, by the grower. In addition, there are usually some costs of converting to organic production. In the long run, the costs are offset by the higher price the grower receives for the coffee. But certification requires an initial investment before any price increase occurs. It thus potentially excludes many small growers who cannot afford certification. This is particularly ironic, because the smaller growers are more likely to be producing in a way that approximates organic production. Many small growers plant under shade, use minimal fertilizers and pesticides because they're too expensive, and couldn't increase their incomes through technification because they couldn't afford the initial investment; now they are also being excluded from being rewarded for their ecologically sound production methods by the cost of certification. The other side of the irony is that very large producers, who could afford to technify their production, could also afford to convert some of their best land to organic production and take advantage of the higher prices this brings.[13] In theory, large producers could benefit from both of these opposing developments, while small producers with limited capital are excluded from both.

The exclusiveness of certification works differently for fair-trade coffee. Fair-trade certification is less costly than organic, and the cost of certification is typically paid by the importers and roasters who want to use the fair-trade seal on the coffee they sell. However, one of the main criteria for producers to be certified as fair-trade producers is that they be small growers organized into democratically run co-ops. Fair trade thus does nothing for the workers on large coffee plantations, who often are poorly paid and live in conditions much worse than small coffee growers. Fair-trade certifiers for other tropical products such as tea and bananas deal with plantations that allow workers to join democratic, independent unions and bargain over wages and working conditions. However, these are products produced primarily on plantations; certifiers have chosen to focus on small growers for coffee because they produce the majority of the world's coffee (Rice and McLean 1999).

Bluewash is a derivative of greenwash. Greenwash is a term that was developed in the 1970s to refer to the advertising practices of large corporations, particularly the oil companies, which found themselves under attack for their poor environmental records. These corporations developed aggressive public relations strategies that involved spending small amounts of money on environmental projects and large amounts of money publicizing the fact. This counteracted the negative image that the corporations had achieved for environmental damage they had caused, and allowed them to continue their environmentally unsound practices. Bluewash (derived from the color of the UN flag) involves the same strategy in response to criticisms of poor social and human rights records. The increasing popularity of fair-trade and organic coffees presents opportunities for bluewash. Two examples from Starbucks illustrate this. In 1995, protests were organized against Starbucks because of the deplorable living conditions of workers who picked coffee on plantations from which Starbucks bought some of its Guatemalan coffee. Starbucks responded by developing a code of conduct for its coffee suppliers and widely publicizing this fact. However, this has had very little impact on the lives of coffee pickers in Guatemala. First of all, this is an internal company policy, and there is no third party verification. Further, Starbucks has refused to drop suppliers who violate the code. Second, Starbucks buys through exporters in Guatemala and importers in the United States, and admits that it doesn't know where all of its coffee comes from. It has to rely on the word of the exporters that the coffee comes from plantations where the code of conduct is followed. It has plausible deniability if any violations do come to light. When critics called attention to the fact that regular violations were occurring, Starbucks responded with another program in association with Appropriate Technology International, to improve the processing facilities available to small farmers in Guatemala. The problem is that this program does absolutely nothing for the coffee pickers on the large plantations, who are the worst treated.[14] Starbucks gets a positive public image, and the coffee business goes on in Guatemala as usual. This is bluewash. More recently, Starbucks' announcements about its recent commitments to sell fair-trade coffee (which was also certified organic), discussed above, have followed a similar strategy. Although these commitments did not change the way in which well over 95 percent of Starbucks coffee is produced and purchased, the company has gone out of its way to publicize them, and company spokespersons are quick to cite them whenever Starbucks' purchasing practices are criticized.[15]

The growth of specialty, organic and fair-trade coffees, and the direct contacts they have opened up between Third World producers and First World consumers, are positive outcomes of increasing globalization. However, organic and fair-trade coffees are caught up in a series of contradictions that arise from their incorporation of non-market logic into a globalized world market. In these conditions, it seems unlikely that they can offer a real alternative to the market power of the TNCs. They are likely to remain small and relatively marginalized niche markets, even as some of their rhetoric is appropriated by the TNCs for use as marketing gimmicks and bluewash. This does not mean that you shouldn't buy organic or fair-trade coffee; undoubtedly they have helped many coffee growers and workers survive through the coffee crises of the 1990s. But organic and fair-trade coffees, by themselves, are not a solution to the crises. More far-reaching measures are needed. The concluding chapter outlines the kinds of measures that will be needed to restore some balance and fairness to the coffee commodity chain.

Notes

1. Christopher London, personal communication, August 23, 2000.

2. Of course, the decline in coffee quality was not the only reason for decreasing consumption. Aggressive marketing by soft drink companies, particularly Pepsi and Coca-Cola, also drew consumers away from coffee.

3. Specialty coffee sales include sales of whole bean specialty coffee as well as sales of brewed coffee in coffee shops. They also include sales of flavored coffees, as well as the various types of specialty coffees sold through supermarkets (discussed below).

4. This is not to say that the same small trading and roasting companies continued in existence over this period by switching from industrial to specialty coffee; as in all economic sectors, small businesses are continually being formed and going out of business. However, many of the "coffee people" employed in small businesses that went out of business in the 1970s began new specialty trading and roasting companies in the 1980s.

5. There are exceptions to this in the coffee producing countries where there is also significant coffee consumption, most notably, Brazil, but also other Latin American countries such as Colombia. But in many coffee growing countries, coffee is grown for export and is not consumed locally.

6. Despite the differences in these two growing styles, there is no necessary correla-

tion between growing style and the scale on which the coffee is grown. Industrial coffee can be grown on large farms or plantations intensively planted with high-yielding varieties, or by smallholders using more traditional methods. Specialty coffee can be grown on large modern farms (sometimes even on the prime portions of large farms which also produce industrial coffee), or by small peasant coops.

7. Mark Pendergrast, "The Starbucks Experience Going Global," *Tea and Coffee Trade Journal* February 2002, pp. 17–24; Chris Lee, "The Fight for Number Two," *Tea and Coffee Trade Journal* June 1999, pp. 27–36; *Seattle Times* November 4, 2001; *Business Wire* October 3, 2002; Starbucks Web site, www.starbucks.com/aboutus/timeline.asp.

8. Information on organic and fair-trade coffees in this section, unless otherwise cited, is drawn from Rice and McLean, 1999.

9. I'm indebted to Christopher London and April Linton for pointing this out to me.

10. See, for example, Donald Schoenholt, "The Fair Trade Ideal," *Tea and Coffee Trade Journal* November 2001, pp. 103–5.

11. Christopher London, personal communication, August 23, 2000.

12. Oxfam U.K. 2001; James 2000; Levi and Linton 2003; *Business Week* September 9, 2002; "Close, But No Cigar," statement by Deborah James, Global Exchange Fairtrade Director, October 22, 2001, available from the Global Exchange Web site, www .globalexchange.org/economy/coffee/news2001.

13. This is a parallel of the movement of some large transnational agribusiness TNCs, such as Dole, into organic production.

14. *Seattle Times* October 24, 1995, p. E1; February 28, 1997, p. D1; *Toronto Star* September 28, 1997, p. F1; *Journal of Commerce* March 7, 1997, p. 1A.

15. To be fair to Starbucks, it is better than the TNCs. It is more socially responsible and pays higher prices for the higher quality coffees it sells. Starbucks makes an easier target because of its high visibility, and because it is primarily a coffee company, while coffee is a minor product of the giant food processing TNCs that dominate the market. However, Starbucks also trades on its socially responsible image, making it seem more hypocritical when such facts come to light.

Conclusion

Toward a Reregulated Market

This book has presented an historical analysis of the coffee commodity chain. I hope that it proves useful in two ways. First, it provides some historical context for understanding the current coffee crisis. It uncovers the roots of the crisis, in changes in the structure and governance of the chain over the post–World War II period. Further, it links those changes to changes in the structure of the larger world economy of which it is a part. An understanding of this history is needed in order to find a way out of the crisis. Second, it illustrates the usefulness of the commodity chain approach for analyzing the structure of the world economy, by applying it to one of the historically most important commodities traded on the world market. Given this dual purpose, the conclusion has two parts. The first proposes a long-term solution to the coffee crisis, and the second sums up the lessons of this analysis for the further development of the commodity chain approach.

A Modest Proposal to Resolve the Coffee Crisis

As the preceding analysis has shown, the coffee crises of the 1990s and early 2000s have been caused by structural imbalances in the coffee commodity chain. As long as these imbalances are not addressed, the crises are likely to continue. Temporary shortages may cause price spikes, during which prices will be high for a brief period, as in 1994. But the long-term outlook is for continued misery for millions of people in the coffee growing regions of the world. Specialty, fair trade, and organic coffees are important ways for some consumers to support coffee growers; and they have helped many, but still only a minority, of the people who work to produce our coffee. A real resolution of the crisis requires structural change. In this section of the conclusion, I will outline the kinds of

213

structural changes that I believe are needed.

The most apparent imbalance in the coffee commodity chain today is between supply and demand—there is a structural oversupply of coffee in the world. I have used the term *structural* oversupply to emphasize that this is not a situation of temporary overshoot by producers that will be corrected by market forces. If that were the case, the correction would have already happened, after several years of disastrously low prices. Even if, in the next few years, coffee production does begin to decline as many small growers are driven out of business and off their land, this will produce only a temporary shortage and a temporary price boom. As soon as prices rise above the cost of production again, the oversupply will return. This is the sense in which it is structural—over the long term, supply and demand are unlikely to come into equilibrium.

In chapter 4, the structural oversupply condition of the 1980s was traced to a combination of four factors: the response of coffee growers to periodic high prices, but particularly to the coffee boom of the mid-1970s, which led to overplanting; the technification of coffee production which greatly increased the yields of land already planted in coffee; the structural adjustment programs of the World Bank and IMF, which forced countries to increase their production of coffee and other commodities in order to service their debts; and the rules of the ICA, which gave producing countries an incentive to produce at levels above their quotas, in order to argue for increased quotas. By the 1990s, only one of these factors had disappeared—the ICA quota rules. The response of coffee growers, particularly in Vietnam and Brazil, to the high prices of 1994 is a major factor in the current crisis; the pressure to export and earn foreign exchange is, if anything, more severe; and technification has continued. And without the restraining effects of the ICA quota system, the combination of the other pressures has created a kind of "race to the bottom," a competition among coffee producers to produce the cheapest coffee possible.

The supply-demand imbalance, however, is only the most apparent one. A more fundamental underlying imbalance is one of power, between small coffee growers at one end of the chain and huge transnational corporations at the other. The TNC coffee manufacturers are, on the one hand, oligopolistic suppliers of coffee to the major consuming markets, and, on the other, oligopsonistic buyers of the coffee being produced by the small growers. This strategic position in the coffee chain has allowed the TNCs to ratchet up the prices of coffee products in the consuming markets while driving down world market prices for green coffee, opening up a huge profit margin. The TNCs are able to use their financial power and their access to the futures markets to protect themselves from price fluctuations, and even to use the volatility of the market to their advantage. The small coffee growers have no such protection.

The small growers did, at one time, have some degree of protection from the volatility of the market and the power of the TNCs. This protection came from their states, which were involved, individually and collectively, in regulating the market. Collective regulation, in the form of the ICAs, stabilized world market prices and kept them at a reasonably equitable level. Within the international context of the ICAs, state regulation of the internal production system enabled producing countries to meet their obligations under the ICAs, stabilize the prices paid to growers, and provide a number of services to them. Undoubtedly, in some countries, this state regulation turned predatory, as inefficient or corrupt marketing systems resulted in very low prices to growers. However, when the World Bank and IMF used the period of low prices in the early 1990s as a rationale for attacking all state coffee agencies indiscriminately, in the name of freeing the market, they threw out the baby with the proverbial bathwater. There clearly were reasons to reform a number of these agencies; there was little reason to eliminate all of them. In many cases, private exporters (some the subsidiaries of the TNC trading companies) have proven to be just as predatory as the old state marketing boards. The states were the only organizations in the producing countries with sufficient power to counterbalance the power of the TNCs. The states served as a buffer between the small growers and the power of the TNCs, and the elimination of this buffer has resulted in the huge power imbalance that exists in the coffee chain today.

The power imbalance is a cause of the supply-demand imbalance, because without state intervention, the small growers have no means of coordinating their production decisions or of bargaining with the TNCs to obtain fair prices. In such a "free" market, tree crop price cycles will occur. The power of the TNCs (based on market position and access to finance and information) will allow them to respond to temporary shortages and high prices by setting their wholesale prices *even higher*. As growers respond to the high prices, the TNCs (aided by the World Bank and IMF) will encourage competition between coffee growing countries to produce more coffee, more cheaply, which will bring on a prolonged period of oversupply and low prices. This, in a nutshell, is what has been happening since 1989. Any real resolution of the coffee crisis will have to come to terms with these structural imbalances.

The ICO is now moving to address the supply-demand imbalance with a coffee quality program. The current race to the bottom has produced some very cheap, very poor quality coffee. Coffee trees are being poorly maintained, which lowers productivity and quality. Coffee trees are stripped, rather than selectively picked, mixing together ripe and unripe cherries, which negatively affects the taste of the coffee. Coffee is being improperly cleaned, leaving sticks and partially fermented beans in the product. Coffee is being improperly dried, resulting in mold formation, which again affects taste. The coffee quality initiative seeks to impose minimum quality standards on all exported coffee. By rendering the lowest quality coffees now being produced unexportable, this initiative would decrease the supply on the market and bring it back into balance with demand, thereby raising the price. The quality program is a worthwhile solution for the short term, but it will not solve the problem in the longer term unless the power imbalance is addressed. Growers will bring their production up to the minimum quality standard, and the race to the bottom will resume, from a slightly higher level.

Ultimately, I believe, the solution must involve a return to some form of market regulation—a new International Coffee Agreement. Export controls worked in the past, but they proved ineffective in the face of the structural tendencies toward oversupply. In the current market situation, production controls are needed. World demand for coffee is relatively stable and unresponsive to price; it can be predicted fairly accurately well in advance. The problem is to bring potentially volatile production into rough balance with stable demand. Ideally, total world production could be set at a level slightly above total consumption, so that some coffee could be stored to cover shortages when the next natural disaster strikes. Excess production could be managed through a system of export controls or a centrally managed coffee stockpile. Although export controls proved insufficient in the face of structural oversupply in the 1980s, they would be effective in combination with production controls. Although a centrally managed buffer stock would not work in the long run with uncontrolled production, it could be effective in combination with production controls. Once the controls were in place, production could be gradually increased to keep pace with slowly increasing world consumption.

First, ICO members would have to agree upon a price range for the world market price of coffee that was both reasonable for consumers and fair for producers. Keeping in mind that a grower must maintain and harvest one tree for one year to produce a pound of coffee, a price in the range of the current fair trade price, $1.26 per pound, is not unreasonable. Since world demand can be predicted fairly accurately, world demand and the agreed-upon price range would determine a total world quota for coffee exports. So far, this is exactly the procedure that was used under the old ICAs. From this, a total world level for export production[1] could be determined, at, say, world demand plus 0.5 percent, in order to have coffee on hand in the case of sudden shortages, caused by frost or drought in Brazil, or other natural disasters. Export quotas would force producers to store their overproduction, or the storage of this buffer supply could be centrally managed by the ICO.

Allocating total world production among producing countries would be the most politically challenging task in a new ICA. It would be difficult precisely because coffee is a key crop and source of livelihood for so many people in developing countries, and each government would want to maximize its economic benefits by having a larger production quota. Part of the problem with the old ICAs was that "historic" market shares were frozen into the agreements and became very difficult to change; the prolonged period of an unregulated market has erased that history. Current levels of demand for the four main types of coffee could provide a guide for this allocation, and producers within each type would then have to decide on how to divide up production among themselves. Production controls would necessitate a cutback of production in many participating countries, and financial assistance would be required to manage the transition. The most feasible source of initial funding for the transition would be the windfall profits of the coffee TNCs. Once the plan was in operation, modest export taxes imposed by producing states could support coffee agencies providing extension services to growers, with a proportion of these taxes contributed to an adjustment fund. The adjustment fund would allow the production of different types of coffee to be changed in response to changes in world demand for these different types. Changes in world demand would be indicated by changing prices in the world market; the prices of those types for which demand was increasing would rise, while prices for those types less in demand would fall. Grants from the fund could be given to countries producing types for which world demand was declining (e.g., robustas) to allow them to phase out some of their production. Countries receiving increased production quotas would also increase their contributions to the adjustment fund. New countries that wanted to start exporting coffee could buy a share of the global quota by contributing to this fund, and this money could be used to phase out comparable production elsewhere. This adjustment fund would be similar to the Diversification Fund that was part of the 1968 ICA (see chapter 3), except that grants from the fund would be driven by market "selectivity" rather than by diversification project proposals submitted by producing countries. In any case, cutbacks in coffee production should not take the form of "diversification" into other related crops, such as cocoa or tea, which are also in oversupply on world markets as a result of World Bank/IMF pressures to expand exports during the 1980s and 1990s. Rather, production controls should probably be extended to some of these crops as well.

The major consuming countries would all have to participate in and enforce this regime, so that very little coffee could be sold outside it. They would have to agree to import coffee only from producers who were participants in the agreement. Otherwise, there would be an incentive for "pirate" producers to arise and subvert the controls by underselling the participating producers. Controls would also be needed to stop "tourist coffee" from passing through any consuming countries that remained outside the agreement and into the quota markets. Once again, this is similar to the system of ICO certificates of origin that was in effect under the quota system in the 1980s. That system was ineffective in stopping "tourist coffee" under conditions of structural oversupply, but should work with production quotas in place. Finally, consuming state participation would be needed in order to collect taxes on the windfall profits of the coffee TNCs, to get the adjustment fund started.

Coffee growers would realize higher prices through this system. With production controls in place, they should be encouraged and assisted, through the state coffee agencies, to invest some of their profits in improving the quality of their coffees and in shifting to environmentally sustainable production. They should also be assisted in investing some of the profits in other economic activities that will reduce their dependence on coffee as a cash crop.

Is this plan politically feasible? Although it will be difficult to find grounds for agreement under current conditions, I believe that it is. Most of the elements of the plan proposed here have been included in some form in some previous ICAs; others, like production controls, have been discussed in previous negotiations. The producing countries are being hurt badly by the current crisis. Another Polanyian double movement is underway, as coffee growers press the producing states to do something to resolve the crisis. They have taken a first step in agreeing to the ICO quality improvement program. If they really understand the structural roots of the crisis, and realize that any future price spikes will be brief and will only lead to renewed crisis under the current conditions, I believe that they will be able to come to agreement on production quotas.

Are the major consuming countries likely to agree to re-regulate the world coffee market? The European states and Japan were prepared to agree to a new ICA in 1993, but the United States again blocked an agreement. Japan and the European countries generally provide much higher levels of official development assistance (relative to GDP) than the United States. Recognizing the seriousness of the current crisis, they would probably agree to a new regime to aid producing countries. WTO negotiations have stalled as Third World countries have refused to discuss extending the free trade regime until they see some benefits from it. A new ICA would be one way of providing such benefits. The United States, and the transnational coffee giants that have considerable influence over U.S. policy, were the major obstacles to agreement in 1989 and 1993, and they would again be the major obstacles. However, a combination of collective pressure from coffee producing states, supported by some developed countries, as well as pressure from U.S. citizens, could convince U.S. policy makers to acquiesce to renewed regulation.

U.S. consumers have already responded overwhelmingly in surveys that they would be willing to pay more for clothing if they were guaranteed that it wasn't made in sweatshops (Bonacich and Appelbaum 2000, 298). They would probably also be willing to pay more for coffee if they could be assured that their money was going to support small farmers and coffee workers, and their families. Sales of fair-trade coffee have been growing rapidly since it was introduced in the United States in 1998; it already has a small but significant market share in Europe. Consumer pressure has forced Starbucks and Sara Lee to begin offering fair-trade coffees. Pressure by consumers and citizens who understand the devastating effects of the current crisis could change U.S. government policy to support a new ICA. Consumers who are already buying specialty, fair-trade, and organic coffees because they care about how their coffee is being produced, and about the people who are producing it, need to be educated about the root causes of the current crisis, and the kinds of changes that are needed to deal with it. Hopefully, this book will make a small contribution to this education.

Developing the Commodity Chain Approach

The analysis presented in this book demonstrates the usefulness of the commodity chain approach for analyzing the structure of commodity production and trading systems and their evolution over time. It also demonstrates the usefulness of this approach for analyzing changes in the structure of the world economy, and the ways in which these changes are manifested in and shaped by changes in the structures of particular commodity chains. The analysis of the coffee commodity chain also highlights three areas in which the commodity chain approach needs to be further developed: the analysis of governance structures, the analysis of financial flows, and comparative analysis.

The governance structure of the coffee commodity chain is not adequately described by any of the ideal types that have been developed so far, by Gereffi and Gibbon. This suggests the need to develop a more complete typology of governance structures. Rather than positing ideal types of structures, we may need to focus in on characteristics that vary across governance structures, such as: what types of TNCs set the rules, what types of rules do they set (e.g., regarding the "quality" of the product or the production process used), what types of products are involved (agricultural vs. mineral vs. manufactures), and so forth. If we can isolate a few key characteristics of governance structures, such as these, we may be able to create a more complete typology out of different combinations of these characteristics. Further, we need to allow for the possibility that different segments of the commodity chain may have different governing agents and different governance structures. This was certainly the case for coffee, at least during the period of the ICAs. Although the coffee chain currently does seem to be converging toward a buyer-driven type of governance structure, as Gereffi predicts, it is still fundamentally different from the apparel chain in that the coffee TNCs directly produce the final coffee products.

Few commodity chain analyses that have been done so far have attempted to "follow the money" in the way that I have in this analysis. In part, this is because the data are very hard to get. The availability of relatively good data over a fairly long period of time for coffee is itself a legacy of the producers' collective action that established the ICAs. Most commodity chain analyses have assumed that the profits flow to the most highly monopolized stages, where there are the highest barriers to entry. Often this is the case, but we still need to quantify the flows in order to assert this. As it turned out in coffee, there was a period when state regulation diverted flows of surplus from the most monopolized to the least monopolized stage of the chain—from TNCs to small coffee growers. So governance structures can change the flows of surplus, and we need to understand how income and profits are distributed among the different participants in commodity chains in order to analyze how financial flows can be changed. I believe that quantification can also serve a political purpose. It demonstrates graphically where consumers' dollars are going. In the case of coffee, and probably in many other commodity chains today, the vast majority of those dollars are flowing into the coffers of the TNCs, and very few of them are making their way back to the people who actually produce the goods that consumers buy. This could be a great tool for consumer education about the overwhelming economic power of the TNCs and the necessity of balancing that power with concern for the environmental, social, and human rights aspects of production. Ultimately, TNCs only care about these latter aspects of production when they are forced to, by consumers or state regulations.

Finally, commodity chain analysis should be further developed through the use of comparative analysis. Most of the commodity chain analyses that have been done so far focus on one commodity, as this one does. But when focusing on only one commodity chain, it is difficult to see what it has in common with other chains, and what its distinctive features are. By comparing the structures of different chains, we can begin to see how differences in their structures cause differences in their outcomes. Why were coffee producers more successful at taking collective action to regulate the market? It seems to have been a conjuncture of the particular geographical distribution of coffee production with the particular geopolitical concerns of the major coffee importing states, and the convergence of a Polanyian double movement caused by declining prices in the late 1950s with decolonization movements worldwide and the Cuban Revolution in particular. But maybe there was something about the particular structure of the coffee commodity chain that set it apart from other similar chains, something that I have not been able to identify in this analysis, because I haven't done detailed comparisons with other chains.[2] Further, I believe that comparative analysis is the only way to begin to develop a typology of governance structures, as I argued above was needed.

Commodity chain analysis is a valuable analytical tool, and this analysis of coffee should provide sufficient grounds for its further development.

Notes

1. Producing countries that consume coffee would also have to produce enough to meet domestic demand. Their production quotas would consist of an exportable portion and a domestic portion. They could produce an amount of coffee equal to the total quota, and decide for themselves which coffee to export, and which to keep for domestic consumption. Typically, the higher quality coffee is reserved for export, and the lower quality is consumed domestically.

2. See Talbot (2002) for an initial attempt at this type of comparative analysis.

Bibliography

Akiyama, Takamasa. 2001. "Coffee Market Liberalization since 1990." In *Commodity Market Reform: Lessons of Two Decades,* eds. Takamasa Akiyama, John Baffes, Donald Larson, and Panos Varangis, 83–120. Washington, DC: World Bank.

Akiyama, Takamasa, and Panayotis Varangis. 1989. "Impact of the International Coffee Agreement's Export Quota System on the World's Coffee Market." PPR Working Paper WPS-148, International Commodity Markets Division, International Economics Department, World Bank, February.

———. 1990. "The Impact of the International Coffee Agreement on Producing Countries." *World Bank Economic Review* 4:157–74.

Andersen, Regine. 2000. "How Multilateral Development Assistance Triggered the Conflict in Rwanda." *Third World Quarterly* 21:441–56.

Andrews, Margaret. 1992. *Avenues for Growth: A 20-Year Review of the U.S. Specialty Coffee Market.* Long Beach, CA: Specialty Coffee Association of America.

Arrighi, Giovanni. 1994. *The Long Twentieth Century: Money, Power and the Origins of Our Times.* London: Verso.

Arrighi, Giovanni, and Jessica Drangel. 1986. "The Stratification of the World-Economy: An Exploration of the Semiperipheral Zone." *Review* 10:9–74.

Bates, Robert. 1997. *Open-Economy Politics: The Political Economy of the World Coffee Trade.* Princeton, NJ: Princeton University Press.

Bevan, D. L., P. Collier, and J. W. Gunning. 1990. "Fiscal Response to a Temporary Trade Shock: The Aftermath of the Kenyan Coffee Boom." *World Bank Economic Review* 3:359–78.

Bilder, Richard B. 1963. "The International Coffee Agreement: A Case History in Negotiation." *Law and Contemporary Problems* 28:328–91.

Bohman, Mary, and Lovell Jarvis. 1990. "The International Coffee Agreement: Economics of the Non-member Market." *European Review of Agricultural Economics* 17:99–118.

Bonacich, Edna, and Richard Appelbaum. 2000. *Behind the Label: Inequality in the Los Angeles Apparel Industry.* Berkeley: University of California Press.

Brown, Christopher. 1980. *The Political and Social Economy of Commodity Control.*

New York: Praeger Publishers.

Cardenas, Mauricio. 1991. *Coffee Exports, Endogenous State Policies, and the Business Cycle.* Unpublished Ph.D. Dissertation, Department of Economics, University of California, Berkeley.

Castells, Manuel, Shujiro Yazawa, and Emma Kiselyova. 1995–1996. "Insurgents Against the Global Order: A Comparative Analysis of the Zapatistas in Mexico, the American Militia, and Japan's AUM Shinrikyo." *Berkeley Journal of Sociology* 40:21–59.

Castle, Timothy. 2001. "A Cup Fraught With Issues." *Specialty Coffee Retailer,* November, www.retailmerchandising.net/coffee/2001/0111/0111issu.asp.

Chalmin, Philippe. 1987. *Traders and Merchants: Panorama of International Commodity Trading.* Chur, Switzerland: Harwood Academic Publishers.

Chase-Dunn, Christopher, and Peter Grimes. 1995. "World-Systems Analysis." *Annual Review of Sociology* 21:387–417.

Chossudovsky, Michel. 1996. "Economic Genocide in Rwanda." *Economic and Political Weekly,* April 13, 938–41.

Clancy, Michael. 1998. "Commodity Chains, Services, and Development: Theory and Preliminary Evidence from the Tourism Industry." *Review of International Political Economy* 5:122–48.

Commodity Research Bureau. 1983. *Commodity Yearbook 1983.* New York: CRB.

Cordell, Arthur J. 1969. "The Brazilian Soluble Coffee Problem: A Review." *Quarterly Review of Economics and Business* 9:29–38.

Cramer, Christopher. 1999. "Can Africa Industrialize By Processing Primary Commodities? The Case of Mozambican Cashew Nuts." *World Development* 27:1247–66.

Daviron, Benoit. 1996. "The Rise and Fall of Governmental Power on the International Coffee Market." In *Economics of Agricultural Policies in Developing Countries,* eds. Michel Benoit-Cattin, Michel Griffon, and Patrick Guillaumont, 81–100. Paris: Editions de la Revue Française d'Economie.

Davis, Jeffrey M. 1983. "The Economic Effects of Windfall Gains in Export Earnings, 1975–78." *World Development* 11:119–39.

Dinham, Barbara, and Colin Hines. 1984. *Agribusiness in Africa.* Trenton, NJ: Africa World Press.

Dolan, Catherine, and Humphrey, John. 2000. "Governance and Trade in Fresh Vegetables: The Impact of U.K. Supermarkets on the African Horticulture Industry." *Journal of Development Studies* 37:147–76.

Economist Intelligence Unit. 1987. *Coffee to 1991: Controlling a Surplus.* London: Economist.

Edmunds, John. 1982. "A Comment on Greenstone's 'The Coffee Cartel: Manipulation in the Public Interest'." *Journal of Futures Markets* 2:19–24.

Edwards, R., and A. Parikh. 1976. "A Stochastic Policy Simulation of the World Coffee Economy." *American Journal of Agricultural Economics,* 58:152–60.

Food and Agriculture Organization. 1947. *The World's Coffee.* Rome: FAO.

Fierro Carrión, Luis. 1991. *Los Grupos Financieros en el Ecuador.* Quito: Centro de Educación Popular.

Finlayson, Jock, and Mark Zacher. 1988. *Managing International Markets: The Developing Countries and the Commodity Trade Regime.* New York: Columbia University Press.

Fisher, Bart. 1972. *The International Coffee Agreements: A Study in Coffee Diplomacy.* New York: Praeger Publishers.

Fitter, Robert, and Raphael Kaplinsky. 2001. "Who Gains from Product Rents as the

Coffee Market Becomes More Differentiated? A Value Chain Analysis." *IDS Bulletin* 32:69–82.

Ford, Derek. 1978. "Commodity Market Modeling and the Simulation of Market Intervention." In *Stabilizing World Commodity Markets: Analysis, Practice, and Policy,* eds. F. Gerard Adams and Sonia A. Klein, 35–61. Lexington, MA: Lexington Books.

Friedmann, Harriet. 1978. "World Market, State, and Family Farm: The Social Bases of Household Production in the Era of Wage Labor." *Comparative Studies in Society and History* 20:545–80.

———. 1982. "The Political Economy of Food: The Rise and Fall of the Postwar International Food Order." *American Journal of Sociology* 88 (Supplement): 248–86.

———. 1991a. "Changes in the International Division of Labor: Agri-food Complexes and Export Agriculture." In *Towards a New Political Economy of Agriculture,* eds. W. Friedland, L. Busch, F. Buttel, and A. Rudy, 65–93. Boulder, CO: Westview Press.

———. 1991b. "New Wines, New Bottles: The Regulation of Capital on a World Scale." *Studies in Political Economy* 36:9–42.

———. 1993. "The Political Economy of Food: A Global Crisis." *New Left Review* 197 (January/February):29–57.

Friedmann, Harriet, and Philip D. McMichael. 1989. "Agriculture and the State System: The rise and decline of national agricultures, 1870 to the present." *Sociologia Ruralis* 29:93–117.

Galloway, L. Thomas. 1973. "The International Coffee Agreement." *Journal of World Trade Law* 7:354–74.

Geer, Thomas. 1971. *An Oligopoly: The World Coffee Economy and Stabilization Schemes.* New York: Dunellen.

Gellert, Paul K. 2003. "Renegotiating a Timber Commodity Chain: Lessons from Indonesia on the Political Construction of Global Commodity Chains." *Sociological Forum* 18:53–84.

Gereffi, Gary. 1994. "The Organization of Buyer-Driven Global Commodity Chains: How U.S. Retailers Shape Overseas Production Networks." In *Commodity Chains and Global Capitalism,* eds. Gary Gereffi and Miguel Korzeniewicz, 95–122. Westport, CT: Praeger Publishers.

———. 1995. "Global Production Systems and Third World Development." In *Global Change, Regional Response: The New International Context of Development,* ed. Barbara Stallings, 100–42. Cambridge: Cambridge University Press.

———. 1999. "International Trade and Industrial Upgrading in the Apparel Commodity Chain." *Journal of International Economics* 48:37–70.

Gereffi, Gary, and Miguel Korzeniewicz. 1990. "Commodity Chains and Footwear Exports in the Semiperiphery." In *Semiperipheral States in the World Economy,* ed. William Martin, 45–68. Westport, CT: Greenwood Press.

———, eds. 1994. *Commodity Chains and Global Capitalism.* Westport, CT: Praeger Publishers.

Gereffi, Gary, Miguel Korzeniewicz, and Roberto P. Korzeniewicz. 1994. "Introduction: Global Commodity Chains." In *Commodity Chains and Global Capitalism,* eds. Gary Gereffi and Miguel Korzeniewicz, 1–14. Westport, CT: Praeger Publishers.

Gibbon, Peter. 2001. "Upgrading Primary Production: A Global Commodity Chain Approach." *World Development* 29:345–63.

Gilbert, Christopher L. 1996. "International Commodity Agreements: An Obituary Notice." *World Development* 24:1–19.

Giovannucci, Daniele. 2001. "Sustainable Coffee Survey of the North American Specialty Coffee Industry." Specialty Coffee Association of America, July. www.scaa .org/survey.cfm.

Goodman, David. 1991. "Some Recent Tendencies in the Industrial Reorganization of the Agri-Food System." In *Towards a New Political Economy of Agriculture*, eds. W. Friedland, L. Busch, F. Buttel, and A. Rudy, 37–64. Boulder, CO: Westview Press.

Gourevitch, Peter. 1978. "The Second Image Reversed: The International Sources of Domestic Politics." *International Organization* 32:881–912.

de Graaf, J. 1986. *The Economics of Coffee*. Wageningen, Netherlands: Centre for Agricultural Publishing and Documentation.

Greenberg, Russell, Peter Bichier, and John Sterling. 1997. "Bird Populations in Rustic and Planted Shade Coffee Plantations of Eastern Chiapas, Mexico." *Biotropica* 29:501–14.

Greenfield, Gerard. 2002. "Vietnam and the World Coffee Crisis." *Focus on Trade*, Number 75, March. Distributed by Focus on the Global South, http://focusweb.org.

Greenstone, Wayne. 1981. "The Coffee Cartel: Manipulation in the Public Interest." *Journal of Futures Markets* 1:3–16.

Haggard, Stephen. 1990. *Pathways from the Periphery: The Politics of Growth in the Newly Industrializing Countries*. Ithaca, NY: Cornell University Press.

Haggard, Stephen, and Beth Simmons. 1987. "Theories of International Regimes." *International Organization* 41:491–517.

Herrmann, Roland. 1986. "Free Riders and the Redistributive Effects of International Commodity Agreements: The Case of Coffee." *Journal of Policy Modeling* 8:597–621.

Hidrobo, Jorge A. 1992. *Power and Industrialization in Ecuador*. Boulder, CO: Westview Press.

Hilke, John C., and Philip B. Nelson. 1989. "Strategic Behavior and Attempted Monopolization: The Coffee (General Foods) Case," In *The Anti-Trust Revolution*, eds. John E. Kwoka and Lawrence J. White, 208–40. Glenview, IL: Scott, Foresman and Co.

Holloway, Thomas H. 1975. *The Brazilian Coffee Valorization of 1906: Regional Politics and Economic Dependence*. Madison: The State Historical Society of Wisconsin.

Hone, A. 1993. *Soluble Coffee: Technical and Marketing Opportunities and Constraints for Origin Producers*, NRI Marketing Series Volume 8. Chatham, U.K.: Natural Resources Institute.

Hopkins, Terence, and Immanuel Wallerstein. 1994. "Commodity Chains: Construct and Research," and "Conclusions About Commodity Chains." In *Commodity Chains and Global Capitalism*, eds. Gary Gereffi and Miguel Korzeniewicz, 17–20, 48–50. Westport, CT: Praeger Publishers.

Instituto Brasileiro do Café. 1978 and 1979. *The Coffee Market, 1976/77* and *1978*. New York: IBC.

International Coffee Organization. 1982. *International Coffee Agreement 1983*. London: ICO.

International Coffee Organization. Various years. *Quarterly Statistical Bulletin*. London: ICO.

International Coffee Organization. Various years. ICO documents; documents are cited by series code (EB = Executive Board documents, ICC = International Coffee Council documents). For EB documents, the series code is followed by document number/year, e.g., EB 3338/92 is Executive Board document no. 3338, issued in 1992. For ICC documents, the series code is followed by the session number and document number, e.g., ICC 49-3 is document number 3 from the 49th session of the

ICC, May 1988. London: ICO.

International Trade Centre UNCTAD/GATT. 1992. *Coffee: An Exporter's Guide.* Geneva: ITC.

International Trade Centre UNCTAD/WTO. 1996. *Coffee: An Exporter's Guide—Supplement.* Geneva, ITC.

James, Deborah. 2000. "Justice and Java: Coffee in a Fair Trade Market." *NACLA Report on the Americas* 34:11–14.

Kaplinsky, Raphael. 1998. "Globalisation, Industrialisation and Sustainable Growth: The Pursuit of the Nth Rent." IDS Discussion Paper 365, Institute of Development Studies, June.

———. 2000. "Globalisation and Unequalisation: What Can Be Learned from Value Chain Analysis?" *Journal of Development Studies* 37:117–46.

Korzeniewicz, Roberto, and William Martin. 1994. "The Global Distribution of Commodity Chains." In *Commodity Chains and Global Capitalism,* eds. Gary Gereffi and Miguel Korzeniewicz, 67–91. Westport, CT: Praeger Publishers.

Krasner, Stephen. 1973a. "Business-Government Relations: the Case of the International Coffee Agreement." *International Organization* 27:495–516.

———. 1973b. "Manipulating International Commodity Markets: Brazilian Coffee Policy 1906–1962." *Public Policy* 21:493–523.

———. 1974. "Oil is the Exception." *Foreign Policy* 14, (spring): 68–84.

———. 1976. "State Power and the Structure of International Trade." *World Politics* 28:317–47.

———, ed. 1983. *International Regimes.* Ithaca, NY: Cornell University Press.

———. 1985. *Structural Conflict: The Third World against Global Liberalism.* Berkeley: University of California Press.

Kratochwil, Friedrich. 1993. "Norms vs. Numbers: Multilateralism and the Rationalist and Reflexive Approaches to Institutions—a Unilateral Plea for Communicative Rationality." In *Multilateralism Matters: The Theory and Praxis of an Institutional Form,* ed. John G. Ruggie, 443–74. New York: Columbia University Press.

Kuchiki, Akifumi. 1990. "The Pricing Mechanism of Primary Commodities Since the 1970s." *The Developing Economies* 28:95–110.

Levi, Margaret, and April Linton. 2003. "Fair Trade: A Cup at a Time?" *Politics and Society* 31:407–32.

London, Christopher E. 1997. "Class Relations and Capitalist Development: Subsumption in the Colombian Coffee Industry, 1928–92." *Journal of Peasant Studies,* 24:269–95.

Lucier, Richard. 1988. *The International Political Economy of Coffee.* New York: Praeger Publishers.

Marazzi, Leonarda. 1984. "Commodity Exchanges: Implications for International Trade." *Trade and Development: An UNCTAD Review,* 5:99–120.

Marshall, C. F. 1972. "Coffee: The Market in 1971 and the Present Position." *Bank of London and South America Review,* no. 63:127–34.

———. 1979. "Coffee in 1978: A Precarious Balance." *Bank of London and South America Review* 13, no. 1:2–6.

———. 1980. "Coffee in 1979: The Effect of the Bogotá Group." *Bank of London and South America Review* 14, no. 1:2–6.

———. 1983. *The World Coffee Trade: A Guide to the Production, Trading, and Consumption of Coffee.* Cambridge: Woodhead-Faulkner.

Masini, Jean, Moises Ikonicoff, Claudio Jedlicki, and Mario Lanzarotti. 1979. *Multinationals and Development in Black Africa.* Hampshire, U.K.: Saxon House, Teakfield

Ltd. and the European Center for Study and Information on Multinational Corporations.

Mattera, Philip. 1992. *World Class Business: A Guide to the 100 Most Powerful Global Corporations.* New York: H. Holt.

McMichael, Philip D. 1990. "Incorporating Comparison within a World-Historical Perspective: An Alternative Comparative Method." *American Sociological Review* 55:385–97.

———. 1992a. "Rethinking Comparative Analysis in a Post-Developmentalist Context." *International Social Science Journal* 44:351–65.

———. 1992b. "Tensions Between National and International Control of the World Food Order: Contours of a New Food Regime." *Sociological Perspectives* 35:343–65.

———. 1996. "Globalization: Myths and Realities." *Rural Sociology* 61:25–55.

———. 2000. *Development and Social Change,* Second edition. Boston: Pine Forge Press.

Mintz, Sidney. 1985. *Sweetness and Power: The Place of Sugar in Modern History.* New York: Penguin.

Monopolies and Mergers Commission (U.K.). 1991. *Soluble Coffee: A Report on the Supply of Soluble Coffee for Retail Sale within the United Kingdom.* London: HMSO.

Montenegro, Armando, Mónica Aparicio, and Andrés Langebaek. 1989. "Análysis de la Votación que Suspendió el Régimen de Cuotas en la OIC." *Ensayos Sobre Economía Cafetera.* (Bogotá, Colombia) Año 2, no. 4:5–16.

Mwandha, James, John Nicholls, and Malcolm Sargent. 1985. *Coffee: The International Commodity Agreements.* Hampshire, U.K.: Gower Publishing.

Nigh, Ronald. 1997. "Organic Agriculture and Globalization: A Maya Associative Corporation in Chiapas, Mexico." *Human Organization* 56:427–36.

Orlandi, Alberto. 1978. "Prices and Gains in the World Coffee Trade." *CEPAL Review* First half of 1978:161–97.

Osorio, Nestor. 1994. "Free Market or Fixed Rules for Coffee." London: Federación Nacional de Cafeteros de Colombia.

Owens, Trudy, and Adrian Wood. 1997. "Export-Oriented Industrialization through Primary Processing?" *World Development* 25:1453–70.

Oxfam U.K. 2001. *The Coffee Market: A Background Study,* January, www.people .cornell.edu/pages/cel5/OxfamReport.pdf.

Pan American Coffee Bureau. 1966. *Annual Coffee Statistics 1966: Thirtieth Anniversary Edition.* New York: PACB.

Pan American Coffee Bureau. 1967–1975. *Annual Coffee Statistics, 1967–1975.* New York: PACB.

Payer, Cheryl. 1975. "Coffee." In *Commodity Trade of the Third World,* ed. Cheryl Payer, 154–68. London: MacMillan.

Pendergrast, Mark. 1999. *Uncommon Grounds: The History of Coffee and How It Transformed the World.* New York: Basic Books.

Percival, Val, and Thomas Homer-Dixon. 1996. "Environmental Scarcity and Violent Conflict: The Case of Rwanda." *Journal of Environment and Development* 5:270–91.

Perfecto, Ivette, Robert A. Rice, Russell Greenberg, and Martha E Van der Voort. 1996. "Shade Coffee: A Disappearing Refuge for Biodiversity." *BioScience* 46:598–608.

Pieterse, M.Th.A., and H. J. Silvis. 1988. *The World Coffee Market and the International Coffee Agreement.* Wageningen, Netherlands: Centre for Agricultural Publishing and Documentation.

Polanyi, Karl. 1957. *The Great Transformation: The Political and Economic Origins of Our Time.* Boston: Beacon Press.

Rapley, John. 1993. *Ivoirien Capitalism: African Entrepreneurs in Côte d'Ivoire.* London: Lynne Rienner.

Reese, Jennifer. 1996. "Starbucks: Inside the Coffee Cult." *Fortune,* December 9, 190–200.

Renard, Marie-Christine. 1999. "The Interstices of Globalization: The Example of Fair Coffee." *Sociologia Ruralis* 39:484–500.

Rice, Paul D., and Jennifer McLean. 1999. *Sustainable Coffee at the Crossroads: A Report to the Consumer's Choice Council.* Washington, DC: Consumer's Choice Council.

Rice, Robert A. 1996. "Coffee Modernization and Ecological Changes in Northern Latin America: Coffee's Importance in a Quality Region." *Tea and Coffee Trade Journal,* September, 104–13.

———. 1999. "A Place Unbecoming: The Coffee Farm of Northern Latin America." *The Geographical Review* 89:554–79.

Rice, Robert A., and Justin R. Ward. 1996. *Coffee, Conservation, and Commerce in the Western Hemisphere.* Washington, DC: Smithsonian Migratory Bird Center and Natural Resources Defense Council.

Roseberry, William. 1996. "The Rise of Yuppie Coffees and the Reimagination of Class in the United States." *American Anthropologist* 98:762–75.

Ruggie, John Gerard. 1983. "International Regimes, Transactions and Change: Embedded Liberalism in the Postwar Economic Order." In *International Regimes,* ed. Stephen Krasner, 195–231. Ithaca, NY: Cornell University Press.

———. 1992. "Multilateralism: The Anatomy of an Institution." *International Organization* 46:562–98.

Sanderson, Steven E. 1986. "The Emergence of the 'World Steer': International and Foreign Domination in Latin American Cattle Production." In *Food, the State, and International Political Economy: Dilemmas of Developing Countries,* eds. F. L. Tullis and W. L. Hollist, 123–48. Lincoln: University of Nebraska Press.

Schiff, Maurice. 1995. "Commodity Exports and the Adding-Up Problem in LDCs: Trade, Investment, and Lending Policy." *World Development* 23:603–15.

Schivelbusch, Wolfgang. 1992. *Tastes of Paradise: A Social History of Spices, Stimulants, and Intoxicants.* Translated by David Jacobson. New York: Vintage Books.

Schurman, Rachel A. 1998. "Tuna Dreams: Resource Nationalism and the Pacific Islands' Tuna Industry." *Development and Change* 29:107–36.

Singh, Shamsher, Jos de Vries, John C. L. Hulley, and Patrick Yeung. 1977. *Coffee, Tea, and Cocoa: Market Prospects and Development Lending.* World Bank Staff Occasional Papers No. 22. Baltimore: The Johns Hopkins University Press.

Smith, Michael D. 1996. "The Empire Filters Back: Consumption, Production, and the Politics of Starbucks Coffee." *Urban Geography* 17:502–24.

Specialty Coffee Association of America. 1999. "1999 Coffee Market Summary." Long Beach: SCAA, www.scaa.org.

Stopford, John. 1992. *Directory of Multinationals.* New York: Stockton Press.

Strange, Susan. 1983. "*Cave! Hic Dragones*: A Critique of Regime Analysis." In *International Regimes,* ed. Stephen Krasner, 337–54. Ithaca: Cornell University Press.

Tangley, Laura. 1996. "The Case of the Missing Migrants." *Science* 274:1299–1300.

Talbot, John M. 1997. *Grounds for Agreement: The Political Economy of the Coffee Commodity Chain.* Unpublished Ph.D. dissertation, Department of Sociology, University of California, Berkeley.

———. 2002. "Tropical Commodity Chains, Forward Integration Strategies, and International Inequality: Coffee, Cocoa, and Tea." *Review of International Political Economy* 9:701–34.

Tilly, Charles. 1984. *Big Structures Large Processes Huge Comparisons.* New York: Russell Sage Foundation.

Topik, Steven. 1998. "Coffee." In *The Second Conquest of Latin America,* eds. Steven Topik and Allen Wells, 37–84. Austin: University of Texas Press.

Topik, Steven, and Alan Wells, eds. 1998. *The Second Conquest of Latin America.* Austin: University of Texas Press.

UN. Various years. *International Trade Statistics Yearbook.* New York: UN.

———. Various years. *Yearbook of International Trade Statistics.* New York: UN.

UNCTAD. 1978. "Action on commodities, including decisions on an integrated programme, in light of the need for change in the world commodity economy." Document TD/184, in *Proceedings of the United Nations Conference on Trade and Development, Fourth Session, Nairobi, 5–31 May 1976.* New York: UN.

———. 1984. *The Processing and Marketing of Coffee: Areas for International Cooperation.* New York: UN.

———. 1995. *Recent Trends on the World Coffee Market.* New York: UN.

———. Various years. *Commodity Yearbook.* New York: UN.

———. Various years. *Handbook of International Trade and Development Statistics.* New York: UN.

———. Various years. *Yearbook of International Commodity Statistics.* New York: UN.

UN Centre on Transnational Corporations. 1981. *Transnational Corporations in Food and Beverage Processing.* New York: UN.

U.S. Census Bureau. 1990. *1987 Census of Manufactures* Washington, DC: USGPO.

U.S. Census Bureau. *1992 Census of Manufactures,* Industry Series—Miscellaneous Food and Kindred Products, www.census.gov.

U.S. Census Bureau, *1997 Economic Census,* Manufacturing, Industry Series—Coffee and Tea Manufacturing, www.census.gov.

U.S. Census Bureau. 1993, 1994, 1995, 1996, 2000. *Annual Surveys of Manufactures,* Industry Statistics, www.census.gov.

U.S. Department of Agriculture, Foreign Agricultural Service. Various years. *Foreign Agricultural Circular—Coffee.* Washington, DC: USDA.

U.S. Department of Agriculture, Foreign Agricultural Service. Various years. *World Coffee Situation.* Washington, DC: USDA.

U.S. Department of Agriculture, Foreign Agricultural Service. Various years. *Tropical Products: World Markets and Trade.* Washington, DC: USDA.

U.S. Federal Trade Commission 1966. *Cents-Off Promotions in the Coffee Industry,* Bureau of Economics Staff Report. Washington, DC: USGPO.

U.S. Government Accounting Office. 1977. *Coffee: Production and Marketing Systems,* Report to Congress by the Comptroller General. Washington, DC: USGPO.

U.S. House of Representatives, Committee on Ways and Means, Subcommittee on Trade. 1983. "Extension of the International Coffee Agreement Act of 1980." Hearing held September 19. Washington, DC: USGPO.

U.S. Senate. 1990. "Drug Policy in the Andean Nations." Joint Hearings of the Senate Judiciary Committee and the Caucus on International Narcotics Control, Washington, DC, January 18. Washington, DC: USGPO.

Uvin, Peter. 1996. "Tragedy in Rwanda: The Political Ecology of Conflict." *Environment* 38, no. 3:7–15, 29.

Vogelvang, Ben. 1988. *A Quarterly Econometric Model of the World Coffee Economy.* Amsterdam: Free University Press.

Wallerstein, Immanuel. 1974. *The Modern World-System I: Capitalist Agriculture and the Origins of the European World-Economy in the Sixteenth Century.* San Diego, CA: Academic Press.

Waltz, Kenneth. 1959. *Man, the State and War.* New York: Columbia University Press.

Ward's Private Company Profiles. 1994. Detroit: Gale Research Inc.

Waridel, Laure. 2002. *Coffee with Pleasure: Just Java and World Trade.* Montreal: Black Rose Books.

Wasserman, Ursula. 1972. "1972 Geneva Coffee Agreement." *Journal of World Trade Law* 6:612–14.

Weiss, Brad. 1996. "Coffee Breaks and Coffee Connections: The Lived Experience of a Commodity in Tanzanian and European Worlds." In *Cross-Cultural Consumption: Global Markets and Local Realities,* ed. David Howes, 93–105. London: Routledge.

Wille, Chris. 1994. "The Birds and the Beans." *Audubon,* November–December, 58–64.

World Bank 1993. *Bank Lending Policy for Plantation Crops.* Washington, DC: World Bank Operations Evaluation Division.

Wrigley, Gordon. 1988. *Coffee.* Essex: Longman Scientific and Technical.

Yorgason, Vernon. 1976. "The International Coffee Agreement." *Development and Change* 7:207–21.

Periodicals and News Services

Agence France Press

Arizona Republic (Phoenix, AZ)

Associated Press

Boletín Cafetera (Manta, Ecuador: Associación Nacional de Exportadores de Café)

Buffalo News (Buffalo, NY)

Business Times (Singapore)

Business Week (New York)

Business Wire

Carta Cafetera (Bogotá, Colombia: Asociación de Exportadores de Café de Colombia)

Chicago Sun-Times (Chicago)

ED&F Man (Coffee) Ltd., *World Coffee Situation* (London)

Economía Cafetera, (Bogotá, Colombia: Federación Nacional de Cafeteros)

El Tiempo (Bogotá, Colombia)

Financial Times (London)

F. O. Licht, *F. O. Licht's International Coffee Report* (Ratzeburg, Germany)

Forbes (New York)

Houston Chronicle (Houston, TX)

Journal of Commerce (New York)

Landell Mills Commodity Studies, *Commodity Bulletin—Coffee* (Oxford, U.K.)

Latin American Economy and Business (London)

Los Angeles Times (Los Angeles)

New York Times (New York)

PR Newswire

Saint Paul Pioneer Press (Saint Paul, MN)

Seattle Times (Seattle, WA)

Tea and Coffee Trade Journal (New York)

Time (New York)
Toronto Star (Toronto, Ontario, Canada)
Wall Street Journal (New York)
Washington Post (Washington, DC)
World Coffee and Tea (Rockville, MD)

Index

About the Author

John M. Talbot received his Ph.D. in sociology from the University of California, Berkeley. He is currently a lecturer in sociology at the University of the West Indies, Mona campus, Jamaica, where he teaches courses on globalization, research methods, and statistics. His research interests include international political economy and structures of international inequality, the sociology of food, and environmental sociology. In addition to studying coffee, he also enjoys drinking it.